Job Creation, Job Destruction, and International Competition

Dec. 2004

To my treasured friend and colleague with great fondness,

Michael

Job Creation, Job Destruction, and International Competition

Michael W. Klein
Scott Schuh
and
Robert K. Triest

2003

W.E. Upjohn Institute for Employment Research
Kalamazoo, Michigan

Library of Congress Cataloging-in-Publication Data

Klein, Michael W., 1958–
  Job creation, job destruction, and international competition / Michael W. Klein, Scott Schuh, and Robert K. Triest.
    p. cm.
  Includes bibliographical references and index.
    ISBN 0-88099-271-9 (pbk. : alk. paper) — ISBN 0-88099-272-7 (hardcover : alk. paper)
    1. Foreign trade and employment—United States. 2. Free trade—Social aspects—United States. 3. Job creation—United States. 4. Unemployment—United States. 5. Labor market—United States. 6. Manpower policy—United States. 7. Manufacturing industries—United States—Employees. 8. Competition, International. I. Schuh, Scott. II. Triest, Robert K. III. Title.
    HD5710.75.U6K54 2003
    331.12'0973—dc22
                                    2003015610

© 2003

W.E. Upjohn Institute for Employment Research
300 S. Westnedge Avenue
Kalamazoo, Michigan 49007–4686

The facts presented in this study and the observations and viewpoints expressed are the sole responsibility of the authors. They do not necessarily represent positions of the W.E. Upjohn Institute for Employment Research, Federal Reserve Bank of Boston, Board of Governors of the Federal Reserve System, or U.S. Bureau of the Census. This book does not contain or use any confidential Census Bureau data.

Cover design by Alcorn Publication Design.
Index prepared by Nairn Chadwick.
Printed in the United States of America.
Printed on recycled paper.

Contents

Acknowledgments	ix
1 Introduction	1
Job Reallocation and International Trade	4
Reallocation Across and Within Industries	7
Overview and Summary of Results	9
Notes	13
2 Openness	15
Openness Over Time and Across Industries	17
The Volatility of Dollar Exchange Rates	22
The Diversity of Behavior of Industry-Specific Exchange Rates	26
Conclusion	30
Notes	30
3 Job Creation and Job Destruction	33
Gross Job Flows in U.S. Manufacturing	35
Conclusion	46
Notes	47
4 Literature Review	49
International Factors and Labor Markets	50
International Factors and Net Employment	61
International Factors and Gross Flows	72
Notes	80
5 Job Flows and the Exchange Rate	83
Job Flows and Idiosyncratic Shocks	84
The Role of Aggregate Shocks	88
Implications of the Model	91
Conclusion	93
Notes	94
6 Regression Implementation and Results	97
Empirical Implementation	98
Regression Results	102
Conclusions and Interpretations	109
Notes	110

7	**Job Flows and Trade**	113
	Economic Effects of Trade Liberalization	114
	An Overview of NAFTA	117
	Previous Research Related to the Economic Effects of NAFTA	118
	Sector-Specific Effects	121
	Conclusion	145
	Notes	147
8	**Policy Implications**	149
	Summary of Main Findings	151
	Exchange Rate Management	153
	Tariffs and Industrial Policy	154
	Worker Assistance Policies	157
	Conclusion	159
	Notes	161
9	**Directions for Future Research**	163
	Matching Job and Worker Flows	164
	Data Development	165
	Measuring Labor-Adjustment Costs	169
	Summary	171
	Notes	172

Appendix A: Standard Industrial Classification (SIC) System	173
Appendix B: A Formal Economic Model of the Effect of Exchange Rate Changes on Job Creation and Job Destruction	175
Note	178
Appendix C: Data Sources	179
Note	180
References	183
The Authors	193
Index	195
About the Institute	201

Figures

2.1	Distributions of Openness across Industries (1958–1994)	18
2.2	Real Trade-Weighted Exchange Value of the U.S. Dollar (January 1973–October 2002)	23
2.3	Balance on the U.S. Current Account (Q1:1973–Q2:2002)	25
2.4	Distributions of Real Exchange Rates across Industries (1973–1993)	28
2.5	Distributions of Real Exchange Rate Growth Rates across Industries (1974–1993)	29
3.1	Gross Job Flows and the Real Exchange Rate—Job Creation (1973–1993)	40
3.2	Gross Job Flows and the Real Exchange Rate—Job Destruction (1973–1993)	40
3.3	Gross Job Flows and the Real Exchange Rate—Job Reallocation (1973–1993)	41
3.4	Gross Job Flows and the Real Exchange Rate—Net Employment Growth (1973–1993)	41
4.1	Schematic Diagram of the Labor Market	53
5.2	Job Flows in Response to a Depreciation	89
7.1	Macroeconomic Developments in Mexico (Real GDP growth Q1:1981–Q3:2002, Real exchange rate Q1:1980–Q4:2002)	123
7.2	U.S. Employment in the Textile and Apparel Industries (1939–2001)	125
7.3	International Trade Shares in the Textile and Apparel Industries, U.S. Multilateral and Bilateral U.S.–Mexico (1972–2001) 128	128
7.4	Ratio of U.S.–Mexico Bilateral to U.S. Multilateral Trade in the Textile and Apparel Industries (1972–2001)	128
7.5	U.S. Gross Job Flows in the Textile and Apparel Industries (1973–2002)	130
7.6	U.S. Employment in the Chemical Industry (1939–2001)	134
7.7	International Trade Shares in the Chemical Industry, U.S. Multilateral and Bilateral U.S.–Mexico (1972–2001)	134
7.8	Ratio of U.S.–Mexico Bilateral to U.S. Multilateral Trade in the Chemical Industry (1972–2001)	136
7.9	U.S. Gross Job Flows in the Chemical Industry (1973–2002)	136

Tables

2.1	Regression of 1990 Openness on Industry Indicator Variables	20
2.2	Transitions of Four-Digit Industries between Openness Quintiles	21
3.1	Net and Gross Job Flows in the Auto Industry	37
3.2	Job-Flow Regressions on Industry Variables	45
4.1	Studies on the Relationship between International Factors and Labor Markets	62
6.1	Baseline Job-Flow Regression Results	104
6.2	Job-Flows Regression Results with Exchange Rate Decomposition	106
6.3	Job-Flow Responses to a Real Exchange Rate Appreciation	107
7.1	NAFTA Changes for Textiles and Apparel	124
7.2	NAFTA Changes for Chemicals and Allied Products	132
7.3	NAFTA Changes for Automobiles	138
Appendix A.1	Two-Digit SIC Industries	173
Appendix C.1	Notation and Data Definitions	181

Acknowledgments

We benefited greatly from the assistance of many individuals during the preparation of this monograph. From the data collection to the research to the writing and ultimately to publication, the entire project was a collaborative team effort achieved over a period of several years. We wish to express our deepest and sincerest appreciation to everyone involved in the process.

This monograph builds on our research paper published by the *Journal of International Economics* (Klein, Schuh, and Triest 2003). We thank Andrew Rose, the editor of the *JIE*, and two very conscientious anonymous referees for helpful suggestions that improved the article significantly, and contributed to its publication and effectiveness.

We also thank several colleagues for reviewing early versions of our *JIE* article and this manuscript, and for providing insightful suggestions for improvement. In particular, we appreciate Michelle Barnes, who read and commented on the entire manuscript. Linda Goldberg and Pierre-Oliver Gourinchas also contributed many useful ideas to the formulation of the *JIE* article. Participants in numerous professional seminars and conferences also gave helpful suggestions.

This study relies heavily on a large, detailed data base assembled from many diverse data sources that were integrated by a team of outstanding research assistants. We especially thank Jennifer Young, who spent countless hours writing code to assembly and construct the data base, and preparing the graphs. Joshua Congdon-Martin, Catherine Humblet, Radoslav Raykov, and Fred Rosenberg also provided excellent research assistance in gathering and manipulating data.

Several individuals contributed their expertise to the writing and preparation of this manuscript. Marcella Vencil converted the manuscript between word processing software packages and also provided outstanding secretarial assistance in general. Ann Eggleston and Robert Wathen contributed excellent editorial services for the manuscript.

Klein gratefully acknowledges financial support from the W.E. Upjohn Institute for Employment Research. We thank Upjohn and its staff, especially Randall Eberts, Kevin Hollenbeck, and Rich Wyrwa, for their support and patience during this project. Schuh and Triest gratefully acknowledge the extensive support provided by the Federal Reserve Bank of Boston in the preparation of this book and the ongoing research program on labor markets and international factors.

1
Introduction

Seattle had seemed like such a good choice. The organizers who selected it as the site of the November 1999 World Trade Organization (WTO) ministerial meeting cannot be faulted for thinking that the city would showcase the benefits of international trade. After all, one source of the city's prosperity was the Boeing corporation, which depends upon exports for a significant proportion of its total sales. Also, Seattle is an important center of the computer and internet industries, and advances in information technology contribute to eroding the difficulties in trading over great distances and across national borders. Furthermore, perched on the Pacific Rim, Seattle represented a reorientation in trade toward emerging markets.

But, the perceived consequences of trade with emerging markets fueled demonstrations that have now made Seattle more synonymous with antiglobalization street protests than with coffee or computers. Prominent among the issues raised by demonstrators were a number of concerns about the effects of trade on labor markets in industrial countries. Will cheap labor in Southeast Asia wholly displace highly paid workers in the Northwest United States? In the wake of greater liberalization, will multinationals close up shop in the industrial countries and set up factories in countries where they can employ children?

The answers provided by economists to these questions is generally "No." Evidence suggests that international differences in wages reflect differences in productivity between, say, American workers who have the benefits of training and infrastructure and Malaysian workers who do not enjoy these advantages.[1] Furthermore, there are many reasons to believe that international trade serves as an important source of economic advance both for American and Malaysian workers. International trade widens the set of goods available to consumers and, by fostering competition, offers consumers better opportunities. Competition promotes the reallocation of resources to their most productive uses. The efficiency gains obtained through this reallocation contribute to the overall economic welfare of a country.

These overall economic benefits are the source of the intellectual arguments for free trade, and the arguments bear up well in both theory and practice. Advocates of free trade are often dismayed that, even in the face of these arguments and this evidence, free trade remains a controversial issue. One important reason for this controversy is that the gains from trade are often accompanied by adjustment costs, including, importantly, worker dislocation. Historically, economists have tended to emphasize that the gains from trade are large and much larger than any adjustment costs, which in theory and practice have been argued to be transitory and small compared with total economic activity.

Until recently, the magnitude of worker dislocation typically has been gauged by the decline in the level of employment in manufacturing or in a particular industry affected by international factors. However, innovations in research on labor-market dynamics reveal that changes in manufacturing or industry total net employment are much smaller than the underlying increases and decreases in employment occurring simultaneously at individual establishments within industries. These establishment-level employment changes represent gross flows of employment, termed job creation and destruction. Prior research on these gross job flows indicates that labor reallocation is much more intensive and extensive than previously thought. Gross job flows occur at rates often an order of magnitude higher than net employment changes. Thus, relatively small changes in total employment do not reflect anywhere near the full extent of job creation and destruction that impacts individual workers and establishments.

Consequently, a more complete understanding of the overall impact of international factors on labor markets requires the analysis of gross job flows, which we undertake in this volume, as well as complementary analyses of the gross flows of workers among jobs and in and out of the labor force.[2] Moreover, a more complete understanding of labor-adjustment costs, and thus the net efficiency gains from trade, also requires the analysis of gross labor flows. This book delves more deeply into the issues of labor-market dynamics and the adjustment costs associated with international factors. We go beyond economy-wide and even sector-wide analyses of the effects of trade and, instead, focus on its disparate effects between and even within detailed industries.

After studying these issues at a more detailed level, we conclude that changes in international factors—exchange rates, trade agreements, and the like—have a much larger and more complex effect on labor markets than was previously understood. For *any* size of total employment change induced by changes in international factors, the changes in individual jobs at individual establishments are much greater. Many more jobs are destroyed, but many more jobs also are created, than is apparent from the change in total employment. In fact, even when changes in international factors seem to have no effect on total employment at all, these changes are linked to greater job creation and destruction.

The turnover of jobs via greater creation and destruction entails numerous costs and benefits not previously considered in estimates of the overall impact of international trade. Workers whose jobs are destroyed are not necessarily the ones who obtain the new jobs that are created, at least not right away, so unemployment usually rises. Prior calculations of internationally generated labor-adjustment costs have considered these unemployment costs, but they have overlooked others. Every job created and every job destroyed entails a cost to a firm, to a worker, or both. Sometimes the job and worker dislocation have very large, permanent effects on one or both parties. At the same time, the creation of new jobs, and the benefits of international trade, surely bring meaningful economic welfare gains in the long run. In fact, a better understanding of the effects of job turnover may very well increase estimates of gains from trade. Although we raise important new ideas and evidence for consideration, neither our analysis nor the economics profession more generally can yet provide a complete quantification and evaluation of these costs and benefits.

Our central empirical finding provides support for arguments on both sides of the Great Trade Debate. On one hand, openness to international trade and changes in international factors do expose some jobs and workers to a significantly greater risk and cost of dislocation than is often acknowledged by economic researchers and trade policy analysts. To some extent, this validates the concerns so forcefully voiced on the streets of Seattle by trade opponents. On the other hand, the adjustment of labor markets to changes in international factors involves the creation of new jobs and opportunities that improve the overall performance and efficiency of the economy.

Our analysis and results also raise a vital policy-related question: what, if anything, can and should be done about this impact of changes in international factors on labor markets? Opinion polls find relatively weak support for free trade among the public if it is not accompanied by policies to aid workers who are displaced by foreign competition.[3] Economists and trade advocates, on the other hand, tend to favor limited intervention. Regardless of whether one believes trade-related polices are needed, our work indicates that the design of such policies is even more difficult than previously thought. Widespread heterogeneity in how firms and plants are affected by trade, even within narrowly defined industries, renders simplistic policies intended to attenuate the impact of globalization ineffective or possibly even counterproductive.

From the outset, we want to be clear that we do not oppose free trade or flexible exchange rates. However, we do see a need for deeper understanding and concern about the actual economic costs of adjustment to changes in international factors born by workers and firms. All parties—whether for or against free trade—would do well to consider the effects of international factors on gross flows of jobs and workers in their ideas, views, and debates. To fully realize the economic benefits of free trade, it is necessary to face and address the political and economic realities stemming from the true magnitude of adjustment costs associated with trade-induced reallocation. This book is part of a first step being taken toward building a base of knowledge that should improve our understanding of, and policies toward, the effects of international competition on labor markets. Many more steps still need to be taken.

JOB REALLOCATION AND INTERNATIONAL TRADE

The goal of this book is to document and study the diversity of effects of international factors on employment across and within manufacturing industries in the United States. In particular, we are interested in the way fluctuations in exchange rates, changes in overseas economic activity, and the altering of trade restrictions contribute to the simultaneous creation of jobs among some firms and the destruction of jobs among other firms. This internationally generated churning in labor markets is a source of the allocative costs associated with international trade.

Our efforts extend the work of Davis, Haltiwanger, and Schuh (1996), who demonstrated that job reallocation is an intense, pervasive, and regular feature of U.S. labor markets. They found that, on average, almost one in five jobs in manufacturing is either created or destroyed each year. Reallocation is a necessary part of a dynamic economy. Through reallocation, workers move to more productive and more remunerative positions as new opportunities become available and as new jobs are created. Labor-market reallocation has a costly side as well, however. In the wake of job loss, workers could experience protracted periods of unemployment during their search for employment. Successful reemployment may require retraining, which itself demands time and resources, or moving to another part of the country. Workers may also find that they cannot match, in their new jobs, the wages they earned in their old positions.[4]

Of course, many factors contribute to the reshuffling of employment across firms. Some of these factors are specific to a relatively small set of firms or a particular narrowly defined industry; for example, there has been widespread job destruction among firms in the office product industry that specialized in typewriters and failed to make the transition to word-processing products. The effects of changes in other factors are felt more widely; for example, virtually all firms must pay higher borrowing costs when the Federal Reserve raises interest rates. Reallocation costs due to economy-wide factors are higher than more narrowly focused ones for the obvious reason that these costs are broadly felt. More subtly, the costs of reallocation may increase more than proportionally with reallocation simultaneously generated across industries by an economy-wide disturbance since, for example, it is more difficult to find a new job when many other people are also seeking work.

Job reallocation reflects the response of the labor market to a wide range of factors, including changes in the domestic macroeconomic environment, technological change, and changes in the international competitiveness of domestic firms. In this book we are concerned with job reallocation due to international factors. There are two main sets of variables that affect the international competitiveness of firms in the United States: the exchange rate of the dollar and the trade policies in place between the United States and its trading partners. In some ways, the formal analysis of the manner in which these two sets of factors affect job reallocation are quite similar, but there are also important differences between the two. For example, a change in both a tariff and the exchange rate alter the relative price of domestic and foreign goods, but these changes may be viewed as having different degrees of permanence. Therefore, we may expect that a firm's responsiveness to a change in relative prices due to exchange rate movements will differ from the responsiveness in relative prices due to a change in a tariff.

There are purely economic, as well as political, reasons for focusing on the manner in which international competition affects job reallocation. From an economic perspective, international variables in general, and the exchange rate in particular, tend to vary more than many purely domestic macroeconomic variables. In addition, international trade is a natural source of pure allocative forces, as distinct from aggregate forces, influencing labor markets. Not all firms and industries engage in international trade, so changes in real exchange rates or in trade policies directly affect only a subset of the economy. This clear differential across firms and industries contrasts with other aggregate variables, which influence all firms and industries but to varying degrees, producing transitory reallocation that is hard to distinguish from permanent reallocation due to relative price changes (e.g., a change in exchange rates).[5] For these reasons, international variables are good candidates for being important sources of reallocation.

From a political perspective, it is important to note that, rightly or wrongly, trade is viewed as an important source of job churning in the United States. For this reason, there is a tendency to associate concerns about job security with the expansion of trade. This perception threatens free trade because industry groups often advocate protectionism as a recourse to job loss. For example, in the spring of 2002, the Bush administration imposed tariffs on imported steel in response to industry claims of dumping by foreign steel producers. These tariffs harm U.S. consumers directly by raising the price of a good used as an input to production of a range of other goods. The steel tariffs also threaten to lead to a trade war. If this does occur, the most vulnerable would likely be developing countries that seek access to world markets as a way to escape the trap of poverty.

REALLOCATION ACROSS AND WITHIN INDUSTRIES

Job reallocation is a manifestation of changing fortunes across firms as some firms create new jobs while others eliminate positions. Reallocation occurs both across and within industries. Reallocation across industries arises when firms within one broad industrial category respond in a similar fashion to a change in the economic environment while firms within another industrial category respond in the opposite manner. For example, reallocation across industries would occur if all firms in the petroleum and coal products industry added jobs in response to a rise in the price of oil while all firms in the transportation industry cut jobs in response to the same event. Reallocation within industries occurs when some firms within an industry cut jobs while other firms in that industry added jobs. For example, reallocation within an industry would occur if some firms in the industry were affected by a price change or trade restriction and other firms in the same industry were not.

In this book we will show that reallocation in response to changes in the international environment occurs both across and within industries. At the broadest level, total employment in manufacturing responds in a significant way to changes in the exchange rate. This response represents across-industry job reallocation as a stronger real exchange rate contributes to a decrease in manufacturing employment. But this overall movement in manufacturing employment masks a wide variety of responses across manufacturing industries that generates within-industry reallocation. Indeed, a central theme of this book is that the effects of international competition vary across industries and even among firms within seemingly narrow industrial categories. This diversity leads to simultaneous job creation and job destruction within industrial categories. In light of this, we show that it is difficult to offer simple conclusions like, "Trade is good for the machinery industry but hurts the apparel industry." Instead, we offer evidence of a more nuanced picture in which the effects of international trade vary widely. This has some important policy implications. For example, policy responses that attempt to ameliorate the costs of reallocation may be better targeted toward particular workers than toward broad classes of industries, as would occur with tariff protection, since, within industries, the experience of firms may differ widely.

We are able to provide this more nuanced picture of the effects of international factors on reallocation partly through the use of data on gross job flows. Gross job flows in a particular industry consist of the total number of employment positions gained (job creation) and the total number of employment positions lost (job destruction) by all establishments within that industry. A common measure of labor-market churning, called job reallocation, is the sum of job creation and job destruction.

The data presented in this book offer a picture in which simultaneous job creation and job destruction, even in narrowly defined industries, characterizes labor markets for manufacturing industries. Thus, it is important to consider gross job flows and reallocation data rather than just net changes in employment (which represent the difference between job creation and job destruction) for particular industries to gauge more accurately the size of labor-market adjustment. For example, consider a particular net change in employment of, say, a decrease in 100,000 jobs. This can reflect a reallocation of 100,000 jobs if this net change arises solely through job destruction. Alternatively, it can reflect a reallocation of two million positions if 950,000 jobs are created while 1,050,000 jobs are destroyed. Given a cost to reallocation, we would expect the welfare consequences of these two scenarios to differ.

Simultaneous job creation and job destruction within a narrowly defined industry reflects heterogeneity among firms in that industry. One possible source of heterogeneity is structural differences among firms that cause them to react differently to a common change in the economic environment. For example, the overall effect of an exchange rate appreciation on the fortunes of a firm depends upon the international exposure of that firm, which depends on the extent to which that firm exports its products, the extent to which it uses imported goods to manufacture its own products, and the extent to which its products compete with imports. Firms within a narrowly defined industry may exhibit a wide range of international exposure along these three dimensions, making them respond differently to a given change in the exchange rate. This can give rise to simultaneous job creation and job destruction. In addition, simultaneous creation and destruction may reflect spillover effects whereby one firm's increased demand for labor affects the ability of another firm to hire workers at the going wage.

In this book we document the differences across narrowly defined industries in the extent of exposure to international competition. We show that there has been a general increase in exposure to international competition among manufacturing industries since the 1960s. There has also been an increasing divergence in the range of exposure to international competition over this period. We also show that the responsiveness of a particular industry to movements in the exchange rate is linked to the level of its international exposure. Thus, we are able to provide a more complete understanding of the manner in which international factors affect the labor market.

OVERVIEW AND SUMMARY OF RESULTS

The foregoing introduction has raised some of the main themes of our book: the costs and benefits of labor-market reallocation, the contribution of changes in the international environment to reallocation both across and within manufacturing industries in the United States, differences in international exposure even among firms classified in the same narrow industrial category, and the divergence in responses to international factors across manufacturing industries. Each of these themes is taken up and more fully developed in this book. Here we outline our presentation.

Chapter 2 offers some initial evidence on the varying importance of international factors across U.S. manufacturing. The statistics presented in this chapter support the commonly held view that, at least for manufacturing, the last few decades have been marked by increasing openness with respect to international competition. But, more to the point for our study, we also show that there has been a steady increase in the divergence of exposure to international competition over this period. Very little of the variance in international exposure across narrowly defined industries is explained by membership in broader industrial categories. This diversity in openness is one source of the divergent responses to international factors across manufacturing. Another source of the divergent response to international factors is that bilateral trade patterns vary across industries, which gives rise to differences in the relevant exchange rates across industries. The industry-specific exchange rates presented in Chapter 2 are used later in the book in our empirical analysis.

The heterogeneity of responses to international factors gives rise to differences in labor-market dynamics, not only across industries, but within narrowly defined industries as well. As mentioned above, the labor market in U.S. manufacturing industries is characterized by significant churning. This churning can be understood using the concepts of job creation and job destruction, which are introduced in Chapter 3. This chapter also presents some initial statistics on job reallocation in U.S. manufacturing industries, including the responsiveness of overall manufacturing job creation and job destruction to business cycle factors and to international factors. We also show that membership in a particular broad industry group explains little of the behavior of job creation and job destruction for firms in the most narrowly defined industrial categories.

Our use of gross job creation and destruction data represents the way in which the analysis in this book advances our understanding of the impact of international competition on U.S. labor markets. There is, however, an existing literature on the effects of international factors on employment that uses data on changes in net employment. We survey this literature in Chapter 4, putting our contributions in the proper context and linking our work to other research on gross job and worker flows. In addition, we highlight the implications of gross flows for the costs of labor adjustment to international (and other) factors. In particular, we raise the question of whether adjustment costs associated with gross flows might be considerably larger than those associated with net employment growth. If so, the net welfare gains from trade might be considerably smaller than previously thought.

Chapter 5 presents an economic model that shows the relationships between openness, exchange rates, tariffs, and job creation and destruction. This model shows how a change in the value of the exchange rate can give rise to simultaneous job creation and job destruction within one industry. The source of this job churning is differences in openness across firms combined with interactions among firms in an industry. This model provides a framework for our empirical analysis of the effects of the real exchange rate on job creation and job destruction.

In Chapter 6 we examine the extent to which movements in the real exchange rate contributed to job destruction and job creation over the entire period since the end of the Bretton Woods fixed-exchange-rate era in 1973 until the mid 1990s. In this chapter, we explore the possibility that the impact of a given change in the exchange rate on job flows depends upon whether that change is viewed as permanent or temporary. We find that this distinction is quite important. Changes in the trend component of real exchange rates have a significant allocative effect on labor markets, moving job creation and destruction in the same direction, but essentially no effect on net employment growth. If our estimated trends represent the permanent components of industry exchange rates, this result suggests that permanent exchange rate changes influence job reallocation only. In contrast, changes in the cyclical component of the exchange rate have a significant effect on net employment growth, but only through job destruction and not on job creation (hence no effect on reallocation other than the reduction in net employment). If our estimated cyclical components represent the transitory components of industry exchange rates, this result suggests that transitory exchange rate changes merely lower employment without providing an offsetting benefit through new jobs. Furthermore, the magnitude of these effects is scaled by the openness of industries. The exchange rate effects are larger in industries that are more open to international trade. In sum, our quantitative estimates indicate that movements in real exchange rates are an important determinant of labor market fluctuations.

In Chapter 7 we offer a more detailed view of the heterogeneous effects of international competition by studying the North American Free Trade Agreement (NAFTA). We focus on the response of three industries—the textile and apparel industry, the chemical and allied products industry, and the automobile industry—to the changes in trade restrictions enacted in NAFTA. In the early 1990s, NAFTA was a source of intense political debate. Some of the issues raised in that debate are sure to resurface with the reemergence of protectionist pressures at the beginning of this decade. And beyond its topical interest, the discussion in Chapter 7 complements the statistical analysis in Chapter 6 by providing case studies of the effects of a changing environment of international competition on labor markets in manufacturing industries. In particular, the case studies in Chapter 7 demonstrate that changes in trade restrictions or agreements, like real exchange rates, can generate significant reallocation of trade and possibly employment within seemingly narrow industries, and that these effects may not appear at the industry level. This result underscores the potential effects of pervasive heterogeneity in trade activity and trading partners, and hence the diverse responses to international competition that must be taken into account when examining the effects on labor markets.

These diverse responses to international competition mean that international competition both offers new opportunities and presents challenges associated with dislocations and downsizing. Free trade offers important sources of growth. The reallocation that is often required for this growth to be realized, however, can come at a significant cost to individuals whose jobs are lost. We need to be concerned about these costs both for reasons of equity and because political support for free trade is predicated on the provision of an adequate safety net. In Chapter 8 we discuss policies that have been used to mitigate the adjustment costs of trade, as well as newly proposed policies. In that chapter, we discuss the implications for these policies of the results presented in this book. For example, economists typically argue that tariffs subsidize inefficient industries and represent an expensive way to preserve jobs. Our demonstration of the diversity of responses to international competition even within narrowly defined industries suggests that the costs of tariffs are even higher than typically thought because this blunt instrument also subsidizes firms that would survive without assistance. A more efficient program would target displaced workers, but the Trade Adjustment Assistance program currently in place is seen as ineffectual. We discuss some newly proposed policies and mention how our analysis contributes to our understanding of their likely impact.

The policy discussion in Chapter 8 points towards an agenda for research on the important issue of the adjustment costs of trade. In the ninth and final chapter of this book, we offer some concrete proposals for the establishment of new data sets. These data would enable researchers to address some of the issues that cannot be fully analyzed now, even with the data employed in this book.

Notes

1. See, for example, Golub (1999).
2. A good example of an analysis of international trade and gross worker flows is Kletzer (2001), a complementary volume to this book.
3. The Program on International Policy Attitudes found that only 18 percent of the respondents to a survey in October 1999 favored free trade if it was not accompanied by programs to help workers who lose their jobs due to international competition. See <www.americans-world.org/digest/global_issues/intertrade/summary.cfm>.
4. This issue is addressed by Jacobson, LaLonde, and Sullivan (1993a,b)
5. The fact that not all firms and industries that engage in trade do so to the same degree generates identification problems that are similar to the differential responses to aggregate factors.

2
Openness

Growth and Diversity

A central theme in economics concerns the gains from voluntary exchange. An early example of this is David Ricardo's demonstration of the gains from international trade and his development of the concept of comparative advantage in the early nineteenth century.[1] Ricardo showed that the welfare of citizens of a country improves when they are allowed to freely trade with citizens of other countries who have different relative abilities to produce goods and services. Strikingly, this result holds even if the citizens of the other country have an absolute advantage whereby they can produce *all* goods and services more efficiently.

Notwithstanding the long and time-honored position of this argument in economic theory, the alternative view of trade as a competition in which some countries "win" while others "lose" has always had its adherents. The view of trade as competition enjoyed a resurgence in the United States in the early 1990s, after a decade in which the U.S. trade balance reached historic deficits and the U.S. real exchange rate underwent unprecedented swings in value. For example, Lester Thurow's (1992) book that described an economic war among the world players surviving the cold war period was on the *New York Times'* bestseller list for more than six months.[2]

Although most economists do not subscribe to the view of trade as competition, there is widespread recognition that, within countries, an increase in international trade will alter the economic landscape in ways that may benefit some groups of individuals while putting others at a relative disadvantage. Ricardo himself pointed this out, showing the differential effects on workers and landowners of opening up to trade. Of course, a change in any important macroeconomic factor will lead to the relative advance of some groups and the relative decline of others, but international trade seems to hold a special place of prominence in the popular imagination as a source of labor-market reallocation and dislocation, if not of opportunity for workers.

Popular focus on international factors as a source of economic turbulence reflects, in part, the behavior of dollar exchange rates and U.S. trade balances over the past quarter century. Exchange rates between the dollar and other major currencies have been marked by both wide swings in value and notable short-run fluctuations since the breakdown of the Bretton Woods fixed exchange rate system in 1973. Over this same period, the current account of the United States, a broad measure of its net international sales of goods and services, has shifted from small surpluses in the early 1980s to record deficits in the latter part of that decade, to near balance in the early 1990s and then again to large deficits a few years later. At the beginning of the twenty-first century, the U.S. trade deficit was at its highest level, both in absolute terms and as a percentage of national income, since the end of World War II.

These dramatic movements in the value of the dollar and in the external balances of the United States have prompted research into the possible links between international developments and the performance of the labor market in the United States. In fact, this book reflects our contribution toward better understanding of these links. In this chapter, we begin our exploration of this topic with a first look at some relevant data. We begin by discussing the evolution of openness to international trade among U.S. manufacturing industries. We then discuss the evolving external environment facing those industries, with a special focus on the often turbulent behavior of dollar exchange rates.

A common theme in our discussion of openness and the exchange rate is the diversity of experience, even across narrowly defined industries. We will show that the interaction of individual industries with the world economy ranges widely, both in terms of overall interaction and in terms of the specific trade partners relevant for a particular industry. To demonstrate this type of interaction, we must use an industrial classification system. Appendix A provides a brief overview of the Standard Industrial Classification (SIC) system for grouping industries, a system we refer to throughout this book. Readers unfamiliar with this system may want to refer to the appendix before moving on to the rest of this chapter.

OPENNESS OVER TIME AND ACROSS INDUSTRIES

It has been widely noted that the U.S. economy has become more open to international trade over time. But, as with many popular conceptions, the details behind this fact are both less well known and provide a more nuanced picture. In this section we confirm the presence of an overall growth in openness in manufacturing, but we also demonstrate that the change in openness over time varies widely across industries, with openness increasing among some industries while other industries remain largely closed.

"Openness" can be defined in a variety of ways, and no single measure can reflect all relevant dimensions by which an industry interacts with consumers, suppliers, and potential competitors from the rest of the world. For example, Campa and Goldberg (1997) developed a measure of openness of disaggregated manufacturing industries (e.g., food and kindred products or primary metal products) that accounts for exports, imports of competing products, and imports of inputs. They found that all three of these measures, as well as a measure of net external orientation (representing the difference between the industry export share and the imported input share), increased from the early 1970s to the mid 1990s for the United States, Canada, and the United Kingdom. This overall pattern of increasing external orientation is not evident among Japanese manufacturing industries. As with the other three countries, export shares of manufacturing industries grew in Japan. However, in contrast to the United States, Canada, and the United Kingdom, imported input shares declined over time for Japanese manufacturing industries, and the share of imports in the Japanese consumption of imported manufactured goods largely remained steady.

As with many economic variables, there is a trade-off here between having a measure that is comprehensive, at least along one dimension, and one that is feasible to construct. Campa and Goldberg were able to disaggregate manufacturing industries into about 20 categories (for U.S. data, this represents a two-digit SIC disaggregation). But, as discussed in more detail later in this chapter, we find a great deal of heterogeneity, even within industries at this level of disaggregation, with respect to openness.[3] Therefore, to study industries at a more disaggregated level, we utilize a less comprehensive measure of openness, but one that enables us to examine the diversity across more narrowly defined industries, those at the four-digit SIC level. Our measure of industry openness is the ratio

$$\frac{\text{Exports} + \text{Imports}}{\text{Domestic sales} + \text{Exports} + \text{Imports}}$$

which measures the proportion of an industry's total activity devoted to international trade. We are able to construct this indicator of openness for almost 450 four-digit SIC industries over the period 1958 to 1994.[4]

Figure 2.1 demonstrates the general increase in openness over time of U.S. manufacturing industries as well as the increasingly divergent degree of openness among four-digit SIC industries. This figure shows the tenth percentile value, lower quartile value, median value, upper quartile value, and ninetieth percentile value of openness for four-digit industries for each year between 1958 and 1994. This figure confirms

Figure 2.1 Distributions of Openness across Industries (1958–1994)

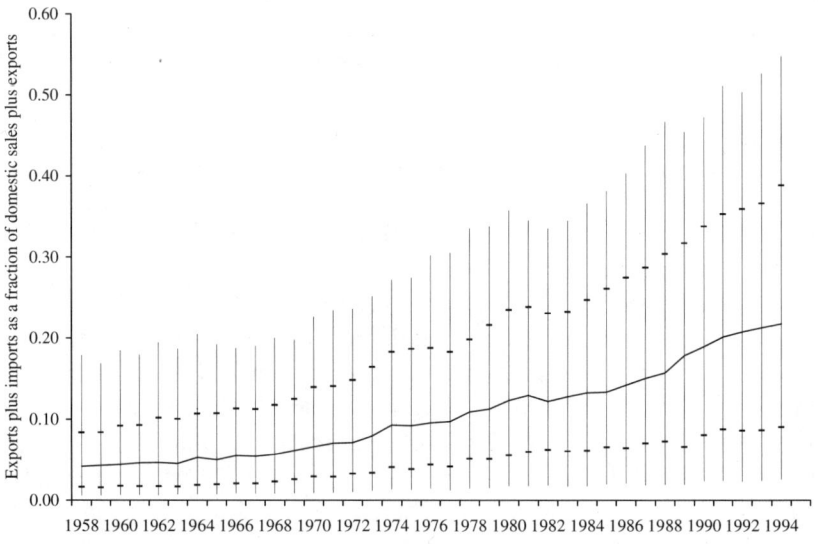

NOTE: Figure displays the time series of percentiles from the annual cross-section distributions of openness over four-digit SIC industries.
SOURCE: Feenstra (1996, 1997).

the upward trend in overall openness over time, with the median value of openness increasing from 4 percent in 1958 to 22 percent in 1994. This growth in the median value of openness proceeded somewhat unevenly over the sample, with relatively little change from the late 1950s until the end of the 1960s when the average annual change in the median value of openness was 3.5 percent. The pace of the growth of openness quickened after 1972. Between 1972 and 1987 the median value of openness grew at an average annual rate of 5.0 percent. This growth has accelerated slightly in recent years, with an annual average growth rate of the median value of openness of 5.25 percent in the years between 1987 and 1994.

Perhaps the most striking aspect of Figure 2.1, however, is not the growth in the median value of openness over time but the increasingly divergent international exposure of four-digit industries. While there are industries throughout the period with essentially no direct international exposure, the value of our openness measure defining the upper quartile of industries almost quadrupled between 1958, when the value was just under 10 percent, and 1994, when its value was 39 percent. Likewise, openness increased for the 90th percentile from 18 to 55 percent over the period. The magnitude of the increase in openness at the top end of the distribution was not matched by the increase among the industries at the lower end. The value of openness at the 25th percentile increased from 2 percent in 1958 to 9 percent in 1994 while its value at the 10th percentile increased from 1 percent to 3 percent over the same time period. As a consequence, the range of openness for the mid 50th percentile increased from 8 percentage points in 1958 to 30 percentage points in 1994 and the range for the mid 80th percentile increased from 17 percentage points in 1958 to 52 percentage points in 1994.

The data presented in Figure 2.1 reveal the range of openness but not the composition of industries constituting high, medium, or low values of openness. One may expect similar levels of openness among industries producing common products. In fact, this is not the case. We regress the values of openness for four-digit industries on three different sets of dummy variables representing more aggregated industry categories: the broad classification of durable/nondurable industries, the larger set of 20 two-digit SIC industry indicators, and the set of 143 three-digit SIC categories. In each case, the measure of the overall fit of the regression (the adjusted R-squared) reflects the extent of openness explained by industry categories. The increase in the value of the overall fit of the regression (the change in the value of the adjusted R-squared) from one regression to another shows the marginal difference explained by a more disaggregated set of industry indicators.

The results from each of these three regressions, using the measure of openness in 1990 for four-digit industries, are presented in Table 2.1. This table shows that there is virtually no difference on average between the openness of durable and nondurable manufacturing industries, with an adjusted R-squared of only 0.02 in a regression using only one dummy variable to distinguish between nondurable and durable manufacturing industries. An interpretation of this result is that only 2 percent of the variation in openness across the 450 four-digit industries is explained by that industry being in either the durable or the nondurable group. The extent to which the variation in openness across four-digit industries is explained by membership in a particular two-digit SIC industry is also relatively small since the adjusted R-squared for a regression using 19 dummy variables to control for the 20 two-digit SIC industries is 0.27. Regressing openness on three-digit industry dummy variables raises the adjusted R-squared to 0.44, well above its value when using two-digit industry dummies but still below one-half.

These results indicate a great deal of heterogeneity in the degree of openness which is largely unrelated to differences among two-digit or even three-digit industry groupings. This suggests that there are likely to be substantial differences in the extent to which real exchange rate movements affect job creation and destruction across industries that constitute a particular two-digit or even three-digit industry.

Increasing heterogeneity over time, as depicted in Figure 2.1, may reflect the fact that the most open industries in 1958 became even more

Table 2.1 Regression of 1990 Openness on Industry Indicator Variables (442 observations)

	Industry indicators		
	Durability	2-digit	3-digit
No. of Variables	1	19	142
$\overline{R}^2$	0.02	0.27	0.44

SOURCE: See Data Sources 2 and 3 in Appendix C.

open over time while the most closed industries at the beginning of the period remained closed. Alternatively, the data shown in Figure 2.1 could also be consistent with significant churning whereby industries that were relatively closed early in the sample period may have become more open over time while other industries experienced little change in openness or even a decline in openness over time. We present a transition matrix in Table 2.2 to address the question of the stability of the ranking of industries by openness over time.

Table 2.2 presents the percentage distribution for quintiles with respect to openness in 1973 of the 442 four-digit SIC industries against the respective percentage distributions for 1993 (the range of years for which we have job flows data for our regression analysis). This table demonstrates that there has been relatively little reshuffling in the ranking of industries' degrees of openness. Fifty-two percent of the four-digit industries stayed in the same openness quintile between 1973 and 1993 and 88 percent either stayed in the same quintile or moved to an adjoining quintile.[5] Note, however, that the cutoff values of openness for each quintile more than doubled during this time period, confirming the overall increase in openness we first noted with reference to Figure 2.1.

These statistics offer an interesting depiction of the growth and heterogeneity of openness in U.S. manufacturing industries. The average degree of openness has increased enormously in recent decades, a result that also is apparent from the work of Campa and Goldberg

Table 2.2 Transitions of Four-Digit Industries between Openness Quintiles

	1993 quintile (range of openness)					
	1	2	3	4	5	
1973 quintile	(0.0–0.07)	(0.07–0.16)	(0.16–0.26)	(0.26–0.40)	(0.40–1.0)	Total
1 (0.00–0.03)	78	17	3	1	1	100
2 (0.03–0.06)	18	40	24	14	5	100
3 (0.06–0.12)	6	26	40	20	8	100
4 (0.12–0.19)	0	10	24	40	26	100
5 (0.19–1.00)	0	6	9	25	60	100

NOTE: The table shows the percentage distribution of industries in each 1973 quintile across 1993 quintiles.
SOURCE: See Data Sources 2 and 3 in Appendix C.

(1997) discussed above. There has been a tendency for all industries to become more open over time, but the biggest increase in openness has been in the industries which were initially most open. This has resulted in an increasingly large degree of heterogeneity in openness to trade across four-digit SIC manufacturing industries. Some four-digit SIC industries have become strongly integrated into the global economy, but others remained largely isolated from international competition. Very little of this heterogeneity is associated with differences between broad industry groups. Even within three-digit SIC industries, there is a large variance in the importance of international trade.

One might suspect that increasing, and increasingly divergent, openness across manufacturing industries has made these industries more sensitive to international factors over time. Perhaps the key international variable that affects manufacturing industries in the United States is the real exchange rate. We next turn to an examination of its behavior over the past quarter century.

THE VOLATILITY OF DOLLAR EXCHANGE RATES

The prices of German, British, Korean, Japanese, or Mexican goods are translated into dollars through euro (formerly deutsche mark), pound, won, yen, or peso exchange rates, respectively. These exchange rates, however, also figure in the determination of the returns of assets denominated in these respective currencies. The volume of trade in assets, comprising the *capital account* of nations, swamps the volume of trade in goods and services, which constitutes the *current account* of nations.[6] For example, the estimated volume of trade in the largest 43 foreign exchange markets is estimated to be $1.5 trillion per day. This is about 60 times the daily value of global trade in goods and services.[7]

Given the relative size of these flows, it is not surprising that dollar exchange rates behave more like the price of an asset than the price of a good. The lexicon used to describe exchange rates includes terms such as overshooting, misalignment, and volatility, terms that are more frequently associated with the prices of other assets, like stocks or bonds, rather than with the price of goods or services. Figure 2.2 illustrates this point by graphing the multilateral trade-weighted value of the real dollar exchange rate index since the breakdown of the fixed-exchange-rate Bretton Woods system in March 1973.[8] The figure includes two multilateral real exchange rates: the widely used but discontinued G-10 rate and the new Federal Reserve broad index. An increase in these exchange rates represents an appreciation of the dollar relative to the foreign currencies. This figure illustrates both the wide swings in the value of the dollar, lasting for five years or more, as well as the month-to-month volatility of the exchange rate.

Figure 2.2 illustrates that, in trade-weighted terms, the dollar ended the century at about the same level at which it began the floating rate period in 1973. But the dollar was subject to wide swings in value during the intervening 27 years. Most noteworthy in this respect is the large run-up in the value of the dollar from late 1978 to early 1985. During this period, the trade-weighted value of the dollar rose by more

Figure 2.2 Real Trade-Weighted Exchange Value of the U.S. Dollar (January 1973–October 2002)

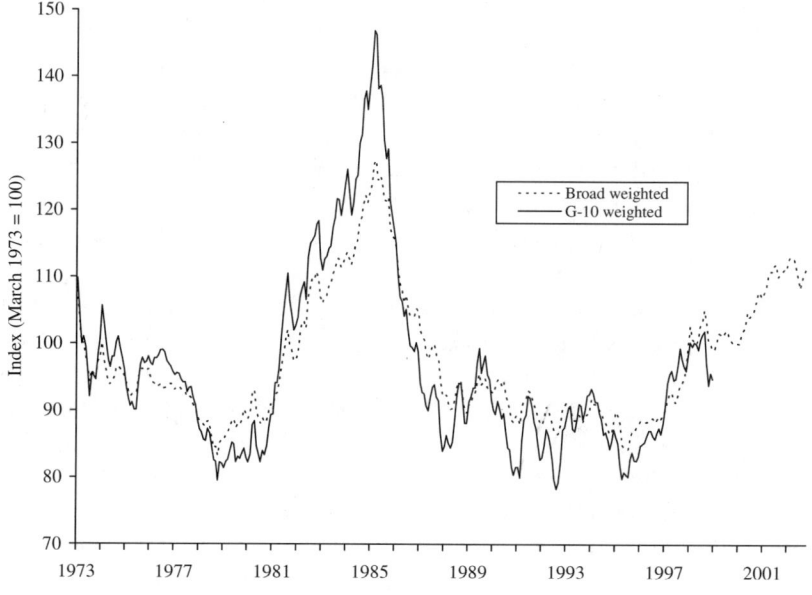

SOURCE: Federal Reserve Board.

than 50 percent. The dollar then reversed course in early 1985, decreasing in value by almost 30 percent between mid 1985 and early 1987. While the dollar more or less lost value steadily for three years after 1975, and more or less gained value steadily in the period between the summer of 1995 and early 2002, the period from 1978 to 1987 stands out as the most dramatic period change for the dollar exchange rate in the post–Bretton Woods era.

Economists' explanation of the movement of the dollar during this period reflects the view that currency values broadly respond to macroeconomic events that influence the flow of capital across national borders. For example, the appreciation of the dollar in the first half of the 1980s is typically seen as a response to the increase in interest rates in the United States during that period, initially due to tight, disinflationary monetary policy and then continuing with the expansion of the federal budget deficit after 1982. Government policy can also have an influence on exchange rates. The depreciation of the dollar, beginning in early 1985 and continuing for the next two years, came in the wake of government intervention in the foreign exchange market. Notable here was the September 1985 Plaza Accord in which the finance ministers and central bank officials of the G-7 (consisting of the seven largest industrial economies) voiced their concern with the strong dollar and undertook intervention in the foreign exchange market to influence currency values.[9] Movements in exchange rates, like movements in the prices of other assets, sometimes defy explanation. For example, the steep run-up in the value of the dollar at the end of 1984 and the rapid decline in the value of the dollar during the spring of 1995 do not easily lend themselves to explanations based upon underlying economic fundamentals or government policies.

Whatever their cause, exchange rate movements alter the price of goods and services traded across national boundaries. Exports sold by American firms become more expensive when the dollar strengthens while imports become cheaper, all else equal. This change in the relative price contributes to a deterioration in the trade balance of the United States, but the effect of currency movements on imports and exports may occur only slowly over the course of a year or more since contracts for foreign trade are signed well before delivery takes place. Furthermore, firms may adjust their domestic currency prices to soften the effect of currency movements on the prices of their goods and services sold abroad.[10]

The relationship between a particular change in the exchange rate and the short-run response of a firm is also complicated by the uncertainty facing managers, who must decide whether the most recent currency movement is part of a long-run trend or merely a short-lived blip. For example, managers may be more reluctant to raise prices and surrender market share in the face of a depreciation perceived as temporary as compared to one perceived as permanent when they incur fixed costs in the establishment of distribution or marketing networks.[11] In our empirical analysis in Chapter 6, we attempt to address this issue by decomposing exchange rate movements in a way that captures these considerations.

While short-run decisions may mitigate the contemporaneous response of trade to exchange rates, the time path of the U.S. current account in Figure 2.3 nevertheless presents a broad correlation between

Figure 2.3 Balance on the U.S. Current Account (Q1:1973–Q2:2002)

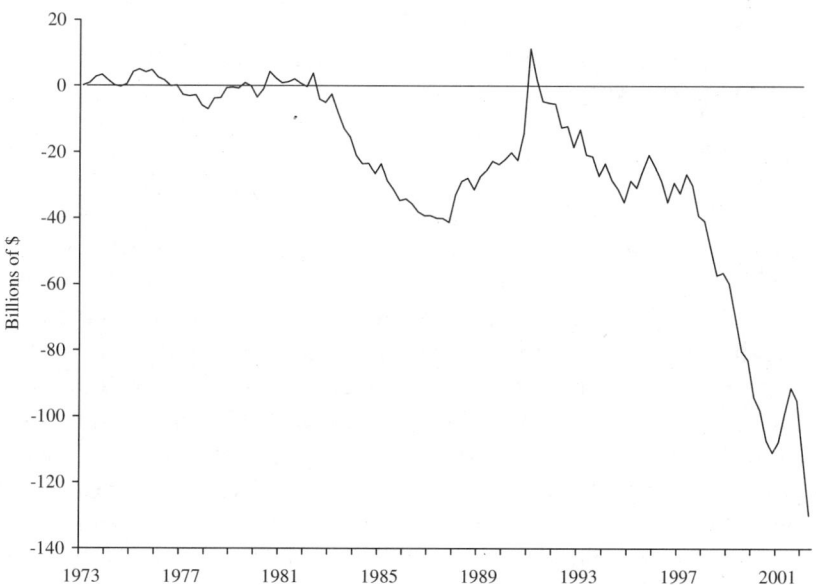

SOURCE: Bureau of Economic Analysis.

dollar movements and the U.S. current account. The appreciation of the dollar in the first half of the 1980s accompanied the increasing current account deficit at that time. The subsequent dollar depreciation contributed to the reversal of this deterioration and to the eventual, albeit short-lived, current account surplus in the early 1990s. The recent renewed increase in the current account deficit is largely a reflection of the differential in the growth of income between the United States and its major trading partners in the 1990s. The ongoing U.S. expansion has fueled a demand for imports while the relatively slower growth among many trading partners has not led to a commensurate surge in U.S. exports. The post-1995 strength of the dollar has also contributed to the increasing trade deficit of the United States.[12]

While it is well known that particular bilateral dollar exchange rates, as well as the multilaterally weighted value of the dollar, have exhibited dramatic shifts in value over the floating exchange rate period, the differences across industries in the relevant trade-weighted values of the dollar are less well known. In the next section, we turn to this issue.

THE DIVERSITY OF BEHAVIOR OF INDUSTRY-SPECIFIC EXCHANGE RATES

As described in the previous section, multilateral exchange rates are weighted averages of many bilateral exchange rates, with the weights reflecting the volume of bilateral trade between each country and the United States. The multilateral exchange rates plotted in Figure 2.2, for example, are weighted averages of the bilateral exchange rates between the U.S. dollar and the currencies of the United States' major trading partners. The G-10 index, which was readily available and common in older studies of exchange rates and labor markets, uses trade weights for the 10 largest U.S. trading partners based on trading patterns between 1972 and 1976.[13] The Federal Reserve's broad index includes many more U.S. trading partners and updates trade share weights more frequently.[14] Although the two measures generally move together over time, the magnitude of their difference varies significantly over time. This fact suggests that the choice of trading partners included in a multilateral exchange rate may be a quantitatively important matter.

This last point is especially relevant for understanding the effects of exchange rates on industry-level trade. In any particular industry, the most appropriate weights to use in constructing a multilateral index would reflect trading patterns for the goods produced by that industry rather than trading patterns for all goods and services, as in the common aggregate multilateral exchange rates. For example, the yen-dollar bilateral exchange rate would be given greater weight in constructing a multilateral exchange rate appropriate for the automobile industry than it would in a general economy-wide index or in an industry that traded very little with Japan. Furthermore, industries vary widely in the composition of countries with which they trade.

Following this idea, we have constructed industry-specific real exchange rates. For each detailed (four-digit SIC) manufacturing industry, we constructed a multilateral exchange rate series with the weights on the bilateral exchange rates based on trading patterns for the industry's output over a lagged two-year period.[15] In calculating the exchange rates, we used approximately 60 countries, a much broader range than those included in the G-10 index, reflecting the increased importance of trade with newly industrialized and developing countries. For any particular industry, however, the number of exchange rates included in the industry-specific multilateral exchange rate is much smaller because most industries only trade significantly with a relatively small number of countries. Because of trade-weight updating and the large number of countries included, our industry-specific multilateral exchange rates are similar in spirit to the Federal Reserve economy-wide multilateral exchange rate.

The distributions of industry-specific real exchange rates is shown in Figure 2.4. All of the exchange rates are indexed such that they equal 100 in 1973. For any given year, the 10th, 25th, 50th, 75th, and 90th percentiles of the distribution of the industry-specific real exchange rates are shown. This figure demonstrates that there is considerable heterogeneity across industries in the time path of the relevant real exchange rate.[16] Each industry-specific real exchange rate is a multilateral index, with weights on the component bilateral exchange rates reflecting the relative importance of trade with other countries in that industry's output. Industry-specific exchange rates will follow dif-

Figure 2.4 Distributions of Real Exchange Rates across Industries (1973–1993)

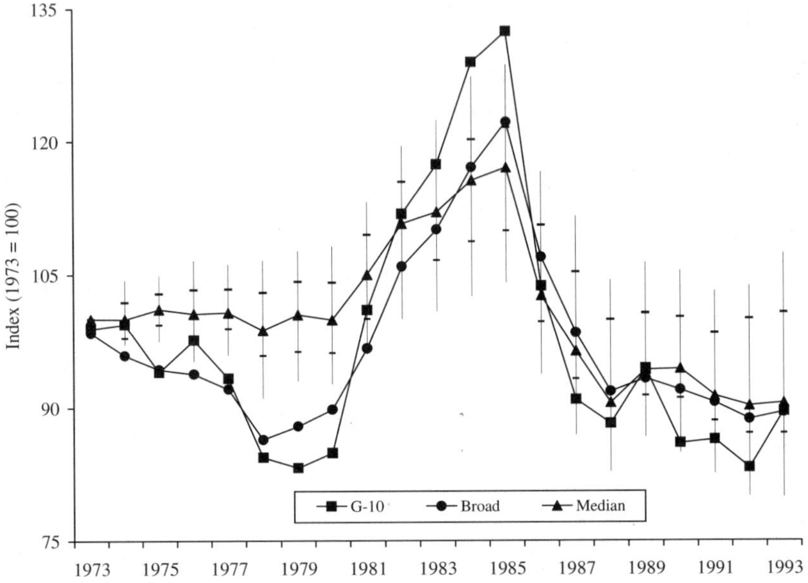

NOTE: Figure displays the time series of percentiles from the annual cross-section distributions of real exchange rates over four-digit SIC industries.
SOURCE: See Appendix C, Data Sources.

ferent patterns over time because either the combination of bilateral exchange rates and/or the trading partner weights differ across industries.

The two multilateral exchange rates in Figure 2.2 also are shown in Figure 2.4. It is striking that even the swings in the Federal Reserve's broad index are more pronounced than the swings in most of the industry-specific real exchange rates; the G-10 fluctuations are greater still. Both the Federal Reserve broad and G-10 exchange rates show the dollar depreciating during the 1970s, sharply appreciating in the early 1980s, and then suddenly depreciating in the mid-to-late 1980s. In contrast, the median of the industry-specific exchange rates stays roughly constant in the 1970s, and then shows a dollar appreciation that is considerably smaller than that experienced by the two economy-wide indexes.

The differences between the G-10 real exchange rate and the others is explained primarily by two factors: the G-10 index uses a narrower range of bilateral exchange rates, and the trade weights used in constructing the G-10 index were fixed over time. However, the differences between the Federal Reserve broad multilateral exchange rate and the industry multilateral exchange rates are more important to decipher. The differences may be explained partly by the fact that data limitations prevent us from using the exchange rates from literally every country with which every industry traded. Nevertheless, given the broad range of exchange rates and their movements, it appears that the economy-wide multilateral exchange rate may not provide an adequate representation of exchange rate movements for all industries at all times.

This last point is made more clearly by Figure 2.5, which is similar to Figure 2.4 except that it shows the distributions of the growth rates

Figure 2.5 Distributions of Real Exchange Rate Growth Rates across Industries (1974–1993)

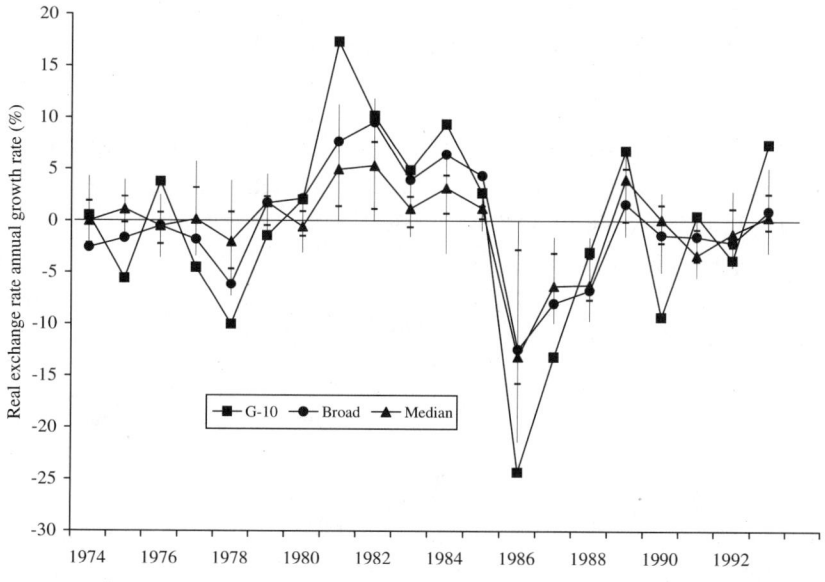

SOURCE: See Appendix C, Data Sources.

of the industry-specific real exchange rates instead of their levels. This figure makes it evident that, in addition to being more volatile than the industry-level exchange rates, the economy-wide exchange rates cannot reflect the heterogeneity in the direction of change of the exchange rate. Specifically, in many years, some industry-specific real exchange rates appreciate at the same time that others depreciate. This fact highlights the importance of heterogeneity across industries in the importance of different trading partners. It also underscores the importance of using industry-specific real exchange rates because our theoretical model in Chapter 5 demonstrates that gross job flows are linked to the growth of the exchange rate rather than to its level.

CONCLUSION

This chapter has provided a context for the analysis that follows. The dramatic swings in the value of the dollar, and the corresponding movements in the U.S. trade account, make international factors one of the usual suspects in most accounts of the fate of workers in the manufacturing sectors of the United States. The research surveyed here suggests that this perception may be warranted, but the focus of this research is, for the most part, on manufacturing broadly or on a subset of industries within manufacturing. In the next chapter we begin our analysis by showing that, even within seemingly narrow industries, there is a range of responses by firms to a changing international environment. This points to a more nuanced effect of international factors on labor markets in the United States.

Notes

1. See Ricardo (1963). This book was first published in 1817.
2. Irwin (1996) provides a history of the debate over free trade since the time of Ricardo.
3. We also find a great deal of heterogeneity across two-digit industries with respect to job flows, a point we discuss in Chapter 3.
4. Our data on exports and imports comes from Feenstra (1996, 1997), who updated data from Abowd (1990). The use of export share and import share alone, without information on the share of intermediate imported goods, while theoretically

ignoring a potentially important channel, may not represent much loss of information. Campa and Goldberg found a high correlation between their three measures of external exposure and, because of this, use only two, rather than all three, measures of openness in subsequent research in which they use openness in wage and employment regressions (see Campa and Goldberg 2001).
5. These percentages are calculated from Table 2.2 as follows. The percentage staying in the same quintile is the average of diagonal entries. The percentage staying the same or adjacent quintiles is obtained by first summing the same and adjacent quintiles in each row, then averaging over these row sums.
6. The current account consists of exports and imports of goods and services (also known as the trade account), payments to factors of production in the form of investment income, and net unilateral transfers. To give some idea of the relative size of these magnitudes, the 2002 *Economic Report of the President* 2002 reports, in Table B-103 (p. 398) that, in 2000, exports were $772 billion, imports were $1,224 billion, receipts on assets abroad were $353 billion, payments on foreign assets in the United States were $368 billion, and net unilateral transfers were $54 billion.
7. The figure for the volume of capital flows is from the Bank for International Settlements' triennial survey, published in October 1998, and it is cited in the February 1999 *Economic Report of the President 1999*, p. 224.
8. The figure depicts a weighted average of bilateral dollar real exchange rates calculated by the Federal Reserve Board. The weights reflect the amount of bilateral trade between each country and the United States. The real exchange rate is the product of the nominal exchange rate and the relative prices of baskets of goods and services in the United States and its trading partners. For example, the real exchange rate between the United States and Japan is the product of the yen/dollar exchange rate and the ratio of the Producer Price Indices of the United States and Japan. A graph of the multilateral trade-weighted nominal exchange rate index would be virtually the same as Figure 2.2 since the correlation between the nominal dollar exchange rate and the real dollar exchange rate for industrial countries is on the order of 0.9 or greater. But, as discussed below, trade-weighted exchange rates for particular U.S. manufacturing industries, where the weights reflect the amount of bilateral exports and imports for those industries, can differ significantly from the overall trade-weighted exchange rate for the United States.
9. It is not at all clear, however, that the dollar's path would have been markedly different in the absence of government intervention. The efficacy of governments' efforts to manage exchange rates is the subject of a great deal of research. Economists are especially interested in the role of *sterilized intervention* whereby governments attempt to alter currency values without adjusting monetary policy. Research tends to suggest that sterilized intervention does not have a systematic effect on exchange rates. For a good overview of these issues, see Dominguez and Frankel (1993).
10. There is a wide literature on this exchange-rate pass-through effect. For an early and influential article, see Knetter (1989).

11. See, for example, Froot and Klemperer (1989).
12. Of course, both the exchange rate and the trade account are jointly determined and reflect the influence of other, underlying, macroeconomic factors. Still, for particular U.S. manufacturing industries, an appreciation of the dollar will, all else equal, likely contribute to a decline in demand. The model in Chapter 5 develops this point more fully.
13. The countries included in the index are Belgium/Luxembourg, Canada, France, Germany, Italy, Japan, the Netherlands, Sweden, Switzerland, and the United Kingdom.
14. Details of the construction of this new multilateral exchange rate index is described in Leahy (1998).
15. We follow essentially the same methodology as Gourinchas (1998) in constructing the exchange rates: see, in that article, pages 165–166, especially footnote 16.
16. The spread in the real exhcange rate distribution tends to grow over time, at least initially, because the exchange rates are indexed to a common value for 1973.

3
Job Creation and Job Destruction

A First Look

In any given year, the fortunes of establishments diverge. Some establishments grow and add jobs while others shrink and offer fewer opportunities for employment. It is common to consider the ebb and flow of employment as a response to the business cycle and, consequently, to think of the changing number of jobs as generally reflecting movements in the overall amount of employment in the economy. This view, however, provides only a partial picture of churning within the labor market. A more complete picture reflects widespread and simultaneous creation and destruction of jobs, even within narrowly defined industries.

In this chapter we introduce the measures of labor-market churning that we employ throughout the rest of this book—job creation, job destruction, and job reallocation—as well as the traditional measure of labor market activity, changes in net employment. An innovative aspect of our analysis is the use of gross flows of jobs—that is, creation, destruction, and reallocation—to assess the impact of international factors on labor markets.[1] As discussed in more detail in the next chapter, the vast majority of studies of the labor-market effects of international factors use data only on change in the level of employment. These data, however, miss the churning that takes place within narrowly defined manufacturing sectors and, consequently, do not provide a full depiction of the consequences for the labor-market of a changing international environment.

Our data were developed by Davis, Haltiwanger, and Schuh (1996) using the Longitudinal Research Database (LRD) from the U.S. Bureau of the Census.[2] The basic observation in the LRD is the number of jobs (employment) at an individual manufacturing establishment, or equivalently "plant," in a particular year. Because establishments are linked in the data set year to year, the change in establishment employment can be calculated each year. Thus, establishments can be identified as having a net increase in jobs (therefore experiencing job creation, but no job destruction), a net decrease in jobs (therefore experiencing job destruction, but no job creation), or no net change in jobs (therefore having neither job creation nor job destruction).[3] These data are summed over all establishments within a four-digit industry to yield the amount of gross job creation and destruction within that industry. We use four-digit-level gross job-flow data because this is the most disaggregate level at which the trade (export and import) data are available.

These gross job-flow data provide us with a measure of the rate of reallocation within an industry. Job reallocation is defined as the sum of the rates of job creation and job destruction. The rate of net employment change is the difference between the rate of job creation and the rate of job destruction. A given rate of net employment change is consistent with a wide range of values of job creation and job destruction. For example, a net employment change of –2 percent can be generated by no job creation and a job destruction rate of 2 percent, or by a job creation rate of 10 percent and a job destruction rate of 12 percent.

However, the welfare consequences of these two scenarios are probably quite different. Job creation and job destruction have different implications for the labor-market status of workers, unemployment, human capital accumulation, and wages—factors that are fundamentally important for calculating the welfare costs of labor adjustment to international competition. In particular, job destruction is closely linked to the dislocation of workers from jobs, and the evidence indicates that dislocated workers typically suffer severe losses of human capital and permanent income. Moreover, job destruction tends to be permanent and occurs disproportionately in larger, older, high-wage plants. Thus, job destruction is likely to involve permanent dislocation of high-wage and/or older workers, human capital destruction, and permanent income loss—all of which are likely to lead to higher structural unemployment.[4]

We next describe the construction of gross job-flow measures from establishment-level data. Some initial statistics on gross job flows describe the overall characteristics of job flows in U.S. manufacturing.

This analysis is complemented by statistics that offer some initial information on the heterogeneity in the year-to-year behavior of job creation and job destruction within narrowly defined industry categories. These statistics suggest that an analysis that considers only net employment changes across broader industrial categories misses an important component of job reallocation due to simultaneous job destruction and job creation within industries.

Overall, this chapter sets the stage for much of the material presented in the rest of this book. An understanding of the distinction between gross job flows and changes in net employment informs the literature review of the international determinants of employment, presented in the next chapter, since most of this literature focuses on net employment changes rather than gross job flows. The simultaneous creation and destruction of jobs in seemingly narrowly defined industries documented here informs the choice of a theoretical framework, which is presented in Chapter 5. This model provides us with an empirical specification which is presented and tested in Chapter 6. In that chapter we present evidence of a significant role for exchange rates in affecting gross job flows. Some evidence in this chapter foreshadows those results by showing that gross job flows for manufacturing as a whole respond in a significant manner to movements in the multilateral dollar exchange rate.

GROSS JOB FLOWS IN U.S. MANUFACTURING

We begin this section with a brief description of methodology used by Davis, Haltiwanger, and Schuh (1996) to construct the gross job-flow data; for more details, see especially their data appendix. We then offer some initial evidence on the extent of simultaneous creation and destruction among manufacturing establishments. The data show that, on average, about one in five manufacturing jobs is either created or destroyed each year. This extensive labor-market churning is surprisingly diffuse across manufacturing. We present evidence that membership within narrow industrial groups accounts for little of the cross-sectional variation in gross job flows.

Data Definitions

To illustrate the calculation of job creation and destruction rates, define L_{pit} as the level of employment in a particular manufacturing establishment, plant p, which is classified as a member of industry i, in year t. Denote its first-difference as $\Delta L_{pit} = L_{pit} - L_{pi,t-1}$.[5] Job creation occurs in a particular manufacturing establishment if ΔL_{pit} is positive while job destruction occurs if ΔL_{pit} is negative. Thus, establishments that increase their level of employment over a given time period will be recorded as having, for that period, job creation equal to ΔL_{pit} and a value of job destruction equal to zero, while, for establishments that reduce their employment, job creation is zero and job destruction is equal to $-\Delta L_{pit}$.

Aggregating the employment changes across all establishments within a particular four-digit SIC industry gives us the *level* of job creation and job destruction in that industry. The size of the establishment is defined as the average of current and lagged employment, or $1/2(L_{pit} + L_{pi,t-1})$. Then the *rates* of job creation and destruction in industry i in year t, denoted C_{it} and D_{it} respectively, equal

$$C_{it} = \frac{\sum_{p \in M^+} \Delta L_{pit}}{\frac{1}{2}\sum_{p \in (M^+ \cup M^-)} (L_{pit} + L_{pi,t-1})}$$

$$D_{it} = \frac{\sum_{p \in M^-} |\Delta L_{pit}|}{\frac{1}{2}\sum_{p \in (M^+ \cup M^-)} (L_{pit} + L_{pi,t-1})},$$

where M^+ is the set of establishments for which $\Delta L_{pit} > 0$ and M^- is the set of establishments for which $\Delta L_{pit} < 0$. The reallocation rate within industry i in year t, R_{it}, is defined as the sum of its creation and destruction rates ($R_{it} = C_{it} + D_{it}$). The net change in employment of industry i in year t, N_{it}, is the difference between its job creation rate and the job destruction rate in that year ($N_{it} = C_{it} - D_{it}$). This last calculation shows that a particular rate of net change in employment is consistent with a wide range of different rates of job creation and job destruction, a point alluded to above.

Gross Job Flows in the Auto Industry

To illustrate these concepts, consider the data on net employment change and on gross job creation and destruction for the motor vehicles and car bodies, or "auto," industry (SIC 3711). Table 3.1 reports these data in levels and rates for each year from 1980 to 1990, along with the averages for the period. The first two columns contain the level and growth rate, N_{it}, of net employment change, whereas the remaining columns contain the levels and rates, C_{it} and D_{it}, of job creation and destruction. The average level of total employment in the auto industry during this period was slightly more than 270,000.

The table shows that employment declined 4.1 percent, or 12,586 employees, per year on average during this period. In contrast, the gross job flows were much larger. The number of new jobs created each year was on average roughly twice as large as the net change in industry employment. At the same time, job destruction averaged

Table 3.1 Net and Gross Job Flows in the Auto Industry

	Net employment change		Creation		Destruction	
	Level	N_{it}	Level	C_{it}	Level	D_{it}
1980	−79,835	−23.6	11,535	3.4	91,371	27.0
1981	−21,666	−7.6	24,800	8.6	46,466	16.2
1982	−28,831	−11.0	19,095	7.3	47,926	18.3
1983	−7,446	−3.0	23,357	9.6	30,803	12.6
1984	46,661	17.7	52,425	19.9	5,764	2.2
1985	26,418	8.8	39,816	13.3	13,397	4.5
1986	−6,768	−2.2	19,597	6.3	26,364	8.5
1987	−30,292	−10.4	18,962	6.5	49,254	16.9
1988	−23,924	−9.0	16,170	6.1	40,094	15.1
1989	−6,036	−2.4	17,490	7.0	23,526	9.4
1990	−6,727	−2.7	15,242	6.3	21,969	9.0
Average	−12,586	−4.1	23,499	8.6	36,085	12.7

NOTE: The rates N_{it}, C_{it}, and D_{it} are in percent and defined in the text. The level of total employment (L_{it}) used to derive the levels data in the table comes from the NBER Productivity database, which contains data from the Annual Survey of Manufacturers from the Census Bureau. In 1990, total employment in the auto industry was 239,500.

approximately three times the net change in industry employment. Thus, approximately 50,000 jobs were either created or destroyed on average, about four times more than were lost on net each year.

Not only are gross job flows large relative to net employment change, but jobs are being simultaneously created and destroyed within the industry each and every year. In 1980, for example, 91,371 jobs were destroyed (27 percent of employment) and net employment fell 79,835 (23.6 percent), but 11,535 new jobs were created (3.4 percent) that same year. Conversely, 5,764 jobs (2.2 percent) were destroyed in 1984, a year when total employment grew 17.7 percent. In fact, the rates of job creation and destruction never dropped below 2 percent of employment in any year during this period. Regardless of whether the industry as a whole was expanding or contracting, there was always a simultaneous expansion of the number of jobs at some establishments and contraction of the number of jobs at some other establishment within the industry. In general, a substantial number of jobs are simultaneously created and destroyed in virtually every year.

Gross Job Flows in All Manufacturing

The data for the auto industry presented in Table 3.1 give some hint of the simultaneous job creation and destruction that occurs within manufacturing, even in years in which there is a relatively large swing in overall employment. Statistics for manufacturing as a whole provide a more complete picture of the extensive churning that takes place. These statistics summarize information from a panel of annual data of about 450 four-digit manufacturing industries, covering the period 1973, the year that the dollar began to float against the currencies of the major U.S. trading partners, to 1993, the final year for which data on job flows are available.[6]

The average value of the annual job creation rate in manufacturing over the period 1973 to 1993 was 8.8 jobs created per 100 positions each year, while the comparable average rate of job destruction was 10.2 jobs destroyed per 100 positions each year (Schuh and Triest 1998). Thus, the average annual rate of job reallocation in manufacturing was 19 percent between 1973 and 1993 while, during this period, the manufacturing sector saw an average net decline of 1.3 jobs per 100 positions (numbers do not add up due to rounding).

These statistics mask the wide swings that have sometimes occurred over our sample period in job destruction and job creation rates for manufacturing. Figures 3.1–3.4 present the time series variation in gross job flows. The four panels of this figure present annual data on job creation, job destruction rate, job reallocation rate, and net employment growth rate for the manufacturing sector during the period 1973 to 1993.[7] This figure also demonstrates the wide variation in gross job flows over time. For example, the reallocation rate exceeded 20 percent in half the years of the sample, reaching a high of 24 percent in 1983. These figures also demonstrate differences between the two components of gross job flows, job creation and job destruction. A comparison of the top two panels shows that the job destruction rate is more volatile than the job creation rate, with the job destruction rate exceeding 15 percent in three years—1975, 1982, and 1983.

Figures 3.1–3.4 also provide evidence on the correlation between manufacturing gross job flows and the business cycle. Shaded bars in the figure represent periods of recession. The data in the figure suggest that the job destruction rate is strongly countercyclical, while the job creation rate is procyclical. The figure also depicts the G-10 multilateral real exchange rate over the sample period; we use the G-10 rate for this figure and the subsequent regression analysis below, to facilitate comparison with prior research on the effects of exchange rates on labor markets. Note that each gross job-flow measure is correlated positively with the real exchange rate. The job destruction rate is more closely correlated with the real exchange rate than the job creation rate, but the job reallocation rate is most closely correlated with the real exchange rate. Net employment growth does not track movements in the real exchange rate very closely at all.

The relationships suggested by inspection of the figures are supported by simple regressions using the annual job creation rate in manufacturing, C_t, the annual job destruction rate in manufacturing, D_t, the lagged percentage change in the G-10 real exchange rate, $\%\Delta RER_{t-1}$, and the lagged percentage change in manufacturing industrial produc-

Figure 3.1 Gross Job Flows and the Real Exchange Rate—Job Creation (1973–1993)

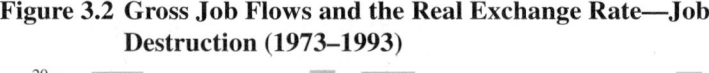

SOURCE: See Data Sources 1 and 6 in Appendix C.

Figure 3.2 Gross Job Flows and the Real Exchange Rate—Job Destruction (1973–1993)

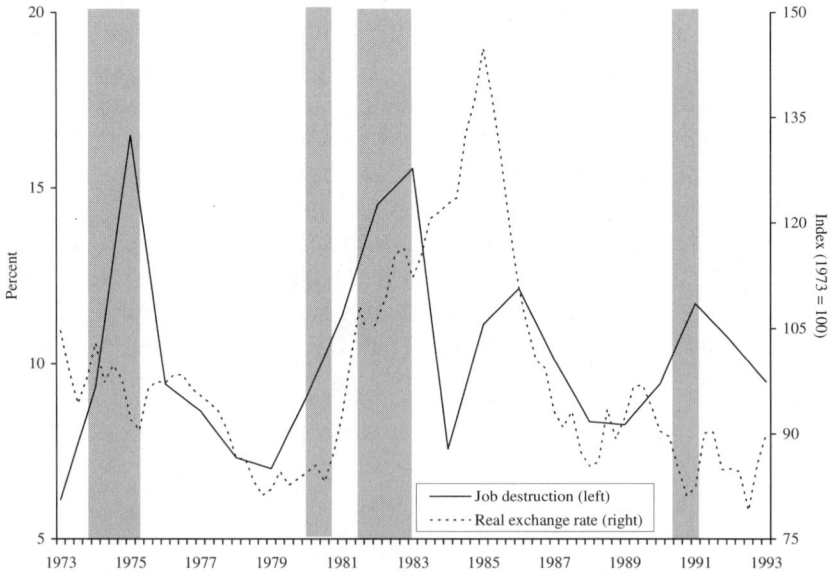

SOURCE: See Data Sources 1 and 6 in Appendix C.

Job Creation and Job Destruction: A First Look 41

Figure 3.3 Gross Job Flows and the Real Exchange Rate—Job Reallocation (1973–1993)

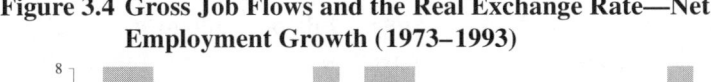

SOURCE: See Data Sources 1 and 6 in Appendix C.

Figure 3.4 Gross Job Flows and the Real Exchange Rate—Net Employment Growth (1973–1993)

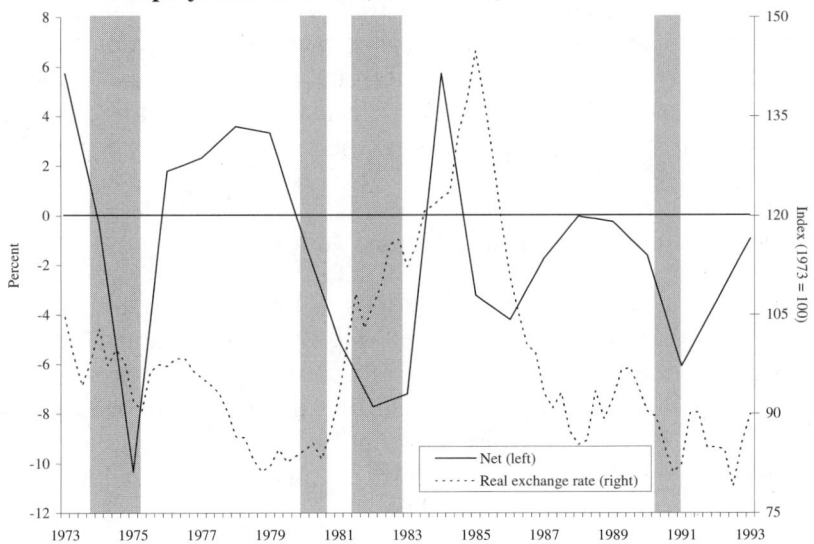

SOURCE: See Data Sources 1 and 6 in Appendix C.

tion, $\%\Delta IPM_{t-1}$. Estimating these equations over the period 1974 to 1993, we find

$$C_t = \underset{(0.51)}{8.28} - \underset{(0.05)}{0.015\% \Delta RER_{t-1}} + \underset{(0.09)}{0.10\% \Delta IPM_{t-1}}$$

$$R^2 = 0.07 \qquad DW = 1.63 \qquad n = 19$$

$$D_t = \underset{(0.56)}{11.12} + \underset{(0.056)}{0.12\% \Delta RER_{t-1}} - \underset{(0.10)}{0.24\% \Delta IPM_{t-1}}$$

$$R^2 = 0.41 \qquad DW = 2.07 \qquad n = 19$$

where standard errors are in parentheses. The coefficients in these regressions are all of the expected sign, and the coefficients in the destruction equation are significant at the 95 percent level. Note that the real exchange rate and industrial production coefficients are insignificant in the job creation equation.

These simple regression results, along with Figure 3.1, suggest a link between the real exchange rate and gross job destruction. They are also a robust precursor of our later results from the more detailed estimation reported in Chapter 6. Most importantly, note that these results imply an economically important impact of real exchange rates on job destruction. For example, from 1982 to 1986, the job destruction rate in manufacturing averaged 12.2 percent, 2 full percentage points above its unconditional sample average of 10.2 percent. The average value of the lagged change in the real exchange rate during that time was 8.9 percent. Thus, more than 50 percent of the average increase in the job destruction rate (8.9 × 0.12 = 1.07 percentage points of the 2 percentage point rise) may be attributable to the real exchange rate appreciation.

Gross Job-Flow Heterogeneity across Industries

Industries are sometimes described as being in a certain phase of their life cycle. Terms like "sunset" industries, or regional tags like "rustbelt" reflect a view that broadly defined industries are being eclipsed, perhaps by "emerging" industries that happen to be located in "booming" regions. This view may not be broadly accurate, however. At any moment there may be both successful, growing establishments and less successful establishments that are downsizing even within narrowly defined manufacturing industries or within a certain region.

The data and statistics presented in the previous section, which reveal a high degree of churning within manufacturing as a whole, cannot, by themselves, provide any information concerning the divergence of fortunes of establishments within certain industries. For example, the average reallocation rate of 19 percent could be consistent with either persistent destruction in one broad industrial category and persistent creation in another, or with shifting patterns of gross job flows across industries. Likewise, the relationship between gross job flows and aggregate economic variables like the real exchange rate and industrial production could reflect either common responses by all establishments in particular broad industrial categories to business cycle and international factors or, alternatively, a more varied pattern of responses across establishments within narrowly defined industries.

At the broadest level, heterogeneous performance within manufacturing as a whole is to be expected since this sector of the economy is populated by establishments producing a wide range of products and serving vastly different markets. Consequently, we would expect the presence of simultaneous creation and destruction within manufacturing. More surprisingly, there is evidence of heterogeneous creation and destruction behavior within narrow industrial categories in which we might have expected more common performance among establishments.

A simple, albeit stringent, condition to consider is whether there is evidence of simultaneous creation and destruction among establishments within four-digit SIC industries. If all establishments within these categories faced a common fate, then we would expect to find many years in which particular four-digit industries had either no job creation or no job destruction. In fact, this is not the case. Either the creation rate or the destruction rate equals zero in only 0.2 percent of all possible cases (that is, among all 447 industries over 21 years). Easing these criteria, we still find only a small number of cases of lopsided creation or destruction activity. In only about 2 percent of all observations is the rate of job destruction or the rate of job creation less than 1 percent. Furthermore, there are very few cases of low rates of job creation even if we consider only observations when job destruction was large. Job creation was less than 1 percent in only 1.8 percent of the cases when job destruction was above its overall average of 10.7 percent. Likewise, job destruction was less than 1 percent in only 1.1 percent of the cases when job creation was above its overall average of 8.7 percent.

A more systematic examination of heterogeneity in creation and destruction can be obtained by determining the extent to which membership in a particular industrial category explains these gross job flows. We run regressions of the form

$$C_{it} = \sum_{i=1}^{n-1} \alpha_i X_i + \varepsilon_{it}^c$$
$$D_{it} = \sum_{i=1}^{n-1} \beta_i X_i + \varepsilon_{it}^d,$$

where C_{it} is the job creation rate for the ith four-digit SIC industry in year t, D_{it} is the job destruction rate for the ith four-digit SIC industry in year t, X_i is a 0/1 dummy variable corresponding to a particular SIC group, n is the number of industries in that group, and ε_{it} is the regression error.[8] For example, the broadest group is where $X_i = 1$ if the four-digit industry is in a Durable Goods industry and otherwise $X_i = 0$. In this case, $n = 2$.

Table 3.2 reports the goodness-of-fit statistic adjusted for number of degrees of freedom, the adjusted R^2, associated with this regression for testing differences across the durable versus nondurable groups ($n = 2$), as well as the R^2 statistics for regressions for the more disaggregated groups of all two-digit industries ($n = 20$), all three-digit industries ($n = 143$), and all four-digit industries (in this case, $n = 442$ rather than the full 447 because there are not data for all four-digit industries for all 21 years). The adjusted R^2 values reflect the time-series and (in all cases but for the regressions using dummy variables associated with the four-digit SIC categories) the cross-section variation associated with membership in particular industry categories. If, for example, all four-digit industries within any two-digit category had very similar measures of job creation, then we would find a large adjusted R^2 in a regression of job creation on a set of two-digit dummy variables and little difference between this adjusted R^2 and the ones we would obtain for regressions of job creation on a set of three-digit dummy variables or on a set of four-digit dummy variables.

The top part of Table 3.2 reports results for regressions using a pooled sample representing all 21 years for which we have job-flow data. In this pooled data set, job creation rates and job destruction rates vary both over four-digit industries and over time. These results show that virtually none of the variation in gross job-flow rates is accounted for by membership in the broad categories of durable and nondurable goods. Membership in the more narrow two-digit categories accounts for only 6 percent of the variation in both job destruction rates and job creation rates. Membership in a particular three-digit industry, while offering almost seven times as many categories of industries, still accounts for only 12 to 13 percent of the variation in creation or destruction rates. The most disaggregated classification scheme, consisting of a complete set of four-digit dummy variables, still generates adjusted R^2 values of only 18 percent for job destruction and 23 percent for job creation.

The adjusted R^2 in the last column of the top panel of Table 3.2 reflects only time-series variation since, with 441 dummy variables corresponding to the full set of SIC four-digit industries, there is no scope for variation within industrial categories within any year. The large increase in the adjusted R^2 values from 0.13 to 0.23 for creation and 0.12 to 0.18 for destruction, suggests that temporal variation in the job-flow rates of four-digit industries is a much more important contributor to their overall variance than are any persistent differences across four-digit industries in the degree of job churning.

Table 3.2 Job-Flow Regressions on Industry Variables ($\overline{R}^2$ values)

	Industry indicators			
	Durability	2-digit	3-digit	4-digit
No. of variables	1	19	142	441
1973–1993 (9,282 observations)				
Job creation	0.01	0.06	0.13	0.23
Job destruction	0.00	0.06	0.12	0.18
1990 (442 observations)				
Job creation	0.00	0.07	0.18	
Job destruction	0.01	0.06	0.13	

NOTE: Table entries are the adjusted R^2 values from regressions of job-flow rates on a set of industry dummy variables.

We investigate this point further in the bottom part of Table 3.2 in which we isolate the cross-sectional variation in openness by performing a comparable ANOVA using data from a single year, 1990.[9] As with the results in the top panel of this table, the results presented in the bottom panel indicate that little of the cross-sectional variation in job-flow rates among four-digit industries in that year is due to systematic differences between more aggregated industry groups. For example, only 6 percent of the cross-sectional variation in job destruction rates is explained by a four-digit industry's membership in a two-digit category, and only 13 percent is explained by its membership in a three-digit industry category. These results suggest that much of the variation in gross job flows cannot be attributed to common movements across a large proportion of establishments within particular industrial groups, even when these groups are narrowly defined.

CONCLUSION

In this chapter, we have introduced the relationships between stock and flow measures in the labor market and, in so doing, have defined gross job flows. We then show how, in practical terms, gross job-flow measures are constructed from establishment-level data. This demonstration is important for the subsequent analysis in this book because it aids in an understanding of the relationship between the actual measures of job flows that we use and the concept of job churning.

Statistics presented in this chapter demonstrate the pervasive level of heterogeneity in the labor market. For example, we have documented the existence of simultaneous job creation and job destruction in a narrowly defined industry, as well as the relative lack of explanatory power for gross job-flow rates of membership in a particular narrow industry. The previous chapter has shown a similar presence of heterogeneity in openness and trade patterns across narrowly defined industries. In subsequent chapters we will explore whether there is a mapping between international factors and job flows in a way that matches up divergent patterns across industries along these two dimensions. But first, to provide a context for that undertaking, we turn to a discussion of the existing research on the effect of international factors on labor markets.

Notes

1. Gourinchas (1998, 1999) also examined the response of job flows to real exchange rate movements. Our analysis differs from and extends his in several ways, as we explain in the next chapter.
2. These data are available at: <http://www.bsos.umd.edu/haltiwanger/download.htm>.
3. These data do not capture churning of jobs within an establishment since any single establishment is recorded as having job creation and no job destruction, job destruction and no job creation, or neither job creation nor job destruction. Thus, for example, a manufacturing plant that destroyed a number of assembly line jobs and created the same number of engineering jobs would be recorded as having neither job creation nor job destruction. Neither do these data identify movements of particular workers within and between establishments. Thus, for example, a plant may fire a worker and hire a replacement worker for the same job without any change in its stock of jobs.
4. On these points, see Davis, Haltiwanger, and Schuh (1996) or the surveys by Fallick (1996) and Kletzer (1998b).
5. Due to the timing of the data surveys underlying the LRD, this difference represents March-to-March employment changes. Whenever we compare job-flow data with other data that have a different chronological timing, we attempt to correct for the mismatch by using appropriate lags.
6. See Appendix C for details.
7. In this figure, the annual job flows data have been interpolated to a quarterly frequency to permit accurate plotting of business cycle dates.
8. This is an example of ANOVA (ANalysis Of VAriance). Davis and Haltiwanger (1992) used similar techniques to make the analogous point about job reallocation, the level of detailed industries, and other plant characteristics.
9. Results from this particular year are broadly representative of results obtained from any other particular year.

4
Literature Review

This chapter surveys research that attempts to explain and quantify the effects of real exchange rates and international trade on employment. The survey provides a context for the research we present later in this book. Our research on the influence of international factors on gross job flows is directly related to, and an extension of, previous studies of employment dynamics. However, as discussed in this chapter, the preponderance of these studies focus on changes in net employment rather than on job creation and job destruction.

The survey comprises three parts. The first section describes the connection between international trade and labor markets, and it explains how standard trade theory has had a limited view of this connection until recently. The second section reviews the early empirical studies, which focused primarily on the relationship between international factors and net employment. Finally, the third section reviews recent research based on the flow approach to labor markets, which focuses on the relationship between international factors and the dynamic processes of gross job and worker flows.

It is in this last area where our research on international factors and gross job flows contributes to the literature. We introduce labor-flow dynamics into the analysis of international trade and, in so doing, help clarify the costs of adjustment associated with changes in international factors. This analysis also highlights the role of international factors as an important channel for allocative forces that drive labor-market dynamics. We evaluate the importance for labor-market dynamics of the real exchange rate and trade policy relative to other factors that have been more extensively studied.

Before proceeding, we note that a voluminous body of research considers the effects of international factors on real wages, skill-biased technological change, and income distribution. This research is closely related to the questions we pose and attempt to answer in this book, and it should be integrated with them in future research. However, research on wage-related issues is so vast and sufficiently distinct from our concern with dynamic employment responses that we do not take it up.

Thus, a full review of the literature on trade and wages is beyond the scope of this book.[1]

INTERNATIONAL FACTORS AND LABOR MARKETS

Trade and Unemployment

In his Ely Lecture, "The Challenge of High Unemployment," Alan Blinder (1988) identified the field of international trade as one of two where theory had failed to sufficiently address the problem and consequences of unemployment. Blinder wrote:

> Conditions of full employment are necessary to validate standard propositions in trade theory. High unemployment calls many of these propositions into question. Both the positive predictions of trade theory and its normative prescriptions may be wrong. (p. 11)

This assessment did *not* lead Blinder to support barriers to free trade, but he did conclude that it is necessary "to pursue a vigorous full-employment policy so that displaced workers will be quickly reemployed" (p. 11). In Blinder's view, there is a large gap between economists' overwhelming and unswerving advocacy of free trade to obtain long-run welfare gains on the one hand and the striking reality of vehement opposition to free trade by many individuals, firms, and interest groups on the other. In our view, the only way to bridge the gap is to consider explicitly the short-run welfare costs associated with job and worker reallocation, unemployment, and the destruction of human capital.

Economists' conclusions about the welfare gains from trade in the long run derive from the standard Heckscher-Olin-Samuelson (HOS) trade model, where factors of production are assumed to be homogeneous across sectors, and there are no impediments to the intersector mobility of factors. In the HOS model, a change in the terms of trade engenders reallocation of factors across sectors, but at no explicit cost. Aggregate employment is constant across changes in underlying conditions in the static version of this model.

In the 1980s and early 1990s, this theoretical prediction seems to have guided empirical research, which focused on net employment effects in aggregate sectors and, to a lesser extent, detailed industries. In his survey of the literature, Baldwin (1994) reported that "The general findings of these inquiries is that the *net* employment effects of changes in exports and imports have not been significant in OECD [Organization for Economic Cooperation and Development] countries." However, studies surveyed by Baldwin do find that "trade changes have produced significant adverse employment effects in particular industries . . ." (pp. 13–14). The next section corroborates this conclusion in more detail and with respect to real exchange rates. Despite large effects on industry-level employment, the underlying presumption of these studies is that the aggregate welfare gains far exceed the cost incurred by factors, especially workers, that shift industries or sectors. These studies largely ignore the adjustment costs associated with changes in employment patterns across sectors, as well as distributional effects, focusing instead on potential net welfare gains in the aggregate.

Responding to Blinder's challenge, Davidson, Martin, and Matusz (1999) reconsidered the predictions of the HOS model by adding unemployment that arises because trade-dislocated labor must search for a new job in another sector. They found that some of the traditional conclusions, including welfare implications, are modified or changed altogether and depend on whether laborers are employed or unemployed (searching for a job). Their central conclusion is that unemployment rises in large, relatively capital-abundant countries that increase their trade with small, relatively labor-abundant countries, and that the unemployed workers in the large countries suffer welfare losses. This unemployment-augmented HOS model bears similarities to the Ricardo-Viner (RV) trade model where some factors of production are completely immobile across sectors. Thus, the nature and process of factor adjustment to trade are of critical importance in assessing the impact of trade on factor markets.[2]

This important line of research underscores Blinder's fundamental critique of prior research on unemployment: "too much of our theoretical debate has taken place within the confining strictures of *homogeneous* labor" (emphasis added). In reality, factors of production are not all perfectly mobile across sectors. In fact, workers and jobs are heterogeneous within sectors and industries, even within firms and establishments, so the process of matching the right workers and jobs is complex. Because of this pervasive heterogeneity, reallocation of labor across sectors, industries, regions, firms, and establishments is very costly and time consuming.

Although an important step in the right direction, the new efforts to account for unemployment in measuring the net effects of international trade are still incomplete. Increases in unemployment are proportional to reductions in net employment (plus changes in the labor force). However, changes in net employment significantly understate the magnitude of gross job destruction and creation occurring in the economy, as we explain in the remainder of this section.

Labor-Market Flows

A microeconomic-based flow approach to labor markets has become the dominant paradigm for modern macroeconomic theories of unemployment and labor-market dynamics.[3] This flow approach explains the behavior of employment and unemployment by introducing dynamic changes in the number and location of workers and jobs. In the flow approach, heterogeneous firms continuously offer a variety of job opportunities, and heterogeneous workers (each of whom has distinct skills) continuously offer their services. Thus, the labor market is characterized by continuous search—firms seeking the best workers and workers seeking the best jobs.[4]

Figure 4.1 provides a schematic diagram of labor-market stocks and flows. The figure illustrates how workers and jobs flow among stocks, or states, of the labor market. Employment, and other labor stocks, typically have inflows and outflows from multiple sources and thus may change for different reasons at different times. In particular, the flows indicate that the labor market is in a constant state of flux and that it is necessary to study the flows to understand how the stocks change over time.

Consider first the labor-market stocks. Total net employment (E) is the set of all matches (denoted by the saw-toothed intersection) between heterogeneous workers who supply labor (E^s) and the heterogeneous jobs offered by firms that demand labor (E^d). Note, importantly, that the *levels* of labor supply and demand are typically never equal because there are always unemployed workers (U) and unfilled, or vacant, jobs (V) arising from frictions associated with heterogeneity

Figure 4.1 Schematic Diagram of the Labor Market

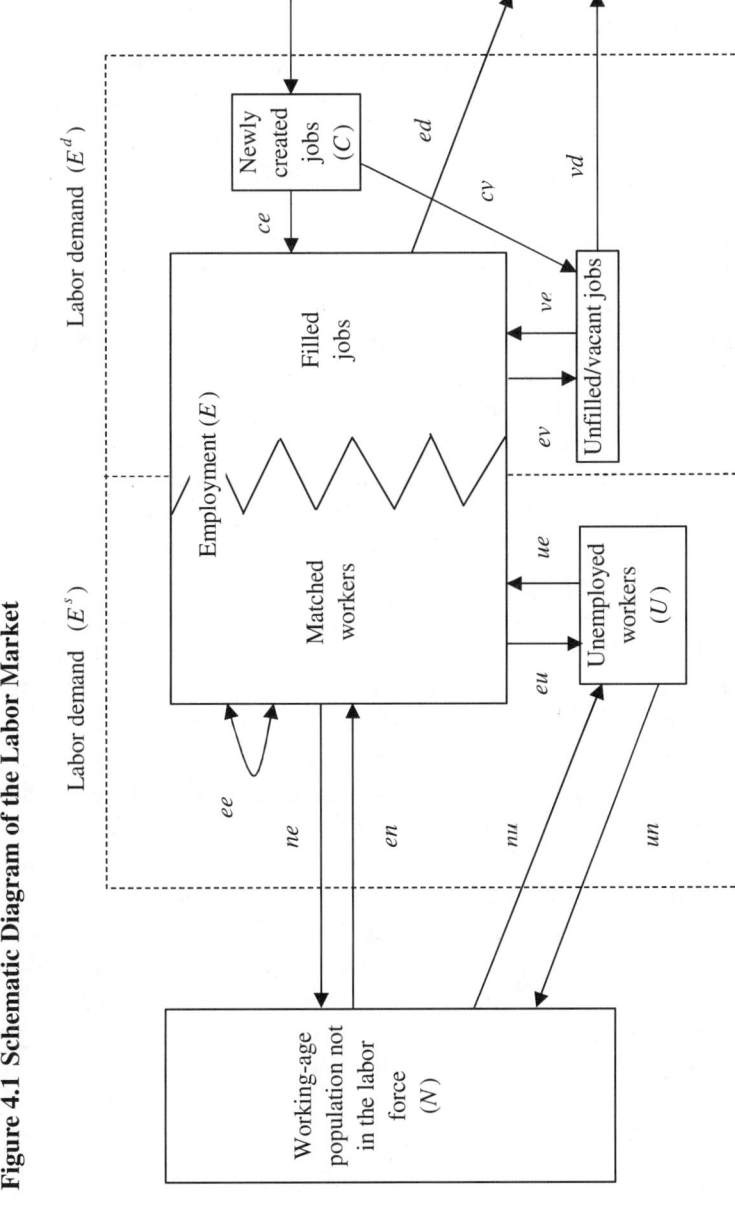

and the costs of matching. Unemployed workers do not fill vacancies instantaneously because it takes time for workers to find the vacancies, the skills of unemployed workers do not match the skill demands of the vacancies, or the geographic location of the workers is different from that of the vacancies.

The level of employment is jointly determined by the net result of two types of labor-market flows, worker flows and job flows. On the supply side of the labor market (E^s), workers flow among three states of the labor market: employment, unemployment, and not in the labor force (*N*). Employment increases when the flows into employment (*ne* and *ue*) rise, or the flows out of employment (*en* and *eu*) fall, or both. Some workers flow from job to job (*ee*) but do not affect employment. On the demand side of the labor market (E^d), jobs flow among firms that continuously create new jobs (*C*) and destroy old jobs (*D*). Employment increases when job creation (*ce*) rises and more vacant jobs are filled (*ve*), or when job destruction (*ed*) falls, and fewer existing jobs become vacant (*ev*).

It is important to understand that worker flows and job flows are not synonymous. For example, if unemployed workers merely replace newly retired workers (i.e., both *en* and *ue* flows rise), employment doesn't change. Furthermore, these worker flows occur without changes in the stock of jobs (labor demand) through greater job creation. Similarly, if a firm replaces newly destroyed jobs with newly created jobs, and its employed workers are simply reassigned jobs within the firm, then worker flows and employment do not change.

In practice, however, labor-market matching is much more complex, and all worker and job flows tend to occur simultaneously. Davis, Haltiwanger, and Schuh (1996, chapter 6) and Bleakley, Ferris, and Fuhrer (1999) showed that there are relatively steady correlations among certain types of flows, but the connections are not one for one. In general, the termination of existing matches via job flows (*ed* or *ev*) generates worker flows (*eu*, *en*, and *ee*), which tend to raise unemployment. Likewise, the establishment of new matches via job flows (*ce* and *ve*) also generates worker flows (*ue*, *ne*, and *ee*), which tend to reduce unemployment. But, even in these instances, the link between labor-market stocks is not one for one. Simply put, employment and unemployment are not inextricably linked.[5]

Abstracting from economic growth, the flow approach says that even when employment reaches an equilibrium or steady state value, the labor market is not at rest. The reason is that gross job and worker flows are not zero when employment is in equilibrium. Individual workers and individual jobs are involved continuously in matching and rematching.

In fact, empirical estimates reported in the literature indicate that gross flows are much larger than net flows such as employment growth, which averages around 2 percent per year in the United States. In manufacturing, job creation and destruction occur at annual rates of about 10 percent each, implying a job reallocation rate of about 20 percent, compared with net employment growth in manufacturing of only about −1 percent (Davis, Haltiwanger, and Schuh 1996). Monthly worker flows into and out of employment and unemployment also occur at annual rates an order of magnitude larger than employment growth (Blanchard and Diamond 1990; Bleakley, Ferris, and Fuhrer 1999). Monthly flows of workers directly from one employer to another (*ee*) are even higher than other worker flows (Fallick and Fleischman 2001).

Figure 4.1 helps explain why we focus on job flows rather than worker flows in our investigation of the effects of international factors on employment. Changes in real exchange rates and trade liberalization directly affect the *demand* for labor; hence, they directly affect the pace of job creation and destruction. These factors also may affect worker flows but only indirectly, if at all. Given existing data, it is quite difficult empirically to identify worker flows resulting from job flows and worker flows occurring for other (supply-side) reasons. For example, job destruction caused by international factors may reduce employment if the workers whose jobs are destroyed move to unemployment (*eu*) or leave the labor force (*en*). However, it will not reduce employment if the worker simply moves to another job (*ee*) that was created at the same time, either by the same employer or by another. Furthermore, workers connected to internationally open firms may move in and out of the labor force (*ne* and *en*) or to and from unemployment (*eu* and *ue*) for reasons having nothing to do with international factors.

Labor-Market Adjustment Costs

Standard trade theory generally does not emphasize the costs associated with adjusting, or reallocating, factors of production.[6] There are two main reasons: the adjustment process is assumed to be transitory and short-lived, and the benefits of trade are thought to far outweigh the adjustment costs. However, the actual evidence in the literature on the nature and duration of adjustment and on the net benefits of trade liberalization is modest and incomplete, as we explain in this section.[7]

In the prevailing view, changes in international factors affect aggregate employment only transitorily because workers eventually are reallocated to other sectors or firms where they are most productive. This process may take some time, but the presumption is that appropriate macroeconomic policy will return the economy to full employment relatively quickly and at a low cost. Because internationally generated labor reallocation raises the efficiency of the aggregate economy, aggregate welfare increases. Thus, at the aggregate level, it appears that flexible exchange rates and more open trade policies provide something for nothing—higher welfare with no overall employment change, at least in the long run.

A study by Magee (1972) provided detailed estimates of the welfare gains from eliminating all U.S. trade-related restrictions in 1971. Magee's efforts are impressive, but this endeavor is so daunting that the estimates must be considered extremely rough and incomplete.[8] Nevertheless, he included estimates of both welfare gains and the short-run labor-adjustment costs associated with the elimination of all trade-related restrictions.

In estimating labor-adjustment costs, Magee took the traditional aggregate, homogeneous labor approach criticized by Blinder. Adjustment costs are calculated solely as the income loss due to unemployment arising from net employment loss in the industries affected by the relaxation of trade-related restrictions. Specifically, Magee calculated adjustment costs as "the implied change in [net] employment, multiply this by a wage rate and an assumed duration of unemployment, and spread this loss equally over the five-year period that I assume industries require to adjust to changes in trade barriers and reach a new long-run equilibrium" (p. 680). Note that this methodology makes two implicit assumptions that are critical to the results. It assumes that the dislocated workers are reemployed rather than replaced in the labor force by new workers or reentrants, in which case dislocated workers might experience long-term structural unemployment or leave the labor force. More importantly, it assumes that the dislocated workers receive the same wage once they are re-employed (or that the entrants earn the same wage). In addition, Magee completely ignores direct costs to firms and workers such as hiring and firing costs, retraining costs, and relocation costs.

According to Magee's calculations, the welfare gains from eliminating all U.S. trade-related restrictions would have swamped the associated costs of adjustment. He estimated that annual welfare gains amounted to approximately 1 percent of Gross National Product (GNP) in 1971, whereas estimated adjustment costs amounted to only 0.01 percent of GNP. This implies that the ratio of welfare gains to adjustment cost losses is approximately 100 to 1.[9]

Baldwin, Mutti, and Richardson (1980) drew similar conclusions. They provided estimates of U.S. welfare gains and adjustment costs associated with a 50 percent multilateral tariff reduction in the late 1970s (as opposed to Magee's 100 percent reduction). Their adjustment cost estimates offered several improvements on Magee's calculations, including controls for detailed demographic characteristics of unemployed workers, positive income effects from export promotion, and estimates of capital adjustment costs. They conclude: "In the aggregate, the calculated gains from trade liberalization *dwarf* the measured adjustment costs by a ratio of almost 20 to 1" (p. 405, emphasis added). Interestingly, it is not the inclusion of capital adjustment costs that produces a smaller gain-to-cost ratio than Magee's, because capital adjustment costs account for only about 12 percent of total adjustment costs.[10]

With welfare gains estimated to be at least 20 times greater than adjustment costs, and perhaps 100 times greater or more, it is not surprising that many economists have essentially ignored adjustment costs associated with changes in international factors. But, if the net gains to trade are so large, why is there such breadth and depth of opposition to introducing trade restrictions? One logical explanation is that adjustment costs are concentrated in a small number of workers and firms who have much to gain from being very vocal, while the benefits are highly diffuse and thus small—perhaps imperceptibly small—to most economic agents. However, another possibility is that adjustment costs are larger than previously estimated or believed. If so, ignoring adjustment costs becomes less tenable.[11]

One reason adjustment costs might be larger is that labor reallocation may involve fixed costs of reallocation in addition to income loss during unemployment. Recent research has begun to recognize the existence and potential importance of per-worker adjustment costs for each trade-dislocated worker, as in Fung and Staiger (1996), Furusawa and Lai (1998), and Davidson and Matusz (2001a). These fixed costs may include time and resource costs of retraining or relocating, among other things. However, these studies focus on net employment changes at the industry level rather than the much larger gross flows at the establishment level. If adjustment costs are proportional to gross job and worker flows, which are roughly an order of magnitude larger than net employment growth, then adjustment costs might turn out to be an order of magnitude larger than previously estimated. To our knowledge, the only other study that raises this issue is Kletzer's (2001) analysis of imports and worker flows.

If adjustment costs are proportional to gross flows, then the net welfare gains from trade would be considerably smaller than previously believed. For example, the gain-to-loss ratios could drop to 10 to 1 in Magee's study and only 2 to 1 in the Baldwin, Mutti, and Richardson (1980) study. The calibrated model of Davidson and Matusz (2001a) indicates that short-run adjustment costs could amount to 90 percent of the long-run gains from trade in some cases. Of course, any projections such as these are hypothetical at this point, and they need empirical verification as well as theoretical consideration. But it seems worth exploring these ideas, given the stakes involved. In any event, the magnitudes of the ratios suggested by gross-flow-based analysis seem to have the potential to better explain the breadth and intensity of opposition to free trade. At a minimum, they suggest that adjustment costs and the redistribution of gains from trade may merit more attention from economists than they have received.

In contrast to standard theory, the flow approach to labor markets inherently emphasizes the simultaneous occurrence of "winners and losers." Gross job and worker flows in response to changes in international factors imply that some individual firms and workers end up worse off while others end up better off. Economists typically assume that aggregate welfare gains from trade are large but that welfare costs typically associated with adjustment to changes in international competition are small. However, a complete and accurate assessment of the true net welfare gains from international openness depends crucially on a complete and accurate assessment of the true welfare losses associated with these adjustment costs.

Unfortunately, there is very little evidence on the magnitude of the welfare losses associated with the labor-market effects of international openness. The vast majority of evidence, summarized in the next section, is based on net employment changes in aggregate sectors, such as manufacturing, or broad industries that may exhibit modest differentials in openness. But the flow approach to labor markets informs us that net employment changes significantly understate the magnitude of gross flows in labor markets, even within detailed industries. Thus, a more complete and accurate estimate of the labor-adjustment costs associated with international factors must focus on the impact of these factors on gross worker and job flows. In particular, even when net employment is unchanged, international factors can induce significant costs of adjustment through job destruction and creation.

Many specific types of labor-adjustment costs arise in connection with job and worker flows induced by international factors. These costs can be summarized broadly in two types. One type is costs to the firm associated with the hiring, training, and firing of workers. The other is costs to fired or dislocated workers, which take several distinct forms: 1) spells of unemployment, 2) loss of firm-specific human capital, 3) costs associated with moving geographic location to find a new job, and 4) general retraining for a new job. The first two take the form of income loss; the latter two are out-of-pocket expenses.[12]

Very few studies quantify these labor-adjustment costs directly because detailed data are not readily available and because it is inherently difficult to quantify these costs. Instead, most efforts focus on inferring the costs indirectly from econometric models of labor-demand and adjustment-cost functions (see Hamermesh and Pfann 1996). Many of these studies use aggregate data, but some actually use firm-level data. However, the most precise and complete estimates come from studies of European economies, which may have higher costs of adjustment to labor flows than does the U.S. economy.

Abowd and Kramarz (1997, p. 1) claimed to "present the first direct evidence on the fixed costs associated with hiring and separations [firing] of various types, the asymmetries in these costs, and the shape of the adjustment cost functions."[13] They used a unique database from France containing matched worker-firm data on a host of labor variables, including among the best available estimates of direct adjustment costs to firms. Abowd and Kramarz found that the cost of firing a worker (average for all reasons) amounts to 56 percent of the average annual labor cost to the firm of that worker. Put another way, the cost is more than one-half, or 6.7 months, of the worker's annual compensation. The cost of firing a worker for economic reasons is even greater, amounting to 126 percent or 15.1 months of annual compensation.[14] In contrast, the total cost of hiring and training a worker amounts to about 5 percent or 0.6 month of annual compensation. French firing costs are approximately linear with respect to the number of workers fired, and there is a fixed cost attributable to personnel departments. This adjustment cost structure likely leads to large, discrete labor adjustment at the microeconomic level.

Another source of direct evidence on labor turnover costs is Del Boca and Rota (1998), a study of 61 primarily small and medium-sized manufacturing companies in Italy. They estimated that hiring costs (including training) range between 2.0 and 2.6 months of labor costs, and firing costs range from less than one month to 20 months of labor costs, depending on the nature of the separation. These cost estimates are somewhat larger than the Abowd and Kramarz estimates for France. Unfortunately, we do not have analogous estimates for U.S. firms.

Empirical evidence on the second type of adjustment cost, the costs suffered by dislocated workers, also is limited largely by data availability. Nevertheless, surveys of this literature by Hamermesh (1989), Fallick (1996), and Kletzer (1998b) all draw the same general conclusions. Workers dislocated from their jobs by international or other factors are likely to experience unusually long unemployment spells and declines in their post-displacement income. The actual unemployment spells and income losses of displaced workers depend heavily on individual worker characteristics, such as age, work experience, and industry. Some displaced workers can even earn higher incomes on their subsequent jobs. More typical, however, is one of the leading studies in this field, Jacobsen, LaLonde, and Sullivan (1993a,b). They found that dislocated workers with high job tenure and significant firm-specific human capital experience average earnings losses of 25 percent of their predisplacement annual income.

In addition to unemployment spells and earnings losses, dislocated workers can also face substantial welfare losses associated with other pecuniary and nonpecuniary costs of adjustment. Workers who must ultimately move to another geographic region to obtain employment may face pecuniary losses, such as moving costs or capital losses on homes, and nonpecuniary losses, such as family separations or broken social ties as well. To our knowledge, there are no concrete estimates of these types of adjustment costs, but they surely factor into a complete calculation of social welfare.

INTERNATIONAL FACTORS AND NET EMPLOYMENT

Virtually all early studies of the relationship between international factors and labor markets focused on net employment, either at an aggregate level, such as manufacturing, or in industries that have relatively intense exposure to international competition.[15] Table 4.1 summarizes these studies, which we discuss in detail in this section. A central question of these studies is whether net employment declines in response to increased international competition. International competition includes the effects of (real) exchange rates, the volume of exports and imports, and trade policies such as tariffs or quotas.

Interest in the relationship between international trade and employment in U.S. manufacturing industries grew in the early 1980s as the trade balance registered record deficits, but trade deficits were far from the only determinant of manufacturing employment during this period. In the early 1980s, the U.S. economy suffered its deepest recession since the Great Depression of the 1930s. An important task facing researchers is to disentangle the effects of international factors from the effects of other contemporaneous events.

Isolating the effects of international competition is often more than just an academic exercise. For example, an industry that petitions the International Trade Commission (ITC) for actions to help alleviate

Table 4.1 Studies on the Relationship between International Factors and Labor Markets

Article	Sample, periodicity	Industries, countries (U.S. unless specified otherwise)	Dependent variable	Regressor	Finding
Grossman (1986)	1973–1983, monthly	Blast Furnaces and Steel Mill Products (SIC 3312)	Hours of employment for production workers	Ratio of tariff-inclusive price of foreign steel to U.S. price index	Significant unitary-elasticity
Grossman (1987)	1969–1979, monthly	Nine import-competing three-digit and four-digit SIC industries (separate regressions)	Hours of employment; average hourly earnings of production workers	Import prices	Significant effects for: employment—one industry, wages—three industries.
Branson and Love (1988)	1970–1986 quarterly	Twenty two-digit SIC manufacturing industries (separate regressions)	Employment of production or non-production workers	Multilateral dollar real exchange rate	Significant in 13 industries: elasticities from 0.13–0.65, with largest for durable goods and production workers.
Revenga (1992)	1977–1987, quarterly	Thirty-eight three-digit and four-digit SIC manufacturing industries (pooled cross-section)	Production workers: number, average number of weekly hours, average hourly earnings	Industry-specific import prices interacted with import share	Employment elasticity = 0.23; with import price × import share, elasticity = 0.16 (at mean import share); elasticity = 0.29 at import share 1 s.d. above mean.
Burgess and Knetter (1998)	1970–1988, annual	Fourteen industries (two-digit SIC) in G-7 countries (95 separate regressions)	Growth rate of employment in particular industries	For each country, average of six bilateral G-7 real exchange rates	Significant coefficient of expected sign in > 25% of regressions, wrong sign and significant in 3%.

Study	Period	Industries/Data	Variables	Exchange Rate	Findings
Campa and Goldberg (2001)	1972–1995, annual	Two-digit SIC industries (panels with all industries, low and high markup, separate)	Number of jobs, total hours, wages, overtime hours, overtime wages	Industry-specific RER, decomposed into transitory and permanent, interacted with exports or intermediate imports	Real exchange rate significant for number of jobs, overtime employment in low-markup industries (interact with both exports and imported intermediate goods).
Goldberg and Tracy (2000)	1971–1995, annual	Two-digit SIC industries, separated by U. S. states	Net employment wages	Industry-specific import and export real exchange rate	Differences across import and export real exchange rate, unambiguous employment response in 13 of 20 industries.
Kletzer (1998a, 2000)		Three-digit CIC[a] industries	Displacement rates (gross worker flows)	Price of imported goods for particular industries, export sales	Export sales significantly lower displacement rates, not so with import prices.
Goldberg, Tracy, and Aaronson (1999)	1977–1997, annual	Current population surveys, 18 two-year panel data sets	Probability of changing jobs for men across successive surveys	Two-digit SIC industry-specific import and export exchange rates.	Exchange rate significantly affects job change probability during appreciation but not depreciation, and sign differs for import and export real exchange rate.
Gourinchas (1998)	1972–1988, quarterly	Gross job flows (LRD) 68 "traded" and 35 "nontraded" industries (of possible 450)	Job creation rate Job destruction rate	Developed from trend of four-digit SIC industry-specific real exchange rate	Appreciation raises both creation and destruction, and depreciation lowers both rates.

[a] Commerce Industrial Classification.

international competition must show that import pressure is the most significant cause of its injury. In two separate studies, Gene Grossman studied the effects of import competition on employment. One of these studies focused on the U.S. steel industry, and the other considered nine U.S. manufacturing industries.

Grossman's (1986) study of the steel industry involved the estimation of employment equations, in which the dependent variable was the average weekly hours of employment of production workers in the Blast Furnaces and Steel Mill industry (SIC number 3312). The regression uses monthly data over the period from 1973 to 1983. One of the regressors was the ratio of the dollar price of foreign steel, inclusive of any tariff costs, to an overall U.S. price index. The tariff-inclusive dollar price of foreign steel is the product of the foreign-currency price of steel, the relevant bilateral exchange rate, and a tariff rate drawn from the University of Michigan model of World Production and Trade. There were two large changes in the tariff rate over the sample period, a tariff surcharge during the Nixon administration and the Tokyo round of tariff reductions, which concluded in 1979.

Grossman found a statistically significant unitary elasticity of the relative cost of foreign steel on the hours of employment of production workers. But when comparing the actual time path of workers' hours and a counterfactual in which the tariff-inclusive domestic currency price of foreign steel is unchanged, he found that, for the most part, actual hours exceed the hours estimated to have prevailed had the price of foreign steel remained unchanged. The exception here, the case where simulated hours fall short of actual hours, is during the period of the rapid dollar appreciation at the end of his sample from mid 1982 through 1983. Thus, Grossman concluded that the source of the significance of the price of foreign steel on employment is changes in the exchange rate rather than changes in tariff rates or changes in the foreign-currency price of foreign steel. He also noted that the exchange rate represents the single biggest determinant of hours of employment by production workers *except for* the secular shift away from employment in SIC 3312; a time trend in these regressions indicated a significant reduction of hours of 9 percent per year.

In subsequent research, Grossman (1987) found less evidence of the effect of import prices in other manufacturing industries. This paper applied the methodology of his earlier work to a study of the effects of the price of imports on average hourly earnings and production-worker employment hours in nine manufacturing sectors. The nine sectors he studied were either three-digit or four-digit SIC industries that are commonly thought of as competing with imports, such as Leather Tanning (SIC 311), Ball and Roller Bearings (SIC 3562), and Radio and Television (SIC 365). The sample consists of monthly observations over the period of 1969 to 1979. He found that a significant reduction in import prices adversely affected employment in only one of these nine industries, Radio and Television. Significant effects of import prices on wages were found for only three industries: Leather Tanning, Ball and Roller Bearings, and Photography Equipment (SIC 386), and the elasticities were generally small.

Grossman's sample period ends in the midst of the great dollar appreciation of the 1980s. Branson and Love (1988) addressed a similar question to Grossman (1987), but their focus was on the effects on employment of the exchange rate during the entire period of the appreciation of the dollar during the first half of the 1980s. Their sample covers the period 1970 to the first quarter of 1986. While Grossman targeted import competition, Branson and Love, by using the real exchange rate and a wider sample of industries, implicitly focused on both import competition and export promotion. Branson and Love estimated separate regressions for each of the 20 two-digit SIC manufacturing industries using quarterly data. The key dependent variable in their study is a multilateral dollar real exchange rate. This is one way in which their work differs from that of Grossman, who used separate sector-by-sector foreign price series. Branson and Love's work is also distinguished from Grossman's research by their running of separate regressions for employment of production workers and employment of nonproduction workers.

Branson and Love found a significant negative coefficient on the exchange rate (that is, an appreciation reduces employment, and conversely) in 13 of the 20 industries they studied. Among the significant coefficients on the real exchange rate, the elasticities range from 0.13 to 0.65, with the larger values found in durable goods industries and among production workers. Especially strong effects are found in the Primary Metals, Fabricated Metal Products, and Non-electrical Machinery industries. These three industries, along with the Transportation Equipment industry, account for two-thirds of the one million jobs they estimated were lost as a result of the dollar appreciation as compared to a counterfactual case of no appreciation in the first half of the 1980s. As with the results presented by Grossman, they attributed a bigger change in employment to the change in the exchange rate than to other factors, such as the change in the price of energy, although they too found that the trend change in employment accounts for more of the reduction in employment than does the change in the real exchange rate.

The estimate by Branson and Love of the loss of one million manufacturing jobs in response to the dollar appreciation of the first half of the 1980s is consistent with the results presented by Revenga (1992). This similarity is striking because Revenga studied only a subset of relatively disaggregated manufacturing firms consisting of 38 three-digit and four-digit SIC manufacturing industries. This subset represented 72 percent of total manufacturing imports and 35 percent of total manufacturing employment in 1985. The period Revenga studies, 1977 to 1987, also differs from the longer sample of Branson and Love but, of course, both samples include the dollar appreciation episode of the first half of the 1980s. The key dependent variable in Revenga's regressions is industry-specific import prices. For each industry, Revenga constructed this variable by using the weighted average of bilateral dollar exchange rates where the weights represent the U.S. imports from the respective countries. She regressed this variable, as well as a number of controls, on quarterly data for both employment (measured either as the number of production workers or as the average number of person-hours per week) and the average hourly earnings of production workers. Among the pooled cross-section regressions that she ran, her most significant estimate is an employment elasticity of –0.23. Given Revenga's estimate of a decline in import prices of about 20 percent over the 6-year period from 1980 to 1985, and total manufacturing employment that annually averaged 19.4 million jobs over this period, the estimate of the annual average job loss is 0.15 million manufacturing jobs.[16] Thus, over this 6-year period, Revenga's estimates suggest a loss of 0.9 million manufacturing jobs, an estimate strikingly close to that of Branson and Love.[17]

Revenga's research also documented the wide variation in exposure to international competition across the industries she studied, a result that is particularly relevant for our research presented later in this book. Revenga reported that the ratio of imports to total output across the industries in her sample ranges from 0.04 (for Meat Products, SIC 2010) to 0.70 (for Apparel, SIC 2380). She divided her industries into three groups based on share of imports. Over the period 1980 to 1987, the fall in employment across these groups is quite diverse, with a reduction of 28 percent in the high import share group, 14 percent in the medium import share group, and 8 percent in the low import share group. Revenga also noted, however, that the standard deviation within each group is quite high, a point consistent with the statistics presented in the previous chapter and one that suggests the importance of considering gross job flows rather than net employment changes. The wide differences across import share groups in the mean values of net employment change motivate Revenga's use of a regression specification that interacts import share with import price. This specification also emerges from the model we present in Chapter 5 and implement in our empirical analysis in Chapter 6. Revenga estimated elasticities of employment with respect to import prices equal to 0.16 for an industry with the mean level of import share (equal to 18 percent) and 0.29 for an industry with an import share one standard deviation above the mean (that is, import share equal to 29 percent). The estimated elasticities of wages with respect to the exchange rate are much lower, ranging from 0.06 to 0.09. Revenga suggested that these differences in the relative size of elasticities reflect a situation where workers are highly mobile across industries but not across skill groups.[18]

The studies mentioned above do not distinguish between import competition from developing and industrial nations. A noteworthy aspect of the expansion of trade between the United States and the rest of the world, however, is that imports from developing nations represented about a quarter of all U.S. imports in 1970 and 1980 and then rose to 32 percent of all imports in 1990 and 38 percent of all imports in 1996. An often-voiced concern is that trade with developing nations represents a greater threat to manufacturing employees in the United States (especially those with relatively low skill levels) than a comparable amount of trade with industrial countries.

Sachs and Shatz (1994) attempted to decompose the role played by trade with developing countries from that of trade with industrial countries in altering employment in the United States. They based their analysis on a data set consisting of the amount of bilateral trade of 51 three-digit U.S. manufacturing industries with each of 150 countries in the years 1978 and 1990. They calculated a counterfactual value of trade that would have occurred had the pattern of bilateral trade in 1990 been the same as the pattern of trade in 1978, assuming a constant relationship between industry shipments and industry final demand across those two years. These estimates are then used to calculate employment patterns in 1990 had the 1978 pattern of trade prevailed in that year. Sachs and Shatz concluded that employment levels in 1990 were 7.2 percent lower for production workers and 2.1 percent lower for nonproduction workers than would have been the case had the pattern of bilateral trade in that year been the same as the pattern of bilateral trade in 1978. They stated that almost all of the difference between the actual and the calculated counterfactual employment is due to a tilt in trade toward developing countries. But, as pointed out in the published comments on this paper by Deardorff (1994), the correlation between trade and labor-market outcomes does not address questions of causality since both trade and employment could be responding to other factors that changed between 1978 and 1990, such as trade liberalization, the (exogenous) growth of labor-abundant foreign economies, and technical change.

This problem of joint causality cited by Deardorff is probably less pronounced for the aforementioned studies of the effect of dollar exchange rates on United States employment. It is more reasonable, when using annual data, to assume that changes in real dollar exchange rates are not driven by contemporaneous events originating in the U.S. labor market for narrowly defined industries.[19] Regression analysis allows one to control for factors such as monetary policy and fiscal policy that jointly affect aggregate labor-market developments and dollar exchange rates. It may be more difficult to control for joint causation between trade patterns and employment, especially over a period of a decade or more.

All of the studies on the effects of exchange rate changes on employment cited above look only at labor-market responses in the United States. Burgess and Knetter (1998) expanded the scope of analysis by considering the effects of the real exchange rate on manufacturing employment in the G-7 countries (Canada, France, Germany, Italy, Japan, the United Kingdom, and the United States). Separate regressions were run for 14 industries in each country (although data are not available for three of the potential 98 industry-country groups). The industry categories, based on an OECD classification, correspond approximately to two-digit SIC industries and cover manufacturing as well as agriculture, mining, finance, construction, transport services, and wood products. The regressions use annual data over the period from 1970 to 1988. The dependent variable is the growth rate of total employees of the particular industry. The exchange rate series used in the regressions are simple averages of the seven bilateral exchange rates for each of the seven countries with respect to the other members of the G-7.

Burgess and Knetter reported significant coefficients on the real exchange rate of the expected sign (that is, an appreciation reduces employment growth, and conversely) in more than one-quarter of the 95 regressions they estimated. The coefficient on the real exchange rate is of the opposite sign and significant in only 3 percent of the regressions. The country with the highest average estimated response of employment growth to the real exchange rate for the full set of industries is the United Kingdom, followed by the United States, followed by Germany and Japan. The estimated speed of adjustment is also faster in the United States and the United Kingdom than in Germany or Japan. Using the full panel, Burgess and Knetter found that the only country with a responsiveness of employment growth to the real exchange rate that is significantly different from the United States' is the United Kingdom.

The research cited above tends to find a significant effect of the real exchange rate on employment, which contrasts with the general tenor of the results of Campa and Goldberg (2001). Campa and Goldberg suggested that the source of the difference between their results and those of either Branson and Love, or of Revenga, lies in the way in which they account for differences in the scope and type of currency exposure across industries. They noted that there are three channels through which the exchange rate affects labor demand: import penetration, export orientation, and the use of imported inputs. The first two of these channels would be associated with a situation where an appreciation lowers labor demand and, consequently, reduces employment. This is the direction of causation that the previously mentioned studies considered, but the third channel, the use of imported inputs, tilts the exchange rate response in the other direction, since an appreciation lowers the cost of production and, given an appropriate cross-elasticity of demand for labor and other inputs, increases labor demand and employment.

Campa and Goldberg captured the different channels through which the exchange rate influences labor demand and employment by using, in their regressions, the product of the exchange rate and a measure of the level of industry exports and, separately, the product of the exchange rate and a measure of the use of imported intermediate goods by an industry. The high correlation across industries of import penetration and imported intermediate use precludes Campa and Goldberg from including the product of the exchange rate and a measure of import penetration as well. They used both a multilateral real exchange rate, which is common across all industries, and a real exchange rate that reflects the trade patterns of particular industries. They reported that the results with either series are similar and, therefore, only presented results using industry-specific exchange rates. The exchange rates are decomposed into their permanent (nonstationary) and transitory (stationary) components, using the technique of Beveridge and Nelson (1981). The dependent variables studied include number of jobs, total hours worked, industry wages, overtime hours, and overtime wages. The regressions on number of jobs, total hours, and industry wages use only the permanent component of the exchange rate, while the regressions on overtime hours and overtime wages use only the transitory component. The observations represent annual data at the two-digit SIC level over the period 1972 to 1995. All the variables in the regressions are first differences but for lagged levels of the dependent variables. Campa and Goldberg ran both time series panels using data from all industries, panels in which they split the sample into low-markup and high-markup industries, and separate regressions for individual manufacturing industries.[20]

The results presented by Campa and Goldberg suggest the importance of splitting the sample by markup, since there are no instances of significant effects of the exchange rate on any of their dependent variables for high-markup industries. But, for the low-markup subsample, there is evidence of a significant effect of both the exchange rate interacted with exports and the exchange rate interacted with imported intermediate goods on the number of jobs and overtime employment. In addition, the coefficient on the product of the exchange rate and exports is significant in the full-sample overtime hours regression. The industry wage regressions include significant coefficients both on exchange rate terms for the subsample of low-markup industries and on the product of the exchange rate and exports for the full sample. The overtime wage regression includes a significant coefficient on the product of the exchange rate and exports for the low-markup sample only.

This distinction in the pattern of significance, between high- and low-markup industries, is also evident in the estimated employment and wage elasticities derived from separate regressions on data for two-digit industries. For example, the five largest estimated elasticities (evaluated using average shares of exports and imported inputs) for number of jobs with respect to the exchange rate are all in industries that are classified as low markup. These industries include Leather and Leather Products (elasticity = –0.20), Petroleum and Coal Products (elasticity = –0.12), Primary Metal Products (elasticity = –0.09), Furniture and Fixtures (elasticity = –0.08), and Fabricated Metal Products (elasticity = –0.07). These estimated elasticities are all significant at the 5 percent level and represent the only significant estimated elasticities for total hours with respect to the exchange rate among the 20 industries. Likewise, these five industries, along with Textile Mill Products, represent the full set of industries with a significant elasticity of total hours with respect to the exchange rate. In fact, arranging industries by the size of the estimated elasticities of total hours yields the same order as in the case of the ranking by the elasticity of number of jobs. But, for each industry, the estimated elasticity is larger for total hours than for number of jobs, with significant estimates ranging from –0.28 (for Leather and Leather Products) to –0.07 (for Textile Mill Products).

Campa and Goldberg found relatively few industries in which there is a significant effect of the real exchange rate on total employment as compared to the results of others, such as Revenga. Even among industries in which Campa and Goldberg found significant results, the estimated elasticities (evaluated at the mean level of the interaction terms) are all less than Revenga's estimate of an elasticity of –0.23 for her pooled sample. There could be quite a few reasons for these differences, including differences in both sample periods and industries studied.[21] Also, there are differences in estimation, notably the decomposition of the exchange rate by Campa and Goldberg. As will be seen, the results we present in Chapter 6 are more supportive of a role for the exchange rate in affecting total employment than is the case with the results presented by Campa and Goldberg.

In another paper, Goldberg and Tracy (2000) analyzed the effect of real exchange rate movements on employment and wages in the United States using data disaggregated by two-digit industry as well as by state. As in Campa and Goldberg, the key regressors are industry-specific import and export real exchange rates constructed by weighting (separately for imports and exports) the bilateral real exchange rates of U.S. trading partners in each two-digit industry for each year and measures of the importance of exports and imported inputs across industries and states. Goldberg and Tracy found that appreciations of the dollar relative to the currencies of export partners are associated with reductions in employment, while appreciations of the dollar relative to the currencies of imported input providers are associated with increased employment. Their results suggest, however, that there is considerable heterogeneity in these effects across industries and states. They found that employment is unambiguously responsive to exchange rate movements in only 13 of the 20 industries examined.

INTERNATIONAL FACTORS AND GROSS FLOWS

The studies cited in the preceding section focus on changes in aggregate net employment, either at the sector or at the industry level. However, aggregate net employment masks the extensive volume of gross job and worker flows underlying labor markets. Consequently, a new literature has emerged recently with a small but growing number of studies of the effects of international factors on labor-market flows. In this section, we review this nascent literature on international factors and gross labor-market flows in two parts. The first part focuses on studies of job flows; the second part focuses on studies of worker flows.

Job Flows

Studies of job flows look for the effects of international factors on job creation and destruction, *ce* and *ed* in Figure 4.1. Unfortunately, data on *cv* and *vd* are not available. The job-flow approach assumes a direct connection between international factors and the total demand for labor at particular production sites or establishments.[22] Individual establishments will create and destroy jobs (i.e., expand or contract the level of employment) in response to changes in international conditions.

The first analysis of job flows and international factors is Davis, Haltiwanger, and Schuh (1996, chapter 3). They reported average rates of U.S. manufacturing job flows for 1973 to 1986 by quintiles of four-digit SIC industries sorted according to their exposure to international trade (their table 3.5). Exposure is defined in terms of import penetration, the ratio of imports to imports plus domestic output, and in terms of export share, the ratio of exports to domestic output. They found:

> Strikingly, the table shows no systematic relationship between the magnitude of gross job flows and exposure to international trade. The only aspect of table 3.5 suggesting that international trade reduces job security is the large rate of gross job destruction among industries with a very high import penetration ratio . . . On balance, the evidence is highly unfavorable to the view that international trade exposure systematically reduces job security. (pp. 48–49)

This apparent lack of a connection between international trade and job flows largely is attributable to the long-run nature of their analysis. They compared the 14-year *averages* of job flows and trade exposure, but one would not necessarily expect to find a connection between average job flows and average trade exposure. Factors determining average trade exposure include resource endowments, geography, transportation costs, exchange rate policies, and free trade political philosophies. In contrast, factors determining average job flows include costs of hiring and firing workers, barriers to entry and exit of firms from markets, the pace of technological change, product and process innovation, and government labor-market policies. There is no well-established theoretical or empirical reason for a connection between these two sets of underlying factors that determine the long-run averages.

On the other hand, there are good reasons to expect a correlation between job flows and *changes* in international factors at higher frequencies. Changes in the exchange rate and changes in trade restrictions (tariffs, quotas, etc.) are likely to induce factor reallocation across firms and industries, unless the changes are very small or very transitory. We would expect the year-to-year movements in job flows and trade exposure to be closely correlated, and thus a time series analysis would be more likely to reveal such correlation.

Gourinchas (1998) offered the first time-series analysis of international factors and gross job flows. He used vector autoregression (VAR) models to estimate the effects of real exchange rates on job creation and destruction during the period of 1972 to 1988 using quarterly job-flow data from Davis, Haltiwanger, and Schuh at the four-digit SIC industry level. Industries are classified as traded, nontraded, or other, using export share and import penetration ratios.[23] He restricted his sample to 103 of a possible 450 industries, focusing on the 68 industries that are the most involved in international trade (his "traded" group) or the 35 industries least involved in international trade (his "nontraded" group). An industry-specific real exchange rate is calculated for each of the 103 industries used in the regressions. These industry-specific exchange rates are the weighted average of real bilateral dollar exchange rates, with weights reflecting the proportion of trade with a particular country undertaken by that industry over the entire sample period. He used the deviation from trend of the logarithm of the level of industry-specific real exchange rates in the regressions.

Gourinchas reported that real exchange rates move job creation and destruction in the *same* direction in traded industries but have little or no effect on job flows in nontraded industries. A 10 percent appreciation (increase above trend) raises job destruction by 0.44 percent and raises job creation by 0.17 percent in traded industries over three quarters, thereby reducing net employment by 0.27 percent and raising job reallocation by 0.61 percent. A 10 percent depreciation produces simultaneous declines in job destruction and creation of the same magnitudes, thereby reducing job reallocation by 0.61 percent. Thus, real exchange rates have allocative effects on jobs whereby appreciations stimulate job reallocation and depreciations inhibit job reallocation, the latter producing a so-called "chill" in reallocative activity. This result contrasts with the typical conclusion from most previous studies of U.S. job flows, which find that aggregate shocks tend to be dominant. That is, job creation and destruction tend to respond to standard macroeconomic shocks in opposite directions, with job destruction rising relatively more than job creation falls. Consequently, Gourinchas's work is among the first to demonstrate the presence of a contemporaneous allocative effect.[24]

In a closely related study, Gourinchas (1999) found that the real exchange rate affects gross job flows even more in France than in the United States, but he did not find evidence of contemporaneous allocative effects. He estimated an analogous VAR system using annual French manufacturing data on net and gross employment for two-digit industries from 1984 to 1992. Once again, Gourinchas identified a selected sample of industries classified as tradable according to their export shares and import penetration ratios. He found that a 10 percent increase in the real exchange rate in tradable industries reduces job creation by 7.1 percent and increases job destruction by 2.4 percent, thus reducing net employment by 9.5 percent.

These results for France differ from his U.S. results in three ways. First, the job-flow responses are an order of magnitude larger in France, reflecting both greater openness and more sensitivity to international factors. Second, job creation and destruction move in opposite directions in France, rather than in the same direction. This response is similar to the bulk of U.S. job-flow studies and suggests the real exchange rates exert more important aggregate effects than allocative effects in France. Third, job creation is more responsive than job destruction, rather than vice versa as in the U.S. data.

Both Gourinchas studies offer dynamic heterogeneous-agent models to explain the empirical results. The model in Gourinchas (1998) extends the matching framework of Mortensen and Pissarides (1994) to include a tradable and nontradable production sector with a relative price that represents the real exchange rate. Fluctuations in the real exchange rate lower the job-matching rate, which induces a simultaneous increase in both job creation and destruction (and therefore job reallocation) with a greater short-run response of destruction. This dynamic pattern fits the U.S. data but not the French data, so the model in Gourinchas (1999) introduces heterogeneous vintage capital, similar in spirit to the work of Caballero and Hammour (1996). Match-specific capital and inefficient contracting prevent wages from adjusting sufficiently to unanticipated real exchange rate movements. Job destruction thus rises immediately, and job creation falls somewhat before eventually rising as unemployed workers are rematched.

The results in this book build on our earlier work (Klein, Schuh, and Triest 2003), which extended and modified Gourinchas's results for the United States. We used essentially the same data except that we include all four-digit industries and explicitly account for the fact that openness varies across industries and time. We also developed a multi-sector model of firms with heterogeneous exposure to international trade. The model allowed us to derive estimating equations for job creation and destruction that control for a host of industry-specific variables not included by Gourinchas, in addition to aggregate variables similar to those included in his VARs. Perhaps most importantly, we showed that the *growth* rate, rather than the level, of the real exchange rate influences job flows. Furthermore, we decomposed the exchange rate into trend and cyclical components.

Our results show that for all U.S. industries, and controlling for industry-level openness, changes in the growth of the real exchange rate influence job destruction but not job creation. A 10 percent appreciation (increase in growth) raises job destruction by 0.33 percent and lowers net employment by a similar amount over three quarters (job creation falls 0.02 percent, but the response is insignificant). These results, which are consistent with the bulk of previous job-flows studies, suggest that Gourinchas's finding of an allocative effect for real exchange rates appears to be attributable to his sample limitations, omission of industry-level controls, and specification of the real exchange rate.

However, by decomposing real exchange rates into trend and cyclical components, we showed that both aggregate and allocative forces are at work through exchange rates. The responses of job flows in the industry with median openness are markedly different for moderate appreciations of the trend and cyclical components of the real exchange rate.[25] A moderate appreciation of the trend real exchange rate has purely *allocative* effects—job creation and destruction both increase by about 0.4 percent, so job reallocation rises about 0.7 percent, but net employment essentially is unchanged. This result is similar to the results reported by Gourinchas. In contrast, a moderate appreciation of the cyclical component of the real exchange rate has primarily aggregate effects—job destruction rises about 0.7 percent and net employment declines by the same magnitude because the effect on job creation is essentially zero. The aggregate effects dominate the allocative effects when the model is estimated using the actual real exchange rate. All job-flow responses are roughly three times larger for the industry at the 90th percentile of the openness distribution.

Davidson and Matusz (2001b) also used the Davis, Haltiwanger, and Schuh (DHS) job-flows data to conduct empirical tests of the ideas advanced in their earlier work with Martin on trade and search generated unemployment.[26] They argued that firms must pay compensating wage differentials associated with job and worker turnover rates. Those firms with low job destruction rates and high job creation rates will have lower wages and thus have a comparative advantage in foreign trade, which Davidson and Matusz define as net trade (exports minus imports) normalized by the domestic market (production plus imports). They reported evidence of a statistically significant negative correlation between average net trade and average job destruction and a somewhat weaker and less significant positive correlation between average net trade and average job creation, at both the two-digit and the four-digit industry level.[27] In a related study, Magee, Davidson, and Matusz (2001) inferred that the distribution of factor income is related to job turnover rates by providing evidence that campaign contributions to political action committees match up well with votes by politicians on trade-related legislation.

Finally, a recent study of four European manufacturing sectors reports little or no connection between international trade and proxies of labor-market flows. Bentivogli and Pagano (1999) used data from Eurostat's Labor Force Survey to construct measures they call job creation, job destruction, and job reallocation. Job destruction is defined as newly unemployed workers (relative to employment), job creation is defined as net employment growth, and job reallocation is defined as the sum of these two. Clearly, these measures are not the same as the DHS plant-level measures of job flows, and they mix job- and worker-flow concepts. For example, newly unemployed workers (flows *eu* and *nu* in Figure 4.1) include not only workers whose jobs were destroyed but also workers who became unemployed for other reasons. Bentivogli and Pagano estimated regression models of the flow proxies and uniformly found that lagged exports to and imports from newly industrialized economies in Asia are completely insignificant in their regressions, while worker characteristics are very significant. They concluded that recent increases in trade with Asian countries are not responsible for adverse labor-market developments in Germany, France, Italy, and the United Kingdom.

Worker Flows

Studies of worker flows look at the impact of international factors on workers who report being displaced from employment: in Figure 4.1, these worker flows include *ee*, *eu*, and *en*. This approach assumes a direct connection between international factors and the demand for individual workers at particular establishments, which may or may not engage in international trade. Workers will flow from employment in a job at a particular establishment to some other state of the labor market in response to changes in international conditions that affect that establishment.[28] These studies use data on workers who report being laid off (displaced) from particular employers.

The worker-flow approach has two distinct advantages in identifying the impact of international factors on labor markets. One is that it can identify the impact at a more fundamental level than job flows, specifically the flow of workers across jobs within establishments. Also, by identifying individual workers, it offers the potential for following workers over time and observing the longer run effects of international factors on workers and labor markets.

However, the worker-flow approach also has two disadvantages. First, it is more difficult to connect the international factors to specific worker flows because workers flow out of employment for many reasons other than job destruction due to international factors. Unfortunately, there is insufficient information about workers' employers in the worker-flow data to be able to control for this problem. Second, the worker-flow data depend heavily on workers' ability to recollect historical circumstances and on their understanding of firms' employment decisions. Both of these difficulties may induce measurement error in the worker-flow data that limits the ability to identify accurately the link between international factors and worker flows.

Two studies by Kletzer (1998a, 2000) considered the effects of international factors on employment and found evidence that import competition contributes to job loss or displacement. She used data from the Bureau of Labor Statistics' Displaced Worker Surveys (DWS), a supplement to the Current Population Surveys (CPS). The DWS ask a panel of participants: "Have you lost a job in the previous 5-year period due to plant closings, your employer going out of business, a layoff without recall, or other similar reasons?" Workers answering "yes" are a subset of all possible job separations, which also include quits and other types of firings.[29] Using econometric models, Kletzer tested whether import competition is a significant contributor to worker displacement and also whether export sales tend to reduce worker displacements.

In both articles, Kletzer regressed the job displacement rate of three-digit Commerce Industrial Classification (CIC) industries on, among other variables, the price of imported goods for that three-digit CIC industry. Her sample consisted of 70 industries from 1979 to the early 1990s. The evidence in Kletzer (2000) is that export sales significantly lower displacement rates, but the results do not strongly support the hypothesis that import prices are a significant determinant of displacement rates. Some industries with extensive import competition exhibit extensive job displacement, but extensive job displacement also occurs in other industries with little or no import competition. In Kletzer (1998a), using a more restricted sample, the effect of import prices on displacement rates is somewhat more significant, although a measure of import share cannot be shown to significantly affect displacement rates, even within this sample. The effect of exports and, especially, domestic demand on displacement rates, is shown to be much stronger. Overall, the Kletzer results are valuable and interesting, but they also highlight the limitations of the worker-flow approach given current data availability.

The analysis of Goldberg, Tracy, and Aaronson (1999) is similar to that of Kletzer but broader in terms of measured job displacement. They used data from the CPS during the period of 1977 to 1997, matching the response of civilian men (aged 18 to 63) from consecutive annual surveys. Respondents are denoted as "job changers" if, between the time of one survey in March and the time of the subsequent survey the following March, they either had more than one employer or had a spell of unemployment. (Note that this definition of job changers is more comprehensive than the displaced workers in Kletzer's work.) Goldberg, Tracy, and Aaronson reported that, across broad industry groups and across the time periods 1977 to 1984 and 1986 to 1996, job changers represent between 15 and 20 percent of the 123,000 matched pairs in their sample.

Goldberg, Tracy, and Aaronson used these 123,000 observations to estimate the effect of exchange rates on the probability of job change. They used a limited dependent variable model in which the dependent variable represents whether or not an individual was a job changer over the course of a year. The regressors include characteristics of the individual (including education, race, age, and marital status), characteristics of the industry in which the individual was employed (including industry fixed effects, industry-specific time trends, and industry-specific import and export exchange rates), and time-varying aggregate regressors (including the real interest rate, Gross Domestic Product [GDP] growth, and the unemployment rate). Their results suggest an asymmetric effect of exchange rate movements on the probability of changing jobs. There is evidence that, during periods of appreciation, the exchange rate influences the probability of changing jobs in manufacturing; an appreciation of the export exchange rate lowers the likelihood of changing jobs, while an appreciation of the import exchange rate raises the probability of changing jobs. Overall, Goldberg, Tracy, and Aaronson reported that appreciations are associated with a small reduction in job instability, although there is no significant effect of depreciations on job stability, nor is there a significant effect when the regression is constrained to have appreciations and depreciations enter symmetrically.

Notes

1. For surveys of this literature, see Feenstra and Hanson (2003), and articles in the summer 1995 issue of the *Journal of Economic Perspectives* (vol. 9, no. 3), including Freeman (1995), Richardson (1995), and Wood (1995).
2. See also the studies by Riordan and Staiger (1993), Sener (2001), and Hoon (2001a,b).
3. For surveys of this literature see Davis, Haltiwanger, and Schuh (1996), Davis and Haltiwanger (1999), Mortensen and Pissarides (1999a), and Hall (1999).
4. For an overview of the search literature, see Mortensen and Pissarides (1999b).

5. During the postwar period, the correlations between changes in employment and unemployment are –0.52 on a monthly basis and –0.83 on a quarterly basis.
6. This point, and the subsequent discussion, apply equally to all factors of production, such as labor and capital, but we emphasize labor here.
7. See Matusz and Tarr (2000) for a complementary survey of this issue.
8. Estimates of both the welfare gains and the adjustment costs likely are underestimated significantly. Welfare gains from economic growth, economies of scale, competition and antitrust, general equilibrium effects, and other miscellaneous factors are omitted. For example, see Melitz (2002) for the latest evidence on the beneficial impact of trade on productivity growth via reallocation. Likewise, adjustment costs from hiring and firing workers, search, and the destruction of human capital are omitted.
9. Magee called his estimates "ball park" and "rough," so we use some rounding to boil down the implications to "rounder" numbers without distorting the main points. For example, the reported adjustment costs range from 0.85 to 0.96 percent of the total welfare gains, which we call "1 percent."
10. Some analogous studies offer estimates for specific industries. Takacs and Winters (1991), which tries to account for some of natural labor turnover, obtained a gain-to-cost ratio of 59 to 1 for removal of "voluntary" import restraints in the footwear industry in the United Kingdom. De Melo and Tarr (1990) obtained a gain-to-cost ratio of 65 for removal of the quotas in U.S. textiles, steel, and automobile industries.
11. Of course, free trade opponents have raised other important issues too, such as concerns about the environment, inequality, and human rights.
12. Of course, labor-adjustment costs are not unique to international factors. All forces that induce labor adjustment through job and worker flows generally will entail these kinds of costs.
13. There are a few prior estimates, such as in Holt et al. (1960) and Oi (1962), but these are relatively simple and they come from a very small number of firms.
14. Conventional wisdom would suggest that these firing costs are lower in the United States, but these numbers are remarkably large for any relatively free-market economy.
15. This section discusses only studies of U.S. net employment because this literature is extensive. There are many analogous studies of foreign net employment and international factors as well. For example, see Dewatripont, Sapir, and Sekkat (1999) for an in-depth study of European employment and international trade. There is also a broader literature on globalization and international unemployment rates, such as Wagner (2000).
16. $19.4 \times (-0.23) \times 0.20/6 = -0.15$.
17. $(-0.15) \times 6 = -0.9$.
18. This result is consistent with a relatively flat industry labor-supply schedule and a relatively steep industry labor-demand schedule. In this case, changes in import prices, which shift the labor-demand schedule, will have proportionally larger effects on employment than on wages. The model we develop in Chapter 5, which

forms the basis of the subsequent empirical analysis, assumes high worker mobility across industries.
19. It is worth noting, in this regard, that the correlation between nominal dollar exchange rates and the respective real dollar exchange rates typically exceeds 0.90.
20. The industries characterized as low markup by Campa and Goldberg include the following 11 industries: Food and Kindred Products (SIC 20), Textile Mill Products (SIC 22), Apparel and Mill Products (SIC 23), Lumber and Wood Products (SIC 24), Furniture and Fixtures (SIC 25), Paper and Allied Products (SIC 26), Petroleum and Coal Products (SIC 29), Leather and Leather Products (SIC 31), Primary Metal Products (SIC 33), Fabricated Metal Products (SIC 34), and Transportation Equipment (SIC 37).
21. Campa and Goldberg noted that Revenga's sample of industries, which, in 1980, represented 72 percent of manufacturing imports but only 35 percent of manufacturing employment, was chosen to focus on the effects of import competition in the United States and, therefore, is not representative of manufacturing as a whole.
22. Labor demand may be affected directly, in establishments that engage in international trade, or indirectly, in establishments that do not engage in international trade but compete with establishments that do.
23. See pp. 162–163 of his article for details.
24. Another is Davis and Haltiwanger (2001), which provided similar evidence for oil price shocks but did not examine the influence of exchange rates.
25. A moderate appreciation is defined as two consecutive years of one standard deviation increases—about 10 percent in the cyclical rate and about 3.5 percent in the trend rate.
26. This paper also used data on worker flows—job acquisitions (related to job creation) and job separations (related to job destruction)—published by the Bureau of Labor Statistics until 1981. Because the methodology and results are similar to those using job-flow data, we focus on these.
27. The regressions are very similar in spirit to the evidence in Davis, Haltiwanger, and Schuh (1996), but with two important differences: 1) the correlations are tabulated at the detailed industry level rather than by quintiles of industries and 2) the focus is on industries' net trade, rather than industries' import and export intensities.
28. Note that the level of employment (job flow) at the establishment may or may not change along with the worker flow, depending on whether the establishment retains the job and replaces the worker, destroys the job without creating a new one, or destroys the job and creates a new one.
29. Kletzer also notes that an individual displaced from a job and rehired into a different job with the same employer is considered displaced. Also, worker displacement may understate actual job loss since it does not capture quits in anticipation of layoffs, quits motivated by wage dissatisfaction or deteriorating working conditions, or changes in the rate of shutdown by firms.

5
Job Flows and the Exchange Rate

A Framework

The data presented in Chapter 3 demonstrate that even narrowly defined industries exhibit simultaneous job creation and job destruction. The focus of this book is to determine the extent to which these gross job flows reflect responses to changes in the international environment, in particular, to movements in dollar exchange rates or changing trade restrictions. The data presented in Chapter 2 suggest the potential importance of international factors for job creation and destruction. As discussed in that chapter, the last quarter century has been marked by both large medium-term swings in currency values and persistent shorter run exchange rate volatility. Also, as shown in that chapter, there is a growing and increasingly diverse exposure to international competition among narrowly defined manufacturing industries in the United States. This combination of widely fluctuating exchange rates and diverse exposure to the effects of these fluctuations may act together to generate job reallocation.

The particular way in which these factors interact to generate simultaneous job creation and job destruction is the focus of this chapter. We begin the chapter with a discussion of how an idiosyncratic change in the fortunes of one establishment can affect the amount of labor employed by both that establishment and other establishments in its industry. We focus on linkages among establishments due to their competition for workers, although we would obtain similar results if, instead, we considered competition among establishments for any common pool of resources used in the production, or the marketing and sale, of their products.[1] We then consider how a change in the exchange rate alters the distribution of labor across industries and, therefore, how this contributes to job creation and job destruction. The change in the exchange rate represents an aggregate shock, one that all establishments in all industries face simultaneously, although its consequences differ across industries depending upon the openness of each.[2] As with the idiosyncratic shock, the full effects of the change in the exchange rate on employment in our model represent both direct effects on labor-demand by establishments and the effects arising from competition for workers among establishments.[3]

In developing our model, we have been mindful of the data available to us. For example, we assume that openness varies across industries but is the same among all establishments within an industry since we have data on industry-level openness but not on the openness of individual establishments. Thus, the model presented here is closely linked to the framework used in our empirical analysis in Chapter 6. A more formal presentation of the model, one that provides an explicit framework for our empirical analysis, appears in Appendix B.

JOB FLOWS AND IDIOSYNCRATIC SHOCKS

The simultaneous job creation and job destruction that we document in the previous chapter suggests that there is a great deal of heterogeneity among establishments, even within narrowly defined industries.[4] It is important that a framework used to organize our thinking about the effects of the international environment on reallocation is structured to reflect this heterogeneity. We introduce heterogeneity in our model by assuming that each establishment within an industry differs from all other establishments in that industry because of an idiosyncratic shock to the demand for its product.[5] This shock is distinct from other factors affecting demand such as the exchange rate, domestic income, or foreign income.

Consider a situation where all establishments within an industry sell a similar, but not necessarily identical, product. We also assume that all establishments in an industry satisfy their labor needs by drawing from a common pool of workers.[6] If one establishment enjoys a particularly high level of demand for its product, then its managers will attempt to hire more workers. But, if the overall employment of the industry as a whole cannot vary, the expansion of workers employed by one establishment must come at the expense of the number of workers hired by other establishments. In particular, the establishment with the expanding desire for workers bids up the industry-wide wage and, in so doing, drives other establishments to shed workers. Thus, the establishment enjoying the positive idiosyncratic shock exhibits job creation while other establishments exhibit job destruction. If, across the entire industry, all establishments faced a proportionately equal positive demand shock then the industry wage would be bid up but there would be no reallocation of labor across establishments and, therefore, no job creation or job destruction in the industry. Thus, the amount of reallocation in an industry is tied to the extent of heterogeneity among its establishments.

The logic outlined in the previous paragraph can be illustrated for the case of an industry consisting of two establishments using Figures 5.1A and 5.1B. Each figure depicts labor-demand schedules for each of the two establishments. The length of the horizontal axis represents the fixed number of workers available for employment in either establishment A or establishment B, and therefore the total number of workers available for both establishments is represented by the distance $0_A 0_B$. The number of workers employed by establishment A is measured by moving to the right from the origin labelled 0_A while the number of workers employed by establishment B is measured by moving to the left from the origin labelled 0_B. The two vertical axes represent both the real wages paid by the establishments, W, and the value to the establishments of hiring an additional worker, the *marginal product of labor*, which represents the increase in the number of units of output an establishment can produce through the contribution of an additional worker. The labor-demand schedule for each establishment reflects the property of *diminishing marginal product,* whereby the marginal contribution of each worker to output is less than that of the worker hired immediately before her. Thus, the labor-demand schedules have negative slopes from the perspective of the relevant set of axes, with the labor-demand schedule for Establishment A represented by the line AA and the labor-demand schedule for establishment B represented by the line *BB*.

The interaction between these two establishments occurs in the market for workers. The simplest way to depict this is to require that both establishments pay the same wage. This reflects a situation where workers are indifferent between working in either establishment and can easily move from one establishment to another in response to wage differentials.[7] The assumption of a common wage enables us to establish the equilibrium number of workers hired by each establishment since this means that the value marginal products of labor will be the same for each establishment. Thus the equilibrium occurs where the two labor-demand schedules intersect. This equilibrium gives us both the division of workers between the two establishments and the wage paid by the two establishments. In Figure 5.1A, two labor-demand schedules AA and BB intersect at the point labeled E. Establishment A hires $0_A L$ workers and establishment B hires $0_B L$ workers (where the number of workers hired by establishment B is measured by the distance leftward from 0_B). The common wage paid by both establishments to their employees is given by $0_A W = 0_B W$.

An expansion in the demand for the product of establishment A shifts its labor-demand schedule out and to the right, to the schedule $A'A'$ in Figure 5.1B. At the original wage, establishment A would now like to hire $0_A M$ workers while establishment B would continue to desire to hire $0_B L$ workers. However, $0_A M + 0_B L > 0_A 0_B$ and, consequently, the establishments bid up the wage to $0_A X = 0_B X$. In this new equilibrium, given by the intersection of $A'A'$ and BB at the point E', the number of workers hired by establishment A has risen to $0_A L'$ while the number of workers hired by establishment B has declined to $0_B L'$. Thus, there is job creation by establishment A equal to LL' and job destruction by establishment B equal to $L'L$. There is, by assumption, no net change in employment (since, obviously, $LL' = L'L$), and the total amount of reallocation equals twice the number of workers represented by the distance LL'.

It is straightforward to show that if each establishment faces a positive demand shock, the one with the proportionally larger increase in demand will exhibit job creation while the other will exhibit job destruction. This simultaneous job creation and job destruction occurs even though, all else equal, both establishments would like to hire more workers. The interaction of the establishments in the market for labor ensures that all else is not held equal; rather, in this case, wages are bid up as both establishments attempt to hire a greater proportion of the fixed pool of workers. This pattern of simultaneous creation and destruction need not hold in the more general case where a shift in the industry-wide demand for labor elicits a supply response for the industry as a whole. For example, both establishments may expand employ-

Job Flows and the Exchange Rate: A Framework 87

Figure 5.1A Labor Demand and the Distribution of Employment across Establishments

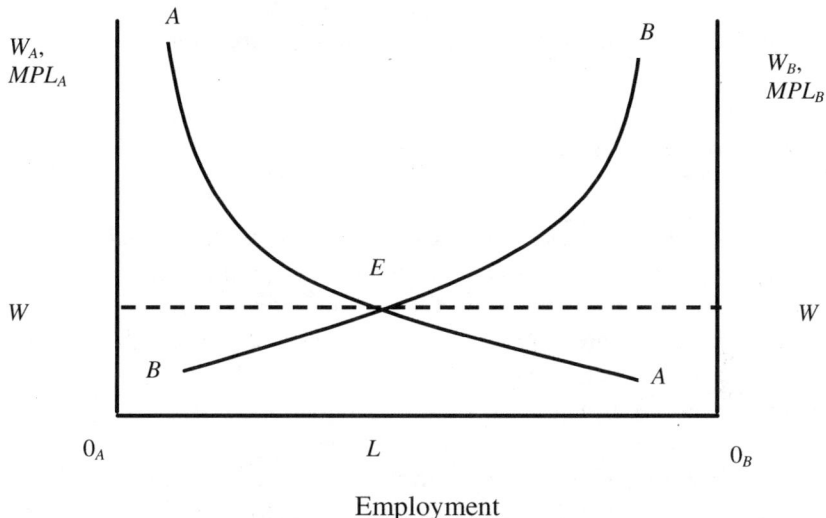

Figure 5.1B Idiosyncratic Shocks to Labor Demand and Job Flows

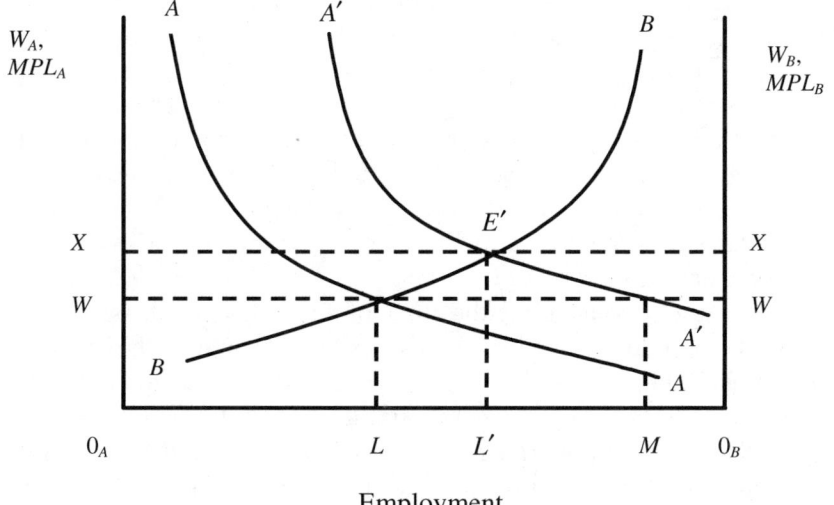

ment and exhibit job creation when they both face positive demand shocks if there is a sufficient labor-supply response. In this case, there is industry-wide job creation and no job destruction. We demonstrate this, and other, generalizations of the model, in Appendix B.

THE ROLE OF AGGREGATE SHOCKS

Idiosyncratic shocks across establishments within an industry are one possible explanation for simultaneous job creation and job destruction within that industry. Job creation and job destruction are also affected by aggregate shocks. An aggregate shock is one that is common to all establishments, such as changes in the exchange rate or changes in foreign income, but the consequences of a given aggregate shock may differ across establishments depending upon their particular structural characteristics. For example, a given change in the value of the exchange rate has a bigger impact on establishments that are more engaged in international trade, or face greater import competition, than it has on establishments that are more internationally insulated.[8] In constructing a framework for investigating the effects of the exchange rate on job creation and job destruction, we assume that all establishments within a given industry share a common level of openness and this distinguishes these establishments from establishments in all other industries. As mentioned in Chapter 2, available data allow us to calculate openness at the level of four-digit SIC industries, but we do not have data that allow us to calculate openness for individual establishments. Thus, our assumption about the homogeneity of openness among establishments within an industry and the heterogeneity of openness across industries leads to a model that can be directly utilized in our empirical analysis.

We begin by considering the effect of the exchange rate on the reallocation of employment across industries, that is, on net job creation in one industry that comes at the expense of net job destruction in another industry. The analysis here is very similar to that discussed above for idiosyncratic shocks, with the exception that the labor-demand schedules represent the overall demand for labor by all (in this case, both) establishments in each industry. The top panel of Figure 5.2 represents

Figure 5.2 Job Flows in Response to a Depreciation

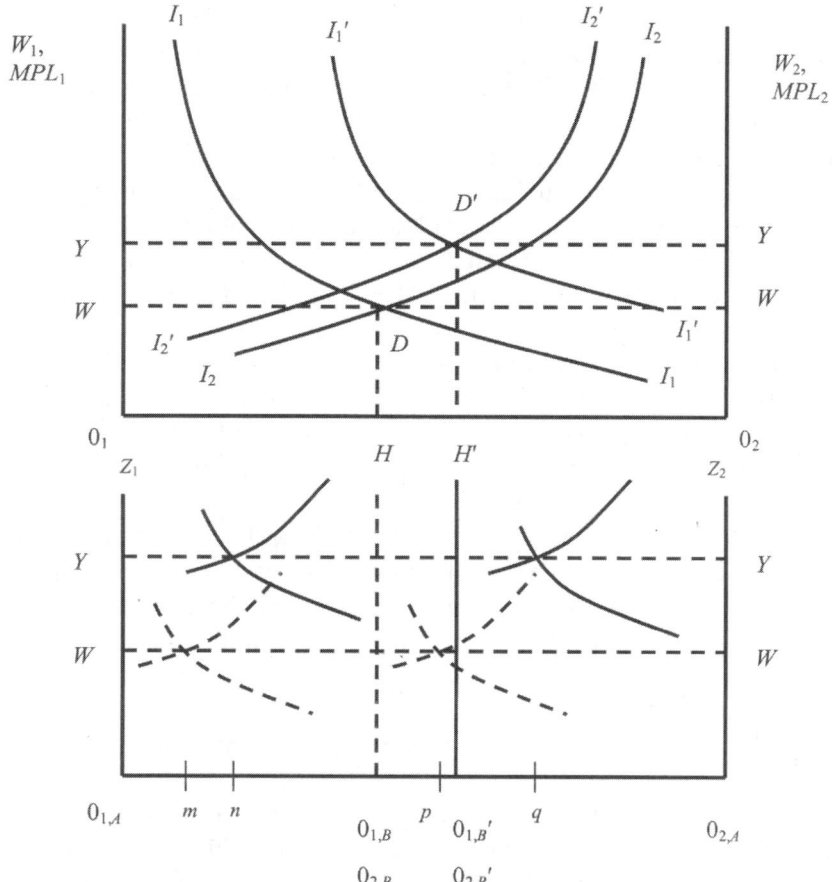

the labor-demand schedules for two industries, industry 1 and industry 2. The structure of this figure is analogous to that of Figure 5.1A. The intersection of the two industry-level labor-demand schedules I_1I_1 and I_2I_2, shows the initial distribution of labor across the two industries, with 0_1H workers in industry 1 and $H0_2$ workers in industry 2, as well as the common wage in each industry of $0_1W = 0_2W$.

A change in the exchange rate alters the demand for workers in both industries. A depreciation raises the number of workers all establishments would like to hire at any wage, while an appreciation reduces the number of workers all establishment would like to hire at any wage. The effect of a given depreciation is depicted by the shifts of the labor-demand schedule for industry 1 to $I_1'I_1'$ and of the labor-demand schedule for industry 2 to $I_2'I_2'$. The amount that each industry's labor-demand schedule shifts reflects the size of the depreciation, which is, of course, the same for both industries, as well as each industry's level of openness. As depicted in the diagram, industry 1 is more open than industry 2 and, therefore, its labor-demand schedule shifts by more. The new intersection, D', differs from the original equilibrium, D, in that the wage paid in both industries has been bid up to $0_1Y = 0_2Y$ and the number of workers in industry 1 has increased to $0_1H'$ while the number of workers in industry 2 has fallen to $H'0_2$.

The lower panel of Figure 5.2 shows what happens in each of the two establishments in each of the two industries. This lower panel consists of two adjoining diagrams of the type depicted in Figure 5.1. The axes for the two establishments that constitute industry 1 are initially defined by $Z_1, 0_{1,A}, 0_{1,B}, H$ while the axes for the two establishments that constitute industry 2 are initially defined by $H, 0_{2,B}, 0_{2,A}, Z_2$ (where $0_{1,B}$ and $0_{2,B}$ represent the same point on the horizontal axis). The four dotted lines in the lower panel represent the establishment-level labor-demand schedules, before the exchange rate depreciates. At this equilibrium the number of workers employed by establishment A in industry 1 is $0_{1,A}m$, by establishment B in industry 1 is $m0_{1,B}$, by establishment A in industry 2 is $0_{2,A}p$, and by establishment B in industry 2 is $p0_{2,B}$.

The exchange rate depreciation shifts the axis that divides the lower panel between the establishments in industry 1 and industry 2 to the right from H to H'. The new sets of axes for industries 1 and 2 are now $Z_1, 0_{1,A}, 0'_{1,B}, H'$ and $H', 0'_{2,B}, 0_{2,A} Z_2$, respectively (where $0'_{1,B}$ and $0'_{2,B}$ represent the same point on the horizontal axis). The four labor-demand schedules shift from the dotted lines to the solid lines. All four schedules shift out (with respect to the appropriate origins) due to the depreciation of the exchange rate. In addition, the labor-demand schedules for establishment B in industry 1 and establishment B in industry 2 move because of the change in the relevant axes arising from the shift of the dividing line between the industries from H to H'. As a consequence of the depreciation, the wage rises from $0W$ to $0Y$. Employment among the four establishments changes to $0_{1,A}n$ for establishment A in industry 1, $n0'_{1,B}$ for establishment B in industry 1, $0_{2,A}q$ for establishment A in industry 2, and $0'_{2,B}q$ for establishment B in industry 2. There is job creation by the two establishments in industry 1, the relatively more open industry, and job destruction by the two establishments in industry 2, the relatively more closed industry.

IMPLICATIONS OF THE MODEL

The model presented above offers two types of determinants of establishment-level job flows, idiosyncratic shocks and aggregate shocks. In this section we draw together some of the lessons of the model. The intuition discussed here complements the formal presentation of the model in Appendix B. The formal model provides us with an explicit framework for our empirical analysis, while the intuition developed here aids our interpretation of the results presented in the next chapter.

We can overlay the consequences of a particular pattern of idiosyncratic shocks, which are unobservable, with the consequences of exchange rate movements for creation and destruction rates across industries to frame our approach to the data. In the model presented above, idiosyncratic shocks are responsible for simultaneous job creation and job destruction within an industry. The source of simultaneous job creation and destruction is a general equilibrium effect rather than an assumed pattern of shocks that mimics the pattern of creation and destruction across establishments. The exchange rate alters the creation and destruction pattern within an industry. Establishments in relatively open industries will tend toward greater job creation and less job destruction in the presence of an exchange rate depreciation while these effects will be reversed in industries that are relatively closed to international competition.[9]

One implication of the model is the importance of an industry's level of openness for determining the consequence of a change of the exchange rate on its level of creation and destruction. Openness can serve as a lens through which the exchange rate affects an industry, with more open industries exhibiting both a greater increase in creation and a greater decrease in destruction in response to a depreciation, and a greater increase in destruction and a greater decrease in creation in response to a depreciation. In the model developed here, the relatively closed industry actually has a qualitatively different response to a change in the exchange rate as compared to the relatively open industry.

Our interpretation of the model can be more broad than this, however. It is reasonable to consider the preponderance of manufacturing industries as more open than the vast majority of service industries.[10] The empirical analysis presented in the next chapter draws only on the experience of manufacturing industries. Therefore, we might expect that a depreciation generally fosters job creation and reduces job destruction among the industries included in our empirical analysis, and conversely for an appreciation, even while these effects are scaled by openness.

While the effects of openness are explicitly included in the discussion in this chapter, we have not focused on the potential for heterogeneity across industries due to differences in their trade patterns and, consequently, differences in their respective trade-weighted real exchange rates. As discussed in more detail in the next chapter, our empirical analysis does explicitly account for heterogeneity in the pattern of trade across industries, utilizing industry-specific real exchange rates calculated as weighted averages of a set of bilateral real exchange rates with the weights reflecting the bilateral trade patterns of an industry.

Finally, we can also move beyond the model's use of the real exchange rate as the sole determinant of the cost of foreign goods relative to the cost of domestic goods. Define a tariff-inclusive real exchange rate, q_T, as

$$q_T = (1+\tau)q$$

where q is the conventional real exchange rate defined above. Taking the total differential of the above expression and then dividing the left side by q_T and the right side by $(1+\tau)q$ gives us

$$\frac{dq_T}{q_T} = \frac{dq}{q} + \frac{d\tau}{(1+\tau)}.$$

The terms dq_T/q_T and dq/q are approximately equal to the percentage changes in q_T and q, respectively, while $d\tau/(1 + \tau)$ is proportional to the percentage change in the tariff rate. In this way, we see that a proportional change in a multilateral tariff rate operates in the model in a way that is identical to a proportional change in the real exchange rate. Tariff rates are often changed in ways that are uneven across industries, however, and this introduces another source of cross-industry heterogeneity in our model. Our discussion of the effects of NAFTA on job creation and job destruction in Chapter 7 draws on the correspondence between tariff changes and real exchange rate changes, as well as the implications of this for job flows as presented in the model here.

CONCLUSION

This chapter has presented a framework for thinking about the manner in which the real exchange rate may influence gross job flows. The model discussed in this chapter attempts to reflect some of the empirical regularities offered in Chapter 3, especially the pervasive heterogeneity of the exposure to international competition across industries. The model is also constructed in a way that will be useful for our empirical analysis by making assumptions on establishment-level and industry-level variation that are consistent with the available data.

The model presented here focuses on two sources of gross job flows, idiosyncratic shocks that reshuffle the distribution of jobs across establishments within an industry and aggregate shocks that alter the distribution of jobs across industries. The main lesson of the model for our empirical analysis is that job creation is generally fostered by an exchange rate depreciation while job destruction generally rises in the face of an appreciation. The model also illustrates the importance of openness for influencing the extent to which these general results hold in a particular industry. In fact, the model shows that some industries that are relatively closed may exhibit job-flow responses contrary to those in industries that are relatively open.

As with all modeling, the theoretical possibility of a particular outcome does not ensure its actual occurrence. In the next chapter we test whether the real exchange rate does, in fact, lead to significant job flows. The discussion in this chapter has provided us with a framework for approaching this empirical issue.

Notes

1. Although, by focusing on a common pool of workers, we have a direct effect of the idiosyncratic shock on labor. Had we focused on a common pool of another resource, the effect on labor would depend upon whether labor and that resource were substitutes or complements in production. For a discussion of the relationship between the demand for labor by firms and their demand for other factors of production, see Hamermesh (1993, pp. 36–42).
2. The independent effects of aggregate and idiosyncratic shocks on gross job flows have been studied by Mortensen and Pissarides (1994), among others.
3. As shown below, the interaction among establishments within an industry in the market for labor, along with a relatively fixed amount of labor within an industry, gives rise to simultaneous job creation and job destruction. Of course, we could just present a simpler model in which we assume that the pattern of idiosyncratic shocks among establishments within an industry yields simultaneous job creation and job destruction. However, we believe that a model with general equilibrium wage effects highlights important and relevant interactions.
4. Recall that the basic unit for the creation and destruction data set is the establishment. Any given establishment will be counted as having only job creation or only job destruction in a particular year; there are no data on simultaneous job creation and job destruction within a particular establishment. The framework we develop here is consistent with this, with any single establishment exhibiting either job creation or job destruction but not both creation and destruction.
5. Alternatively, we could assume that all establishments within an industry differ in their exposure to international competition and, therefore, a change in an aggregate variable, such as the exchange rate, would have different effects across those establishments. We do not pursue this modeling strategy, however, because we want to match our theoretical model to our empirical approach and the most disaggregated measure of openness available to us is at the four-digit SIC industry level, not at the establishment level. As discussed below, our model does assume differences in openness across industries.
6. We can motivate the assumption that all establishments draw from a common pool of workers by appealing to the presence of industry-specific skills among workers. This means that a particular industry employs people from occupational pools of workers that are distinct and segmented from the occupational pools of other industries. More generally, we could assume that some workers, such as secretaries, custodians, and bookkeepers, do not have industry-specific skills while others, such as engineers, sales representatives, and line workers, could only move from one industry to another at some cost of retraining. This weaker

assumption would generate results that are qualitatively similar to the results in the model we present.

7. Relaxing this condition through a cost of relocation or by introducing nonpecuniary benefits of working in one or both firms does not alter the basic results of the analysis.
8. The discussion in Chapter 2 shows that distinctive patterns of trade across industries give rise to divergent industry-specific exchange rates. In this chapter we consider only a common "exchange rate" that is the same across all industries, although an extension to industry-specific exchange rates would be straightforward. Our empirical analysis does, in fact, utilize industry-specific exchange rates.
9. In the model developed above, the exchange rate enters through its role in affecting demand, rather than supply. Campa and Goldberg (2001) developed a model in which the exchange rate also affects the price of imported intermediate goods, along with the prices of exports and imports. Potentially, this could lead to a situation where a depreciation, by raising input prices, drives down the demand for labor. This effect would augment the effects outlined in our model.
10. Manufacturing's share of total U.S. trade was relatively steady during our sample: 0.81 in 1975, 0.79 in 1985, and 0.78 in 1995 (see Table B-104 in the *Economic Report of the President 2000*, February 2000, p. 426).

6
Regression Implementation and Results

The model presented in Chapter 5 offers a theoretical framework for understanding how changes in the real exchange rate contribute to job creation or destruction within an industry as well as to the reallocation of jobs across industries. But, of course, theory alone cannot be used to determine whether, in fact, changes in the real exchange rate actually have an important role in the determination of job creation and job destruction. This is essentially an empirical issue, although one that must be guided by both a coherent theoretical framework and an understanding of the relevant characteristics of the data used in the analysis. In this chapter, we present quantitative estimates of the effects of movements in the real exchange rate on job creation and job destruction.

The manner in which we undertake the analysis in this chapter reflects lessons learned from earlier chapters in this book. The basic form of our analysis, especially with regard to the specification of the regression equation, draws heavily on the framework presented in Chapter 5. Our analysis is also shaped by our understanding of the job-flow and exchange rate data, as discussed in Chapters 2 and 3. The divergence of industry-specific multilateral real exchange rates, shown in Chapter 2, underscores the potential importance of matching the job flows of a particular industry with an exchange rate that matches its trading patterns, rather than using an aggregate real exchange rate for all industries. The divergence of openness among the four-digit SIC industries that constitute particular two-digit SIC industries, discussed in Chapter 3, leads us to control for openness directly rather than estimating separate regressions for each two-digit SIC industry.

The empirical analysis in this chapter also introduces a consideration that we have only alluded to, the importance of the permanence of exchange rate changes for generating job flows. A range of models that include adjustment costs suggest that exchange rate changes that are perceived as permanent will have different effects from those that are perceived as temporary.[1] While we cannot directly gauge the perceived permanence or actual exchange rate changes, we can attempt to estimate the permanent and temporary components of actual exchange rate changes and then use these separately in our analysis.[2] As shown in this chapter, we find that these different components have distinct effects on job creation and job destruction and these differences have important implications for the nature of job flows.

In the next section of this chapter we discuss the manner in which we undertake our empirical analysis. This discussion focuses on the choices we made as we moved from a theoretical framework to an empirical analysis. Section 2 then presents the results of our empirical analysis. The concluding section of this chapter offers some interpretations of these results. Details of the data used in this analysis are presented in Appendix C.

EMPIRICAL IMPLEMENTATION

The model presented in Chapter 5 offers some insights regarding the relationship between the exchange rate and gross job flows. Most primarily, the model presented in Appendix B links changes in the exchange rate (rather than its level) to rates of job creation and job destruction, and this is the specification we use. A central result of the model is that an exchange rate depreciation, all else equal, contributes to an increase in the rate of job creation and a decrease in the rate of job destruction among relatively open industries, while an exchange rate appreciation has the opposite effect on these relatively open industries. Therefore, we would expect to find this pattern of effects among manufacturing industries since they tend to be more open than other sectors of the economy, such as the service sector. The model also suggests that openness enters in a particular fashion, interacted with both the exchange rate and foreign output. Accordingly, our regressions include the product of the exchange rate and openness.

The data presented earlier in this book also offer insights on how to proceed with our empirical analysis. For example, the statistics presented in Chapter 2 show that, while there is tremendous diversity in the importance of imports and exports across U.S. manufacturing industries, very little of this heterogeneity is related to membership in particular two-digit, or even three-digit, industries. Therefore, it may not be warranted to estimate separate regressions for each of the 20 two-digit industry groups since that assumes a degree of homogeneity within those groups that is likely not present. Instead, our regression uses data on all 442 industries and, as mentioned above, controls for differences in openness across industries by including the product of openness and both the real exchange rate and foreign output. Our sample uses annual data for the period 1975 to 1993, giving us more than 8,000 industry-year observations.[3]

Based upon these considerations, we draw on the model presented in Appendix B and specify our regression equation as

$$JF_{it} = \sum_{s=0}^{1} \left[\beta_{1,s} C_{i,t-1-s} + \beta_{2,s} D_{i,t-1-s} + \beta_{3,s} \left(\widetilde{\Omega}_{i,t-s} \widehat{E}_{i,t-s} \right) \right.$$
$$\left. + \beta_{4,s} \widehat{Z}_{i,t-s} + \beta_{5,s} V_s \right] + \left(\alpha_i + v_t + \varepsilon_{it} \right)$$

where i indexes four-digit SIC industries, t indexes years, ^ denotes growth rates, $Z_{i,t-s}$ is a vector of industry-specific variables, and V_s is a vector of aggregate variables.[4] The dependent variables are the four job-flow rates; the job creation rate, the job destruction rate, the rate of job reallocation, and the net employment rate, which are represented as $JF_{it} = \{C_{it}, D_{it}, R_{it}, N_{it}\}$. Lagged values of C_{it} and D_{it}, as well as the other explanatory variables, are included as regressors to account for possible dynamic adjustment. The components of the error term of the regression ($\alpha_i + v_t + \varepsilon_{it}$) represent the effects of unmeasured influences on job creation and destruction at the industry, aggregate, and time-varying industry levels. We specify α_i as a fixed (nonstochastic) effect, and treat v_t and ε_{it} as stochastic.[5]

The coefficients of central interest to us are those represented by β_3 which demonstrate the impact of current and lagged values of the percentage change in the industry-specific real exchange rate, interacted with the level of industry openness, on job flows. Both elements of the product of the regressor for this coefficient, $\widetilde{\Omega}_{it} \widehat{E}_{it}$, reflect information specific to industry i. The industry-specific real exchange rate, $\widehat{E}_{it}$, is constructed by weighting bilateral real exchange rates by the trade shares of industry i. Trade shares are averaged over the preceding two years and then lagged to avoid potential endogeneity problems.[6] The openness variable for industry i, $\widetilde{\Omega}_{it}$, is a five-year moving average of the ratio of total trade (exports plus imports) to total market sales (domestic sales plus imports) for that industry. The use of a moving average minimizes the influence of transitory fluctuations in openness. The moving average of openness is lagged one period such that, for job flows from period t, its most recent value is from period $t - 1$. This allows us to avoid any potential problems due to the possible influence of job flows on measured openness.

As we address the data using the framework developed in the previous chapter, it is important to recognize that the static nature of the model skirts a potentially important issue. In the face of hiring and firing costs, establishments' employment responses to exchange rate changes will likely depend upon their perception of whether those changes are temporary or permanent. We would expect a greater response of workers and establishments to perceived permanent changes in the exchange rate than to those exchange rate movements that are thought to be merely transitory. Furthermore, it is reasonable to expect an asymmetry between the responsiveness of job creation and job destruction to temporary changes in the exchange rate. Employees can be discharged nearly immediately after an establishment has determined that it is optimal to do so, albeit with some firing cost, but expanding employment often requires considerable planning, screening of new employees, installation of new equipment, and sometimes erection of new structures. In addition, there may be fixed costs, periods of learning, and other barriers to entering markets that differ from the costs of scaling back operations in these markets. These types of job creation costs would not likely be incurred for job creation that was expected to be transitory, such as that associated with temporary shifts in the value of the real exchange rate. At the same time, it is common for establishments to engage in transitory job destruction by temporarily laying off workers and then recalling them later.

These factors argue for including separately in the regression the perceived permanent component of the change in the exchange rate and its perceived temporary component. The actual implementation of this idea, however, is not straightforward. At a minimum, it is difficult to estimate a model of the determination of the exchange rate at annual intervals. Compounding this difficulty is that of modeling perceptions of exchange rate movements as permanent or transitory.

One possible recourse is to decompose the exchange rate into its trend and cyclical parts and then to identify the trend as the "permanent" change and the change in the cyclical part of the exchange rate as its "transitory" movements. This decomposition is based on defining the actual real exchange rate of industry i, E_{it}, as the sum of its trend and cyclical components,

$$E_{it} = E_{it}^T + E_{it}^C,$$

where the superscript T denotes the trend component and the superscript C denotes the cyclical component.

We implemented this approach by first fitting the log level of each industry real exchange rate to linear and quadratic time trends. We found an extraordinarily wide variety of trends among the four-digit industry real exchange rates—including opposite signs across industries in both the linear and quadratic parts. We then calculated the cyclical component as the residual between the actual industry exchange rate and its trend component.[7] This decomposition of the exchange rate proves to be important in our regression analysis as we find distinct effects for the coefficients on the trend and cyclical components of the exchange rates, with the differences corresponding to the types of distinctions we might expect given the discussion above.

Our regression specification also reflects the fact that, as discussed in the theoretical model presented in Chapter 5, a range of variables other than the exchange rate influence job creation and job destruction rates. Accordingly, we include industry-specific variables, $\widehat{Z}_{it}$, where

$$\widehat{Z}_{it} = [(\widetilde{\Omega}_{it}\widehat{Y}_{it}^*), \widehat{Y}_{it}, \widehat{\Psi}_{it}^Q, \widehat{\Psi}_{it}^{G_1}, \widehat{\Psi}_{it}^{G_2}, \widehat{\Psi}_{it}^W].$$

Some of the variables in $\widehat{Z}_{it}$ represent the prices of inputs other than labor, variables represented by $\widehat{G}_p$ in the model in Chapter 5. In our regression specification, these include the industry-specific real prices of output, energy, and materials, $\Psi_{it}^Q = (P_{it}^Q/P_t^Q)$, $\Psi_{it}^{G_1} = (P_{it}^{EN}/P_{it}^Q)$, and $\Psi_{it}^{G_2} = (P_{it}^{MAT}/P_{it}^Q)$, respectively. The aggregate (total manufacturing) real wage also is included, and represented by $\Gamma_t = (W_t / P_t^Q)$.[8] Y_{it} is domestic industry demand. The industry-specific foreign demand, Y_{it}^*, is constructed using trade-weighted foreign output data for each trading partner in a manner analogous to the industry real exchange rates. The model presented in Appendix B shows that, as with the real exchange rate, foreign output should be interacted with openness.[9]

Another set of variables in the regression specification is included to ensure that any significance attributed to industry-level real exchange rates is not merely reflecting a correlation between exchange rates and aggregate variables that also influence gross job flows. We include in our econometric specification the aggregate explanatory variables

$$V_t = [N_t, \rho_t],$$

where N_t is total manufacturing net employment growth and $\rho_t = i_t^f - \pi_t$ is the *ex post* real federal funds rate. Total manufacturing net employment captures aggregate real shocks to the traded goods sector. The real federal funds rate captures monetary policy shocks. These aggregate variables capture the main aggregate, macroeconomic determinants of industry-level job flows. It is reasonable to assume that these variables are exogenous to any particular industry and, therefore, to discount any concerns of four-digit SIC industry-level job flows contemporaneously affecting the real federal funds rate or manufacturing net employment.

REGRESSION RESULTS

In this section we present the results of our regression analyses. The first set of results, reported in Table 6.1, is based on a specification that includes the interaction of the four-digit SIC industry-specific real exchange rates and openness, as well as the other control variables discussed above. The second set of results, in Table 6.2, replaces the actual industry-specific real exchange rate with its two separate components, reflecting the estimated trend and cyclical parts of the real exchange rates. In all of these tables, there are separate columns, one for each of the different types of job flows (net employment, N_{it}; job creation, C_{it};

job destruction, D_{it}; and job reallocation, R_{it}). The reported point estimates represent the sums of coefficients for periods $t-1$ and $t-2$ for the regressors C_i and D_i, and for periods t and $t-1$ for all other regressors.[10] Only the coefficients on the growth rates of the exchange rates interacted with openness are shown in Table 6.2 since the other coefficients were very similar across the two specifications.

The important role played by the change in industry-specific real exchange rates, interacted with openness, for gross job flows and net job flows is shown by the results in Table 6.1. An appreciation of the real exchange rate leads to a significant decline in net employment growth. This response is typical of the results reported in the literature on the effect of real exchange rates on *net* employment cited in Chapter 4. But, using gross job-flow data, we are able to gain a more complete understanding of this effect on net employment. A decrease in net employment can come about through a reduction in job creation, an increase in job destruction, or some combination of the two. The results in Table 6.1 suggest that an appreciation affects net employment solely through a significant increase in job destruction, with no change in job creation. Job reallocation also increases significantly but only enough to accommodate the net employment change.

There are important implications of the relative responses of job creation and job destruction to changes in the exchange rate since these two components of job flows likely have significantly different implications for worker flows, unemployment, human capital accumulation, and wages—factors that are fundamentally important for calculating the welfare costs of labor adjustment to international competition. In particular, job destruction is closely linked to the dislocation of workers from jobs, and the evidence indicates that dislocated workers typically suffer severe losses of human capital and permanent income.[11] Moreover, Davis, Haltiwanger, and Schuh (1996) showed that job destruction tends to be permanent and occurs disproportionately in larger, older, high-wage plants. Thus, job destruction is likely to involve permanent dislocation of high-wage and/or older workers, human capital destruction, and permanent income loss—all of which are likely to lead to higher structural unemployment. In contrast, had the empirical results suggested that net employment responses to exchange rate appreciations arose through lower job creation rates, these effects would likely have a smaller impact on workers and wel-

Table 6.1 Baseline Job-Flow Regression Results

Variable	Description	N_{it}	Dependent variable C_{it}	D_{it}	R_{it}
C_i	Gross job creation	−0.10	0.03	0.05	0.16**
		(0.07)	(0.04)	(0.04)	(0.03)
D_i	Gross job destruction	0.10	0.17**	0.02	0.16**
		(0.07)	(0.04)	(0.04)	(0.03)
$\tilde{\Omega}_i \hat{E}_i$	Openness × real exchange rate	−0.35**	−0.02	0.33**	0.30**
		(0.15)	(0.06)	(0.13)	(0.14)
$\tilde{\Omega}_i \hat{Y}_i^*$	Openness × real foreign GDP	0.07	0.07	0.01	0.06
		(0.25)	(0.11)	(0.20)	(0.19)
$\hat{Y}_i$	Real domestic sales	0.12**	0.04**	−0.08**	−0.05**
		(0.03)	(0.01)	(0.02)	(0.01)
$\hat{\Psi}_i^Q$	Real output price	0.07	0.05	−0.02	0.03
		(0.06)	(0.03)	(0.03)	(0.03)
$\hat{\Psi}_i^{EN}$	Real energy price	−0.02	0.03**	0.06**	0.09**
		(0.02)	(0.02)	(0.02)	(0.02)
$\hat{\Psi}_i^{MAT}$	Real materials price	0.02	0.01	−0.00	0.01
		(0.04)	(0.02)	(0.03)	(0.03)
$\hat{\Psi}^W$	Aggregate real wage	−0.14**	0.06*	0.21**	0.28**
		(0.04)	(0.03)	(0.06)	(0.08)
N	Aggregate net employment growth	0.78**	0.40**	−0.34**	0.03
		(0.09)	(0.05)	(0.10)	(0.12)
ρ	Real federal funds rate	0.21**	0.07	0.30**	0.39**
		(0.10)	(0.05)	(0.10)	(0.12)
	R^2	0.26	0.22	0.21	0.13

NOTE: Estimated by ordinary least squares with annual data over the period 1975 to 1993 (8,376 industry-year observations) and fixed effects for four-digit industries. Estimates for N (net employment), C (job creation), D (job destruction), and R (job reallocation) are sums of the coefficients from the $t-1$ and $t-2$ values; all other estimates are the sums of coefficients from the t and $t-1$ values. Standard errors are in parentheses and are corrected for aggregate regressor bias. * and ** denote significance at the 10 and 5 percent levels, respectively.

fare. Lower job creation raises the duration of unemployment and, through this channel, slows the accumulation of human capital, but this is probably not as economically significant as the effects of job destruction.

For reasons discussed in the previous section, a more complete analysis of the effects of the exchange rate on job flows recognizes the possibility that these effects can vary depending upon whether the changes in the exchange rate are perceived to be permanent or temporary. As discussed above, we implement this idea through the inclusion of two separate components of the industry-level real exchange rates in our regression specification, the trend component and the cyclical component. The results presented in Table 6.2 show that net and gross job flows respond quite differently to changes in the growth of the trend and changes in the cyclical components of the industry real exchange rates. An appreciation of the trend real exchange rate leads to significant and roughly equal increases in job destruction and job creation rates. Consequently, job reallocation also increases significantly in response to an appreciation of the trend component of the industry-level real exchange rate, but there is no change in net employment growth. In sharp contrast, an appreciation of the cyclical component of the real exchange rate yields quantitatively similar results to those reported in Table 6.1, with the job destruction rate increasing, the job creation rate unaffected and net employment growth declining.

The statistical significance of these results is matched by their economic relevance. We estimate the quantitative effects of changes in industry-level real exchange rates on net and gross job flows using coefficients presented in Table 6.2. This exercise proceeds by holding constant all other variables, including monetary policy (as measured by the real federal funds rate), changes in domestic and foreign income, and changes in overall net manufacturing employment. Each of these is a significant determinant of gross job flows and would likely be correlated with an appreciation; therefore, this exercise considers the pure effect of an exchange rate appreciation rather than the likely behavior of job-flow rates during the period when the exchange rate is appreciating, a period when other factors would likely also be driving rates of creation, destruction, reallocation, and net employment.

Table 6.2 Job-Flows Regression Results with Exchange Rate Decomposition

	Dependent variable			
Explanatory variable	N_{it}	C_{it}	D_{it}	R_{it}
$\tilde{\Omega}_i \hat{E}_i$ (from Table 6.1)	−0.35**	−0.02	0.33**	0.30**
	(0.15)	(0.06)	(0.13)	(0.14)
$\tilde{\Omega}_i \hat{E}_i^T$ (trend)	0.03	0.70**	0.78**	1.42**
	(0.29)	(0.17)	(0.30)	(0.39)
$\tilde{\Omega}_i \hat{E}_i^C$ (cyclical)	−0.45**	−0.10	0.36**	0.25*
	(0.16)	(0.06)	(0.13)	(0.14)

NOTE: Estimated by ordinary least squares with annual data over the period 1975 to 1993 (8,376 industry-year observations) and fixed effects for four-digit industries. Estimates for N (net employment), C (job creation), D (job destruction), and R (job reallocation) are sums of the coefficients from the $t-1$ and $t-2$ values; all other estimates are the sums of coefficients from the t and $t-1$ values. Standard errors are in parentheses and are corrected for aggregate regressor bias. * and ** denote significance at the 10 and 5 percent levels, respectively.

Table 6.3 summarizes the responses of job-flow rates (in percentage points) to a real exchange rate appreciation representing two consecutive one standard deviation increases in the real exchange rate. These changes amount to 10.8 percent (5.4 percent per year) for the cyclical rate and 3.4 percent (1.7 percent per year) for the trend rate. Responses are shown for the 10th, 50th (median), and 90th percentiles of industry openness over all years (0.02, 0.14, and 0.42, respectively) and are not reported in those cases where the coefficients are not significant.[12]

The results presented in Table 6.3 demonstrate the economically meaningful effect of changes in industry-level real exchange rates on rates of job creation and job destruction. We estimate that a sustained, one standard deviation appreciation of the cyclical component of the industry-level real exchange rate raises job destruction and reallocation, and lowers net employment growth, by more than one-half percentage point in an industry with median openness. This response is significant when compared with a time-series standard deviation of job destruction of 2.8 percent (the average job destruction rate in manufac-

Table 6.3 Job-Flow Responses to a Real Exchange Rate Appreciation

	$\tilde{\Omega}_i$		N_i	C_i	D_i	R_i
	Percentile	Value				
$\tilde{\Omega}_i \hat{E}_i^T$	10	0.02		0.0	0.0	0.1
$\tilde{\Omega}_i \hat{E}_i^T$	50	0.14		0.3	0.4	0.7
$\tilde{\Omega}_i \hat{E}_i^T$	90	0.42		1.0	1.1	2.1
$\tilde{\Omega}_i \hat{E}_i^C$	10	0.02	−0.1		0.1	0.0
$\tilde{\Omega}_i \hat{E}_i^C$	50	0.14	−0.7		0.5	0.4
$\tilde{\Omega}_i \hat{E}_i^C$	90	0.42	−2.0		1.6	1.1

NOTE: The table reports cumulative responses over a two-year period to two consecutive annual one standard deviation increases in the real exchange rate (5.4 percent per year for the cyclical rate and 1.7 percent per year for the trend rate). All estimates are in percentage points. Standard errors are the same as in Table 6.2. Responses are omitted where coefficient estimates are insignificant at the 10 percent level.

turing in our sample is 10.2 percent). Thus, real exchange rate fluctuations account for a substantial fraction of the cyclical movements in job flows. Real exchange rate movements are also responsible for the divergence in job flows across industries. The results in Table 6.3 show that the estimated job-flow responses are about three times larger for a highly trade-intensive industry, one at the 90th percentile of openness, than for an industry at the median level of openness. The job-flow responses of an industry at the 90th percentile of openness, which is about two percentage points, is large in both relative and absolute terms.

An appreciation of the trend component of the real exchange rate also leads to large estimated job-flow responses. A sustained, one standard deviation appreciation of the trend component of the industry-level real exchange rate raises job creation and job destruction rates in an industry with median openness by 0.4 percentage point, and the job reallocation rate increases by 0.7 percentage point. This reallocation response is significant when compared with the time-series standard deviation of reallocation of 1.9 percent (the average job reallocation rate in manufacturing in our sample is 19.0 percent). Thus, trend real exchange rate fluctuations account for a substantial fraction of the variation in reallocation. As with changes due to the cyclical component of the industry-level real exchange rate, movements in the trend component of the real exchange rate lead to divergent responses across manufacturing industries. The job-flow responses to a change in the trend real exchange rate are about three times larger for an industry at the 90th percentile of openness than for an industry at the median level of openness.

Although the main focus of this section is the real exchange rate, it is worth mentioning the results pertaining to other regressors. Industry domestic demand is a very significant determinant of all four categories of job flows, but industry foreign demand, conditional on the real exchange rate and other variables, is totally insignificant. The three aggregate regressors are generally quite significant. The aggregate real wage, net employment growth, and the real federal funds rate significantly affect industry-level net employment and job destruction. The real wage and the real interest rate are significant in the job reallocation equation, and the real wage and net employment growth are significant in the job creation equation. The significance of the real exchange rate is especially noteworthy given the significance of these aggregate regressors. The industry-specific real price of energy significantly affects job creation, job destruction, and reallocation, but not net employment, a result consistent with that found by Davis and Haltiwanger (2001), who focused on the effect of oil prices on job reallocation. Finally, the only important lagged job flow is destruction in the creation equation. This finding suggests that an adverse effect on jobs, distinct from those effects represented by other variables in the regression, first depresses demand and then creation responds with a lag as the economy recovers.[13]

CONCLUSIONS AND INTERPRETATIONS

We have argued in this chapter, as well as elsewhere in this book, that a full accounting of the welfare effects of labor-market adjustment requires going beyond measuring net employment changes. Rather, we need to consider what occurs at the job creation and the job destruction margin. For example, the implications of a given change in net employment on people's lifetime earning profiles depend upon the way in which this change reflects movements in the job creation rate and the job destruction rate. Therefore, it is important to recognize, as shown by the results in Table 6.1, that the effects of industry-level real exchange rate changes on net employment occur solely through their effect on job destruction rather than job creation. It is also important to recognize that the effects of exchange rate changes on particular industries depend upon their level of openness. The estimates presented in Table 6.3 illustrate how exchange rate changes can lead to job flows, not only between manufacturing sectors and the rest of the economy, but also across manufacturing sectors which vary widely in their exposure to international factors.

While these results give us an idea of the overall consequences of exchange rate movements on gross job flows, the different effects of the trend and cyclical movements in the exchange rate on both gross job flows and net employment provide important insights on employment dynamics. These results complement other evidence on job flows. Our finding that changes in the trend component of the industry-level real exchange rate lead to significant effects for job destruction and job creation rates but no change in net employment growth is consistent with others' conclusion that gross job flows are primarily permanent whereas net employment changes are primarily transitory. For example, Davis, Haltiwanger, and Schuh (1996) reported that more than one-half of job creation and nearly three-fourths of job destruction represent *permanent* (at least two years) establishment-level employment changes while, in contrast, most net employment changes over the business cycle are short-lived.

This interpretation of the results on the trend and cyclical components of the exchange rate hinges on the interpretation of these components as permanent or transitory. In a statistical sense, this interpretation seems reasonable since growth in the trend component is persistent and does not change sign frequently. Whether our simple decomposition is reasonable in an economic sense is unclear without a formal model of exchange rates and expectation formation. It is well known that exchange rate movements are extremely difficult to model and predict. Thus, significant changes in exchange rates are likely to be viewed as some mix of permanent versus transitory changes.

The welfare implications of the results presented in this chapter must also take into account the fact that some jobs destroyed by a dollar appreciation may have been only marginally profitable and slated for eventual elimination even if the real exchange rate remained stable. However, the timing of job destruction does have an impact on the welfare of displaced workers. Workers are likely to have an easier time finding suitable reemployment when job destruction is gradual and diffuse than when an external shock causes job destruction to spike and, consequently, a glut of displaced workers are searching for new jobs simultaneously. For this reason, acceleration of job destruction caused by a temporary appreciation of the exchange rate can have adverse consequences on economic welfare.

Notes

1. See, for example, Dixit (1989) and Krugman (1988).
2. As mentioned in Chapter 4, Campa and Goldberg (2001) and Gourinchas (1998) also decomposed the exchange rate and used the separate components as regressors in their analyses.
3. The use of 442 four-digit SIC industries as well as the use of annual data represent two ways in which our empirical analysis is distinguished from that of Gourinchas (1998), who restricted his sample to the 103 industries he identified as the most or least involved in international trade and who used quarterly data.
4. Recall that the gross job-flow data represent March-to-March changes whereas all of the other data correspond to changes over the calendar year. Thus, period t job-flow data match most closely with period $t - 1$ other data, so we make this timing adjustment before estimating the model. About a one-quarter mismatch remains, but it does not appear to seriously affect the timing of relationships between variables at annual frequencies.
5. The presence of v_t implies nonindependence of the regression error term across observations for any given year. Our estimated standard errors correct for this. Failure to correct for nonindependence of regression errors arising from unmeasured aggregate effect in panel regressions with aggregate regressors can result in

substantial understatement of the standard errors associated with those regressors; see Kloeck (1981) or Moulton (1990).
6. We use essentially the same methodology as Gourinchas (1998) in constructing the exchange rates; see, in that article, pages 165–166, especially footnote 16. Given that the trade variables in openness and multilateral exchange rates are lagged, the only potential source of endogeneity with respect to international competition is in contemporaneous (time t) bilateral exchange rates. However, at our highly disaggregated level of industrial detail (four-digit SIC), it is highly unlikely that industry-level activity influences bilateral dollar exchange rates. Nevertheless, as discussed below, we explored instrumental variable estimation for robustness.
7. The quadratic term in the trend allowed us to account for important covariances between the trend and cyclical parts, as well as between the level and growth rate of each of these parts. We are unable to use time-series techniques, such as the Beveridge-Nelson decomposition, to decompose real exchange rates into permanent and transitory components because 20 years of time-series observations are insufficient to use these techniques.
8. As discussed in a footnote below, we also estimated the regressions using an industry-specific real wage as a robustness check. Industry-specific wages have the potential econometric drawback of being endogenously determined with employment, but the results for the exchange rate do not depend upon which wage measure we used.
9. Endogeneity is a potential problem for many of these industry-specific variables, but our results are not sensitive to corrections for endogeneity, as we explain in the next subsection. Also, our results are robust to the use of the aggregate real wage rather than the industry-specific real wage. Details on these variables are included in Appendix C.
10. In order for each equation to include its lagged dependent variable, we impose the testable restrictions that $\beta_1 = -\beta_2$ in the N_{it} equation and $\beta_1 = \beta_2$ in the R_{it} equation. Estimates of the coefficients of the unrestricted N_{it} regression can be calculated by subtracting the D_{it} regression coefficients from the C_{it} regression coefficients; similarly, estimates of the unrestricted R_{it} regression coefficients can be calculated by summing the coefficients of the C_{it} and D_{it} regressions. Performing this exercise reveals that the restrictions have little or no effect on the coefficients on variables other than C_i and D_i.
11. For references, see the surveys by Fallick (1996) and Kletzer (1998b).
12. By 1993 these percentiles were 0.02, 0.21, and 0.53, respectively. Thus, the estimated sensitivity of job flows to real exchange rate movements has increased significantly over time, and the effect has become more diverse over manufacturing industries.
13. We conducted a number of robustness checks of the results presented in Tables 6.1 and 6.2 but do not report them because none of the checks had any qualitative effect on the results (and even the quantitative effects were quite small). The robustness checks included the following alternative specifications: 1) time

effects rather than the aggregate variables, V_t; 2) the subsets of industries identified by Gourinchas (1998); 3) inclusion of real exchange rate levels; and 4) inclusion of industry-specific real wages rather than the manufacturing real wage. We also tried estimating the models using instrumental variables (IV) estimation rather than ordinary least squares to control for the potential endogeneity of contemporaneous bilateral real exchange rates and industry-specific variables. The types of instrument sets we tried included the Hall-Ramey instruments used by Gourinchas, lagged industry-specific variables, and various macroeconomic variables that should be exogenous to industries. The IV point estimates varied widely across instrument sets and often yielded insignificant estimates (both common problems with IV estimation), but our thorough search turned up no specification that altered our qualitative results.

7
Job Flows and Trade

The Case of NAFTA

Although we have focused on the effect of real exchange rate movements in this book, the real exchange rate is but one of a number of factors that affect the international environment facing establishments. The degree of international competition facing establishments depends upon the extent to which international markets are open and free from government-imposed restrictions on trade. Establishments' efforts to export will be adversely affected by tariffs and quotas imposed upon them by foreign governments. Establishments' domestic sales are promoted through the protection from international competition afforded them by their own governments.

The world trading system has progressed by fits and starts toward more openness since the end of World War II. These movements toward freer trade have occurred both at the multilateral level, through the various rounds of the General Agreement on Tariffs and Trade (GATT), and through regional agreements like the 1989 Free Trade Agreement (FTA) between the United States and Canada and, more recently, the North American Free Trade Agreement (NAFTA). These trade negotiations have lowered tariff rates and reduced quota restrictions on industries in member countries. By lifting these politically imposed impediments to trade, agreements such as NAFTA increase the volume of both imports and exports. Our econometric estimates suggest that the increased openness of the economy leaves patterns of labor demand more sensitive to fluctuations in real exchange rates. Trade agreements also have a direct effect on labor demand, however, as plants and firms expand or contract in response to the new trading environment.

This chapter demonstrates that much of our analysis of the effects of real exchange rate fluctuations is relevant to understanding how trade liberalization affects labor markets. The first section discusses the similarities and differences between trade liberalization and real exchange rate movements. We then turn to analysis of a recent trade liberalization: implementation of NAFTA. Following a brief general analysis of NAFTA, we focus on case studies of how NAFTA affected three industries: textiles and apparel, chemicals, and automobiles.

ECONOMIC EFFECTS OF TRADE LIBERALIZATION

Trade liberalization may generate economic effects that are much like permanent changes in real exchange rates. An important common element is that trade liberalization and real exchange rate movements both result in changes in the prices of goods produced in the United States relative to goods produced abroad. For U.S. companies producing goods for export, lower tariffs have an effect that is similar to a permanent depreciation of the dollar relative to the currency of the countries that have reduced tariffs on goods produced in the United States. Both tariff reductions and depreciation reduce the prices charged in the other countries for goods produced in the United States, but tariff reductions differ from a depreciation in that they also reduce the prices in the United States of goods produced by other members of the trade agreement relative to domestically produced goods. So, from the standpoint of foreign firms that export their goods to the United States, implementation of a trade liberalization is much like a permanent real appreciation of the dollar.

In the model presented in Chapter 5, heterogeneity across establishments within industries combined with the general equilibrium effects of changes in exchange rates could lead some establishments to increase employment in response to an exchange rate movement while other establishments within the same industry may reduce their employment. A similar mechanism could result in simultaneous job creation and job destruction within industries following implementation of a trade agreement. Although establishments within an industry in which the United States has a comparative advantage would tend to experience an increase in the demand for their products following a general trade liberalization, some establishments would experience a greater increase than others as a result of heterogeneity. For example, some establishments may be producing products which are already being marketed abroad, while others may not yet be producing products for export. As a result, some establishments' derived demand for labor schedules would shift out more than would other establishments' labor-demand schedules. As the industry's total labor demand increases, wages of the industry's workers would tend to be bid up, resulting in a backward movement along establishments' labor-demand schedules. The net effect might be for overall industry employment to increase but for employment at some establishments within the industry to decrease.

One likely source of heterogeneity over establishments within an industry is the stage of production the plant is engaged in. Although the United States might have a comparative advantage at some aspects of production within an industry, other countries may have a comparative advantage in other aspects. Feenstra and Hanson (2003) noted that increased openness may be associated with a shift in the production of less skilled labor intensive intermediate goods to lower wage countries. This effect of trade might result in reallocation of resources largely within, rather than between, industries.[1] Employment at domestic plants producing intermediate goods would decrease, but employment at other establishments within the same industry might simultaneously increase. Trade liberalization would increase the profitability of specialization according to comparative advantage, and thus tend to promote within-industry reallocation.

The high degree of heterogeneity across industries in their exposure to international trade, which we document in Chapter 2, is as important to understanding the effects of trade liberalization as it is to understanding the effects of exchange rate movements. The magnitude of the impact of trade liberalization on an industry depends on its exposure to trade and the degree to which trade barriers for its output and inputs are reduced. Industries which experience the largest reductions in tariffs, and those which are initially the most open, will be the most affected by trade liberalization. In considering the level of an industry's initial exposure to trade, however, the effect of the initial level of tariffs and trade restrictions on the initial level of openness must be taken into account. Tradable goods sectors with high tariffs (or other politically imposed barriers to trade) may initially appear to have little exposure to trade, but they may potentially experience greatly increased trade as tariffs are reduced.

Although the economic effects of trade liberalization are similar in many ways to the effects of movements in the real exchange rate, our econometric estimates cannot be directly used to predict the effects of trade liberalization on job creation and job destruction. As noted above, trade liberalization is equivalent to a simultaneous depreciation of the dollar from the standpoint of exporters and an appreciation of the dollar from the standpoint of importers, and so it does not match the type of exchange rate movements which our model estimates are based on. Moreover, the degree and sources of heterogeneity over plants within industries applicable for analysis of the effects of trade liberalization may be quite different from those relevant to analysis of movements in real exchange rates.

An important difference between trade liberalization and exchange rate swings is that trade agreements result from explicit policy decisions, and the resulting political debate is sometimes acrimonious. In contrast, an appreciation of the dollar generally takes place without any explicit policy action. Industry groups may lobby for a weak dollar policy or ask for special assistance to counter the effect of the appreciation on their competitive position, but there is typically relatively little, if any, discussion of exchange rate management policy, at least in the United States.

The controversy over trade liberalization is generally focused on negotiations over new trade agreements. The fierce opposition to NAFTA is a case in point. Labor unions promised political repercussions for congressmen who voted for its ratification. The NAFTA debate made its way into American living rooms in November 1993 when Vice President Al Gore debated its merits with Ross Perot, whose prediction of a "great sucking sound" raised concerns about the migration of jobs from the United States to Mexico. Six years later, the streets of Seattle played host to protesters who paralyzed the city while the WTO, the successor to the GATT, met there. Reflecting on this episode, Jay Mazur, the President of the Union of Needletrades, Industrial, and Textile Employees and Chair of the AFL-CIO International Affairs Committee, wrote in *Foreign Affairs*: ". . . the labor movement's message from Seattle could not have been clearer: The era of trade negotiations conducted by sheltered elites balancing competing commercial interests behind closed doors is over . . . Globalization is . . . hurting too many and helping too few" (2000, p. 79). Given the prominence of NAFTA in the recent debate over trade policy, we focus on this trade agreement in the remainder of this chapter.

AN OVERVIEW OF NAFTA

The infamous Smoot–Hawley Tariff Act of 1930 brought U.S. tariffs to their highest levels up to that time. This American protectionism prompted retaliatory tariff acts from other countries. These rounds of tariffs are believed to have contributed to both the severity of the Great Depression and its international transmission.

Trade policy in the post–World War II era reflects the hard lessons learned from the interwar period. Trade liberalization has been a goal of most industrial countries and, increasingly, of developing countries as well. This liberalization has proceeded on two fronts, through multilateral agreements and through regional trading agreements involving smaller sets of countries. Multilateral trade liberalization progressed through rounds of negotiations under the auspices of the GATT. The latest round of negotiations, the 1986 to 1994 Uruguay Round, led to the creation of the WTO. Alongside this multilateral track, nations have also negotiated trade arrangements among more limited sets of countries. These arrangements can be found all over the globe, with "trade clubs" in Europe (among members of the European Union who enacted the 1992 "Single Market"), Asia (including the Association of South East Asian Nations, ASEAN), South America (including MERCOSUR, the abbreviation for MERcado COmún del SUR, a trade agreement among Argentina, Brazil, Paraguay, and Uruguay), and North America (NAFTA).

The NAFTA treaty expanded the 1989 United States–Canada Free Trade Agreement by bringing Mexico into a free trade area.[2] The treaty was signed by the United States, Canada, and Mexico in December 1992 and, after being ratified by the legislatures of the three countries, its implementation began on January 1, 1994. Among other provisions, NAFTA calls for the elimination of all tariffs on industrial products traded among the United States, Canada, and Mexico by 2004.[3]

The main effect of NAFTA is on trade between the United States and Mexico, because there was already virtually free trade between the United States and Canada and trade between Canada and Mexico is relatively limited. The tariff reductions undertaken by Mexico exceed those of the United States since, before NAFTA, Mexican tariffs on United States imports were about two-and-a-half times larger than U.S. tariffs on Mexican imports.[4] Mexico eliminated tariffs on almost half of all industrial goods imported from the United States in January 1994 and, by the beginning of 1999, 65 percent of all U.S. exports of industrial products to Mexico were tariff free. NAFTA also led to the elimination of nontariff barriers and trade-distorting restrictions such as local content requirements that limited the access of U.S. manufacturers to Mexican markets.

PREVIOUS RESEARCH RELATED TO THE ECONOMIC EFFECTS OF NAFTA

It is difficult to conclusively link NAFTA to the creation or destruction of jobs in the United States. As is always the case, the world does not offer controlled experiments whereby one and only one feature of the economy is altered while all else is held equal. This difficulty is especially acute here because of other contemporaneous events. Perhaps most importantly, Mexico suffered a financial crisis in December 1994, when speculative pressure forced a 50 percent devaluation of the peso. As Krueger (1999) emphasized, this depreciation had a much larger impact on the relative price of Mexican goods than did the tariff reductions mandated by NAFTA, which will average only 15 percent even after the reductions are phased in completely.

In the wake of its financial crisis, Mexico suffered an economic crisis; its economy contracted by 7 percent over the first nine months of 1995, although it subsequently rebounded. The United States enjoyed strong growth throughout the second half of the 1990s for reasons not related to NAFTA and, consequently, the employment growth of this period in any given sector partially reflects the overall trends in the U.S. economy. Further complicating any attempt at isolating the effect of NAFTA is the fact that, beginning in 1995, the United States implemented tariff cuts that were agreed to in the Uruguay Round of the GATT and were unrelated to NAFTA. Thus, the United States would have reduced tariffs on Mexican products even in the absence of NAFTA.[5]

Despite the potentially confounding effects of these factors, as well as others, efforts have been made to determine the consequences of NAFTA. At the aggregate level, a study by DRI/McGraw-Hill (now Global Insight) concluded that NAFTA increased U.S. exports to Mexico by $12 billion per year and Mexican exports to the United States by $5 billion per year. The U.S. Commerce Department estimated that the export gains due to NAFTA support 90,000 to 160,000 jobs in the United States. Furthermore, NAFTA had little effect on the overall level of U.S. imports from Mexico, because the pre-NAFTA tariffs imposed by the United States on Mexican goods were generally low and, therefore, their removal was not of great consequence. Finally, the feared "great sucking sound" seems to have been little more than the tiniest of slurps, since U.S. direct investment in Mexico declined between 1994 and 1997 while its direct investment to the rest of the world increased. A study by the U.S. International Trade Commission concluded that U.S. direct investment in Mexico had minimal impact on aggregate investment at home.[6] Recent overviews of the economic effects of NAFTA by Burfisher, Robinson, and Thierfelder (2001), and by Krueger (1999) concluded that the overall impact of NAFTA on the U.S. economy has been relatively small.

One would expect that the impact of NAFTA would differ across geographic areas within the United States as a result of differences in industrial specialization. Some areas may have a concentration of industries that would benefit from the increased opportunities for exporting, while others may have a concentration of industries vulnerable to competition from lower wage areas. Coughlin and Wall (2001) found that implementation of NAFTA is associated with changes in the distribution of exports over states. They estimated that overall U.S. merchandise exports increased by close to 8 percent as a result of NAFTA, but that the change varied widely over states. Thirteen states increased exports by 20 percent or more as a result of NAFTA, while the effect was negative for 12 states. The wide variation in the change in exports over regions suggests that the impact on local labor markets, and associated magnitude of job reallocation, exceeded that suggested by the national average of 8 percent export growth.

One expected benefit of trade liberalization is lower production costs. As competitive pressure increases, less productive plants need to either improve productivity or shut down. In some cases, the expanded market may also make it possible to realize greater economies of scale. Free trade in raw materials and intermediate products reduces the cost of the inputs into production, resulting in lower costs. Trefler (2001) focused on the effect of the 1989–1996 Canada–U.S. Free Trade Agreement (that preceded NAFTA) on Canadian manufacturing.[7] He found that industries which experienced large tariff reductions suffered a 15 percent decline in employment. Offsetting this, however, is a large increase in labor productivity associated with turnover of low-productivity plants and increased technical efficiency at surviving plants. Tybout and Westbrook (1995) examined the effect of trade liberalization in the 1980s on Mexican manufacturing. They found that average cost decreases were largest in relatively open manufacturing industries. For export-oriented industries, the average cost decreases were associated with decreased input prices. In the case of industries with import competition, productivity improvements played a significant role. Scale effects were relatively unimportant in explaining productivity improvements.

One of the principal concerns of opponents of trade liberalization is the effect of trade on the distribution of wages. Although workers in high-wage countries are viewed as most at risk, workers in protected sectors of less developed countries may also be adversely affected. Revenga (1997) found that trade liberalization has been associated with real wage decreases in Mexican manufacturing. Some of the economic rents arising from trade protection had accrued to workers in the form of higher wages, and these were dissipated as the degree of protection was decreased. Hanson and Harrison (1999) found that the Mexican trade liberalization resulted in an increase in wage inequality. The liberalization in trade was especially strong in low-skill industries, exposing Mexican producers to competition from countries with more abundant supplies of unskilled labor.

It is surprisingly difficult to find a direct link between protection from trade and wages in the United States. Gaston and Trefler (1994) examined how trade protection affects U.S. manufacturing wages.

They found that protection is associated with lower wages, holding worker characteristics constant.

SECTOR-SPECIFIC EFFECTS

Eventually, NAFTA will lead to the full liberalization of trade among the United States, Canada, and Mexico.[8] All tariffs among these countries will be eliminated by 2004 for industrial products and by 2009 for all other products. NAFTA also will bring about the elimination of nontariff barriers and other distortions to trade, such as quotas and licenses.

This section considers the effects of NAFTA for three key manufacturing sectors experiencing significant trade liberalization: the textile and apparel industries (combined), the chemical industry, and the automobile vehicle industry. In these industries, NAFTA led to the reduction of large Mexican tariffs on imports from the United States and Canada, as well as to the reduction of tariffs on Mexican exports to the United States and Canada, both of which were lower than the Mexican import tariffs initially. We look at the extent of tariff reductions and elimination of nontariff barriers in these sectors, as well as their possible effects on trade.

In this section, we adopt a more narrative approach than we utilized in our analysis of the effects of real exchange rate movements on job creation and job destruction. Given the limited time span since the implementation of NAFTA began, and the significant macroeconomic developments that occurred during the same time period, the fruitfulness of formal econometric analysis may be very limited.[9] What we can do is look at net employment levels for narrowly defined industries and review reports of industry activity with an eye toward the potential effects of NAFTA on gross job flows. Specifically, we examine the correlation between developments in the foreign trade activity of industries and their labor market behavior. The foreign trade measures for each industry are:

$$\text{Export Share} = \frac{\text{Exports}}{\text{Total Sales}}$$

$$\text{Import Penetration Ratio} = \frac{\text{Imports}}{\text{Total Sales} + \text{Imports}}.$$

These measures are constructed for both multilateral and bilateral trade. Multilateral trade includes all exports or imports in the industry to all countries, whereas bilateral trade includes only trade between the United States and Mexico. Finally, we also look at the ratio of the bilateral trade measures to the multilateral trade measures to ascertain the relative importance of NAFTA trade to worldwide trade for the industry.

Our approach presents us with a result that is a subtext of the entire book, the diverse response within industries to a change in the international environment. This result offers evidence that "globalization" is both helping and hurting, though whether it is helping too few and hurting too many, as in the view cited above, necessarily depends upon a weighting of the relative welfare gains and losses across individuals.

Before turning to the industry analyses, we offer a brief overview of macroeconomic conditions in Mexico, which are important to bear in mind when evaluating the effects of NAFTA. Figure 7.1 plots the real growth rate of Mexican GDP and the real exchange rate between the Mexican peso and U.S. dollar (adjusted for consumer prices) for the period 1980 to 2002. The most notable feature pertinent to our analyses is the Mexican crisis of 1994–1995, during which the real peso devalued sharply and GDP growth plunged to its lowest level in the sample period. Because the crisis unfolded at precisely the same time NAFTA was implemented, it is extremely difficult to identify the separate effect of NAFTA during the crisis. However, real GDP growth rebounded fairly quickly and was robust throughout the remainder of the 1990s. The real peso took the rest of the decade to return to its precrisis level, but it appreciated fairly steadily during that time.

The trend behavior of Mexican real GDP growth and the real peso are also important for interpreting the effects of NAFTA. Since the late 1980s, both real GDP growth and the real peso have been relatively strong on average, especially compared with the rest of the 1980s. This general strength probably contributed to higher Mexican multilateral

Figure 7.1 Macroeconomic Developments in Mexico (Real GDP growth Q1:1981–Q3:2002, Real exchange rate Q1:1980–Q4:2002)

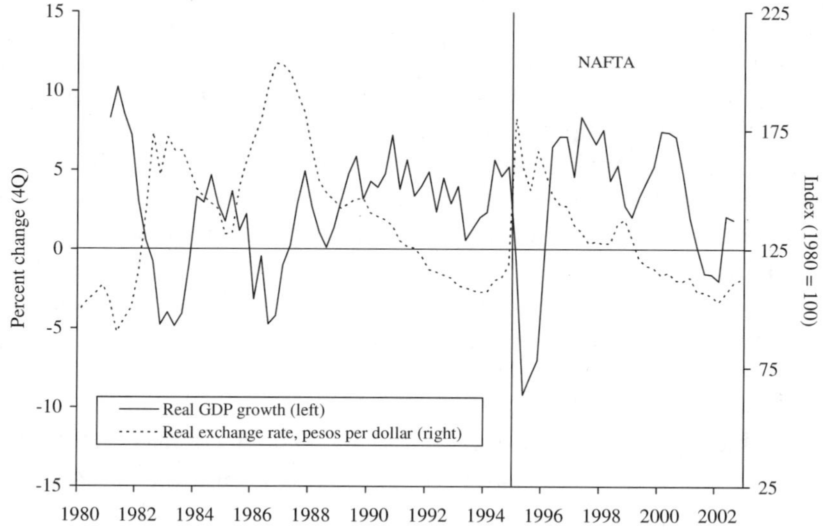

SOURCE: International Monetary Fund, International Financial Statistics.

imports and exports in all industries, on average, and this probably translated into higher bilateral U.S. exports to Mexico and bilateral U.S. imports from Mexico as well.

To summarize, both the cyclical effects of the Mexican crisis and the trend robustness of the Mexican macroeconomy are important factors that influenced Mexican multilateral trade in the years surrounding NAFTA. Thus, we might expect to see a long-run trend increase in U.S.–Mexico bilateral trade as well. Also, there may be a cyclical influence from the Mexican crisis, most likely manifesting itself as a decline in U.S. bilateral exports to Mexico. Indeed, we find both of these effects in the trade data. Any separate effects attributable to NAFTA would appear over and above the effects of the macroeconomic developments.

Textiles and Apparel

The U.S. textile and apparel industries (SICs 22 and 23) are often viewed as susceptible to the destruction of low-wage jobs through international competition. In 1996, U.S. average hourly earnings in these industries were relatively low: $9.62 per hour for textiles and $7.67 per hour for apparel, compared with $12.00 per hour for all manufacturing. Nevertheless, the relatively low earnings in these industries are significantly higher than the earnings of textile and apparel workers in less developed countries with which the United States trades, such as Mexico. Thus, U.S. textile and apparel jobs potentially are threatened by imports and by the relocation of plants abroad. Concern about the welfare of workers in these industries may have contributed to the relatively high tariff protection afforded textile and apparel firms before NAFTA.

Table 7.1 provides an overview of the changes in tariffs and trade rules for the textile and apparel industries as a result of NAFTA. The

Table 7.1 NAFTA Changes for Textiles and Apparel

Country	Category	Change	Developments
Mexico	Tariff	Eliminated 20% apparel and 15% textile tariffs mostly by 1998 and completely by 2002.	U.S. textile and apparel exports to Mexico increased from less than $1.6 billion in 1993 to $2.8 billion in 1996.
	Rule	Allowed domestic sales by *maquiladora* plants.	During 1995 financial crisis, Mexico placed 35% tariffs on non-NAFTA goods.
United States	Tariff	Eliminated 9.1% average tariff by 2000 on: 95% of fabric imports, 83% of made-up textile imports, 99% of apparel imports.	U.S. importers shifted from Asian to NAFTA imports. From 1993 to 1996, Canadian and Mexican share increases from 6% to 14% of total U.S. textile and apparel imports. Benefits U.S. industry because NAFTA members use more U.S. supplies than Asian competitors.

primary impact of the agreement was to eliminate the substantial tariffs on these products levied by both the United States and Mexico by the year 2002. Mexico also removed some trade barriers for NAFTA partners but raised tariffs on non-NAFTA partners.

Prior to NAFTA, the average U.S. tariff on imports of Mexican textile and apparel products was the highest among 22 industrial categories. Thus, U.S. firms in these two sectors faced the largest reductions in protection due to NAFTA among all U.S. manufacturers. Mexico had even higher tariffs in these industries before NAFTA, so Mexican firms in these sectors faced even more dramatic changes in their trade with NAFTA partners. However, to some extent the policy changes toward non-NAFTA partners offset the NAFTA changes.[10]

For historical perspective, Figure 7.2 plots U.S. employment in the textile and apparel industries since 1939. Employment declined fairly steadily in both industries for many years—both in absolute terms and

Figure 7.2 U.S. Employment in the Textile and Apparel Industries (1939–2001)

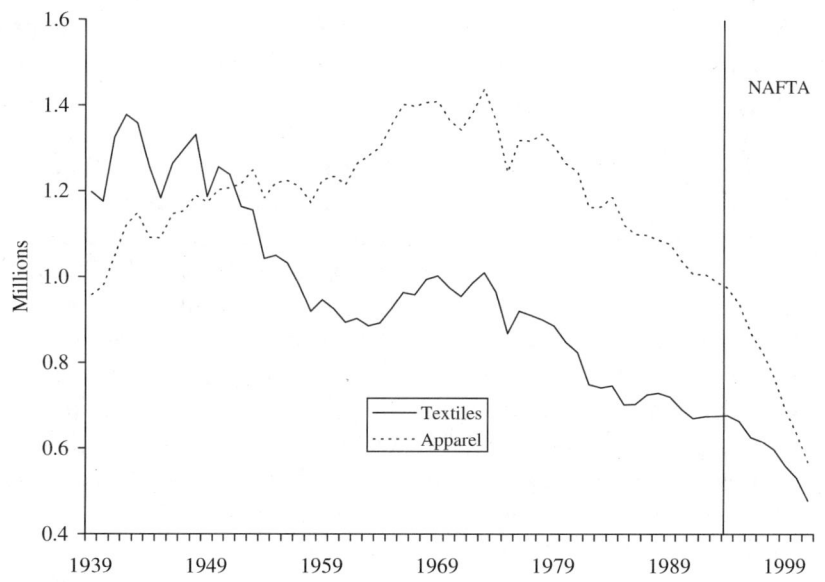

SOURCE: Bureau of Labor Statistics.

as a share of manufacturing employment. These negative trends reflect a variety of long-run technological factors, international trade, and other forces that obviously cannot be attributed to NAFTA.[11] Moreover, the sources of the trends differ between the two industries.

Textile employment has trended downward since World War II. The main driving force has been revolutionary technological advances, which have led to labor productivity growth of twice the rate for all manufacturing. At least partly because of this innovation, the textile industry faced only mild competition from foreign textile producers. From 1970 to 1988, textile imports as a proportion of domestic consumption rose modestly from 4.6 percent to 6.8 percent. Within this industry, firms that adopted the technological advances would have been relatively free from foreign competition, while those firms that did not—or could not—keep up with technology likely declined and destroyed jobs at a faster rate.

In contrast, technological innovation in the apparel industry was much less dramatic and much more incremental. Apparel employment did not peak until the early 1970s, when the industry began to experience stiff competition from foreign apparel producers, particularly those in developing countries with very low wages. From 1970 to 1988, apparel imports as a proportion of domestic consumption jumped from 5.2 percent to 26.1 percent and employment began a trend decline, perhaps because of the adverse effects of increased trade via imports.

The question at hand for both industries is whether NAFTA could be responsible for employment effects above and beyond those attributable to other factors such as trend developments, macroeconomic conditions in the United States and Mexico, and non-NAFTA trade changes. This question is difficult to answer definitively for these industries given the range of factors involved, but also because of the mixed employment responses. Following the implementation of NAFTA on January 1, 1994, textile employment continued to decline at about the same long-run trend rate as it did before NAFTA. In contrast, employment in the apparel industry appears to have declined at a much faster rate than before NAFTA, dropping about 40 percent since 1994. The timing and magnitude of the apparent change in the apparel employment trend suggest the possibility that it may be related to

NAFTA, but one would want corroborating evidence from foreign trade data.

Figure 7.3 portrays the dramatic changes in U.S. international trade of textile and apparel products.[12] Since the early 1970s, the multilateral import penetration ratio (left scale) has risen steadily by almost sixfold, to nearly 35 percent in 2001.[13] The multilateral export share was essentially flat until the late 1980s, when it began increasing steadily, and it has approximately tripled since then. Although multilateral imports have risen somewhat faster in the second half of the 1990s, there is no apparent change in either measure that seems obviously connected with the implementation of NAFTA.

A closer look at the bilateral trade shares between the United States and Mexico, also shown in Figure 7.3 (right scale), reveals changes that are likely to be connected with NAFTA.[14] The most notable development is a sharp increase in the share of U.S. exports to Mexico since the late 1980s. As Krueger (1999) explained, changes in trade between the United States and Mexico before the implementation of NAFTA may reflect anticipation of its passage, but it is more likely that the changes primarily reflect general trade liberalization and favorable macroeconomic developments in Mexico since the late 1980s. Nevertheless, the pace of increase in the bilateral export share quickened significantly since 1994 and may reflect a boost by NAFTA. Most of this faster increase in bilateral exports to Mexico occurred in the textiles industry. The share of U.S. bilateral imports from Mexico is small and did not change as much, but there also appears to be evidence of a significant increase in the upward trend since the implementation of NAFTA.

Whether or not NAFTA was significant enough to affect total U.S. multilateral trade in textiles and apparel, it does seem to have contributed to changes in the bilateral composition of such trade. Figure 7.4 illustrates the compositional shift by plotting the shares of bilateral U.S.–Mexico trade in total U.S. multilateral trade. The shares of U.S. textile and apparel trade with Mexico have been increasing rapidly since the mid 1980s; the bilateral export share roughly tripled to about 30 percent, and bilateral import share roughly quadrupled to about 2 percent. In both cases, the reorientation of exports and imports toward firms trading with Mexico quickened shortly after NAFTA took effect.

Figure 7.3 International Trade Shares in the Textile and Apparel Industries, U.S. Multilateral and Bilateral U.S.–Mexico (1972–2001)

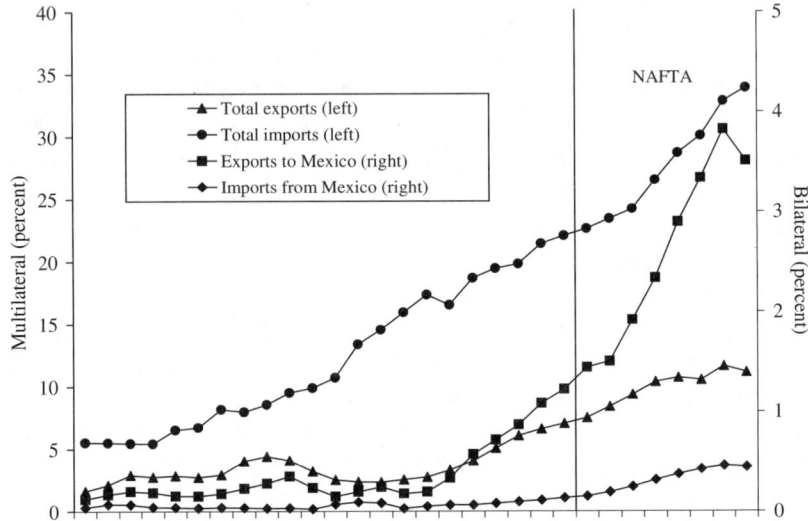

SOURCE: Census Bureau, Bureau of Economic Analysis.

Figure 7.4 Ratio of U.S.–Mexico Bilateral to U.S. Multilateral Trade in the Textile and Apparel Industries (1972–2001)

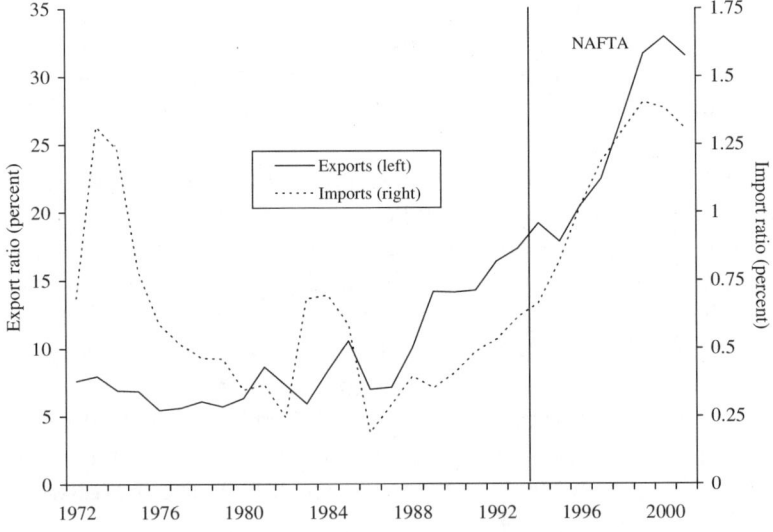

SOURCE: Census Bureau, Bureau of Economic Analysis.

NAFTA seems to have contributed to the shift in American purchases of textiles and apparel from the Far East to North America, making Mexico and Canada the top two suppliers of textiles and apparel for the United States. In 1993, China, Hong Kong, Taiwan, and Korea together accounted for 39 percent of U.S. textile and apparel imports, while Mexico and Canada accounted for 7 percent. By 1996, these percentages shifted to 30 percent for China, Hong Kong, Taiwan, and Korea and 14 percent for Mexico and Canada. This shift, toward firms that tend to use more American products as inputs, was welcomed by the textile industry.

In 1999, Doug Ellis, CEO of Southern Mills, Inc., in Atlanta and president of the American Textile Manufactures Institute (ATMI), was quoted as saying that Asian economies ". . . are still trying to export their way out of their difficulties and, to our detriment, the U.S. is the one they rely on as a buyer of first and last resort." He continued that, because of the use of U.S. textile products in Mexican and Canadian apparel manufacture, "If it weren't for NAFTA, our exports would be in much worse shape."[15] A September 1997 news release by the ATMI echoes this theme, stating ". . . in terms of textile and apparel trade, our NAFTA-forged relationship with Mexico is truly symbiotic, truly mutually rewarding."[16]

Note well, however, the disparity in bilateral export and import shares. Although the import share increased more in percentage terms, the import share is an order of magnitude smaller than the export share. In fact, the small share of textile and apparel imports from Mexico suggests that it is unlikely that NAFTA itself stimulated enough new imports to threaten many jobs in the textile and apparel industry overall. Individual U.S. textile and apparel firms, however, would have been affected relatively more or less if their trade with NAFTA partners was disproportionately high or low.

To the extent they exist, any employment effects of NAFTA are manifested in the net and gross job flows depicted in Figure 7.5.[17] Net employment in the textile and apparel industries has been declining at a much faster rate during the NAFTA period. This net employment reduction probably has been accomplished mostly by an increase in the rate of job destruction, which is estimated to have been at high levels normally associated with past recessions and other major manufacturing contractions. Job creation, on the other hand, has steadied at, or just

Figure 7.5 U.S. Gross Job Flows in the Textile and Apparel Industries (1973–2002)

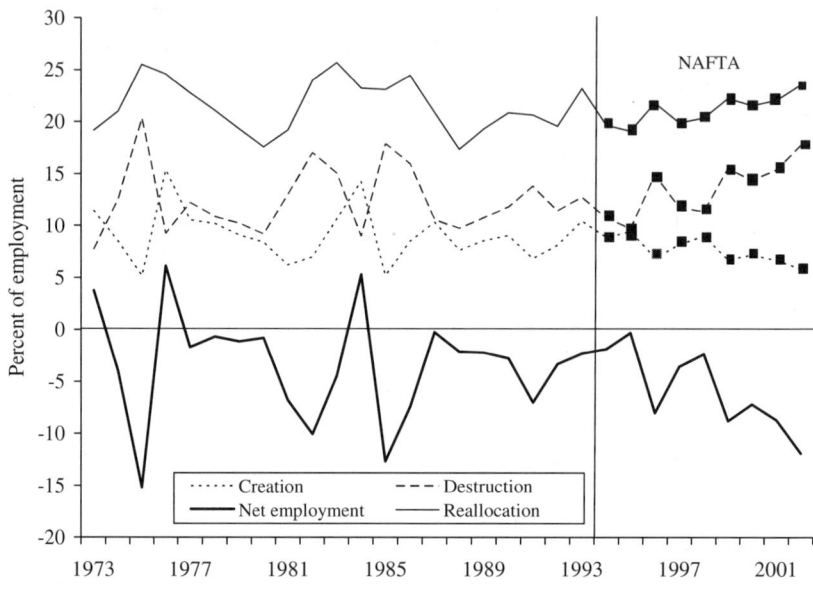

NOTE: ■ Indicates imputed data.
SOURCE: Authors' calculations; Bureau of Labor Statistics, Longitudinal Research Database.

slightly below, its long-run average. Together, these developments brought about a significant increase in the rate of job reallocation among textile and apparel plants.

Linking trade-related changes in the textile and apparel industries to net employment change is tricky at best, and we have only a short sample of data for the post-NAFTA period. Because the share of imports of textiles and apparel from Mexico is very small, the effect of NAFTA on net employment in this industry is almost surely small as well. Many other factors, some of which were non-NAFTA trade-related issues, also likely played important roles. Competition from non-NAFTA countries and the high value of the dollar have been problems for domestic industries, and competitive pressure will likely further increase in the near future with the expiration of quota restrictions on textile imports from China.[18]

Although the net employment effect of NAFTA probably was very small, it is possible that NAFTA and other trade-related changes in Mexico may have contributed more to gross job flows. This conclusion depends importantly, though, on the assumption that sufficient heterogeneity exists among textile and apparel plants. If plants differ enough in their extent of participation in international trade and in the countries with which they trade, we should expect the trade changes to induce gross job flows. The compositional shift toward trade with Mexico, evident primarily from the substantial increase in the share of exports going to Mexico, may tend to induce job creation in plants exporting to Mexico and job destruction in plants exporting to other countries.

What remains hard to explain, solely based on trade developments, is the asymmetry between creation and destruction in the late 1990s. The multilateral trade gap (exports less imports) for textiles and apparel has grown steadily during the past 3 decades, as is apparent from Figure 7.3. Undoubtedly, this ongoing shift in the relative importance of domestic producers has put downward pressure on employment in the industry, but it is unclear why domestic producers responded more on the destruction margin. Perhaps Foote's (1998) argument regarding nonconvex employment adjustment in declining industries is applicable here. In any case, the apparent relative success of U.S. textile and apparel producers who export to Mexico suggests that they may have experienced unusual increases in job creation.

Other more subtle factors may help explain the relative importance of job destruction. As Bernard and Jensen (1995) note, exporters tend to be larger, more technologically advanced, and have higher labor productivity. Thus, a shift in employment toward these producers could, on average, induce a reduction in total industry employment that would be accomplished primarily by job destruction in plants relatively unengaged in foreign trade. A more subtle explanation may arise from differences in the types of textile and apparel products traded among NAFTA partners. For example, if products traded among NAFTA partners were more "sophisticated" and required higher levels of technology and capital intensity, then the compositional shift could also motivate the job flows we observe. Of course, without more specific data, these explanations remain merely speculative.

Chemicals and Allied Products

The chemical and allied products industry (SIC 28) is the third largest U.S. export sector. Its production workers enjoy the highest average wages of any manufacturing sector, about $17 per hour in 1996, reflecting the use of well-trained and highly skilled production workers in an increasingly complex industry. The industry is also quite diverse, manufacturing over 50,000 different substances, and this diversity is reflected in the attributes of its subsectors. For example, the shares of production workers in the two largest subsectors, drugs (SIC 283) at 50 percent and plastic materials and synthetics (SIC 282) at 67 percent, differ significantly from the 60 percent average for all chemical industries.

Table 7.2 summarizes the changes in tariffs and trade rules pertaining to the chemical industry due to NAFTA. Prior to NAFTA, average chemical tariffs were relatively low compared with the other industry

Table 7.2 NAFTA Changes for Chemicals and Allied Products

Country	Category	Change	Developments
Mexico	Tariff	Average reduced from 10.2% in 1992 to 4.0% in 1996.	U.S. chemical exports to Mexico increased from $3.4 billion in 1993 to $5.1 billion in 1996.
	Rule	Eliminated import licenses on chemicals, rubbers, plastics, and pharmaceuticals.	
	Rule	Agreed to protect process patents.	
	Rule	Initiated competitive bidding for Pemex (government oil) and CFE (government electricity) contracts.	U.S. exports of petrochemicals to Mexico grew more than 75 percent to $1.2 billion from 1993 to 1996.
United States	Tariff	Average reduced from 1.0% in 1992 to 0.5% in 1996.	Mexican chemical exports to United States increased from $0.6 billion in 1993 to $1.4 billion in 1996 (although it is unlikely that this small tariff reduction caused the increase).

tariffs discussed in this chapter. Nevertheless, the agreement cut average tariffs in both countries by half or more. Tariff reduction in Mexico was more important, as Mexican tariffs were 10 times larger than U.S. tariffs. But, these averages mask a range of reductions across subsectors. For example, about one-fourth of all chemical products had entered Mexico duty free before NAFTA, while tariffs on certain pharmaceuticals were as high as 20 percent. The new, lower Mexican chemicals tariff reflects the immediate elimination of 20 percent tariffs on close to one-half of U.S. pharmaceutical exports to Mexico.

Equally importantly, NAFTA required Mexico to adopt several changes in rules that significantly liberalized trade. For example, it eliminated import licenses and terminated the virtual monopoly held by the Mexican government on petrochemical production. The latter change opened Mexican petrochemical markets to U.S. and Canadian firms, leading to cross-border vertical integration with Mexican firms supplying basic and primary products for manufacture in the United States into high value-added secondary petrochemicals. The effects of NAFTA on other chemical industries likely were mixed. Some sectors were little affected for technological reasons. For example, prepared paint is costly to transport relative to its price. This leaves little scope for supply from distant firms; indeed, the U.S. paint market comprises many small to medium-sized firms that are geographically dispersed.

Figure 7.6 plots the history of employment in the chemical industry since 1939. Employment grew steadily until the 1970s, when it leveled off at a little above 1 million workers. This time-series pattern is similar to that of total manufacturing employment, except that chemicals employment rose faster in the earlier period, while its manufacturing share has stabilized more recently. In particular, note that chemicals employment has changed little during the post-NAFTA period, hovering at about its average for the past three decades.

As in most industries, foreign trade has been increasing in importance for chemicals, as shown in Figure 7.7. Total multilateral exports and imports (left scale) have trended upward since the early 1970s, with exports doubling to more than 16 percent and imports more than tripling to about 13 percent by 2001. During the NAFTA period both multilateral exports and imports have continued to increase. Exports have increased in line with their long-term trend, but imports have risen significantly faster since NAFTA. However, because the NAFTA

Figure 7.6 U.S. Employment in the Chemical Industry (1939–2001)

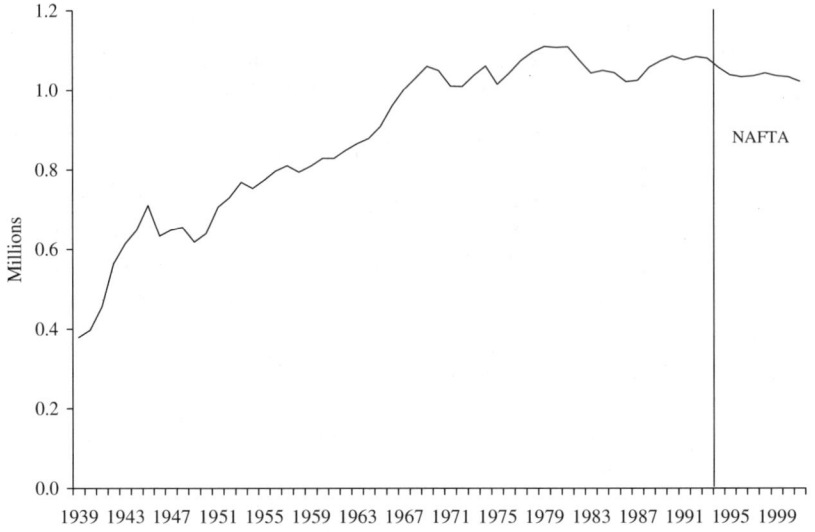

SOURCE: Bureau of Labor Statistics.

Figure 7.7 International Trade Shares in the Chemical Industry, U.S. Multilateral and Bilateral U.S.–Mexico (1972–2001)

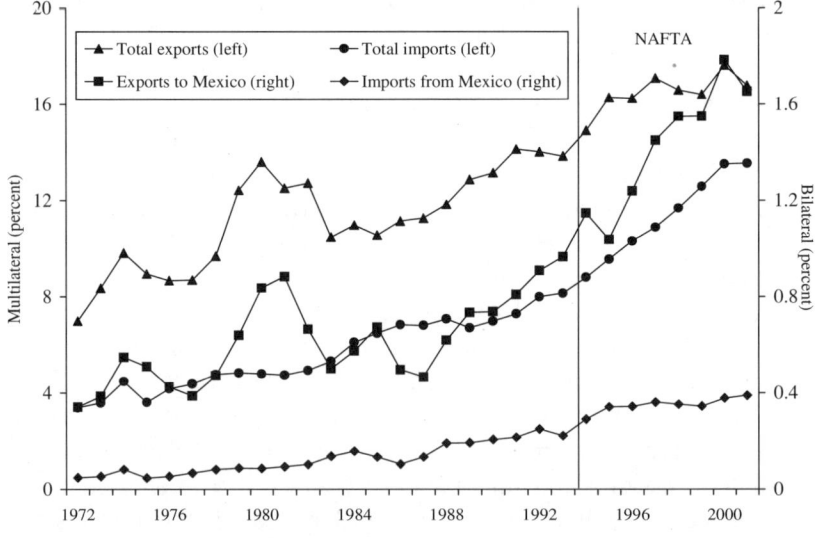

SOURCE: Census Bureau, Bureau of Economic Analysis.

changes pertaining to U.S. chemical imports from Mexico were modest, it seems unlikely that the increasing propensity to import chemicals is attributable to NAFTA. This conclusion is supported by developments in the bilateral trade shares (right scale), also shown in Figure 7.7. Imports from Mexico have not increased at a significantly faster pace like the multilateral imports did. Exports to Mexico have nearly doubled since NAFTA and may have been influenced at least in part by the trade liberalization, but it appears that bilateral exports to Mexico began to increase faster even before NAFTA.

The shares of bilateral trade to Mexico confirm this assessment. As can be seen in Figure 7.8, U.S. chemical imports from Mexico (right scale) peaked shortly after NAFTA, then declined, and now are at about the same level they were at before NAFTA, but they seem to be about in line with their long-run upward trend. These relatively minor changes probably stem from the fact that U.S. tariffs on Mexican chemicals averaged only 1 percent before NAFTA. In contrast, U.S. exports to Mexico seem to have risen more rapidly since NAFTA (left scale). Exports of chemicals to Mexico were approximately 6 percent of total exports of chemicals until NAFTA but have risen to about 10 percent since then. This increase of more than 50 percent compares favorably to the 37 percent increase in exports to non-NAFTA countries during the same period, and Mexico became the third largest foreign destination of U.S. chemical exports by 1998 (Canada is the largest). However, the increases in bilateral export shares, both relative to industry sales and to total industry exports, are relatively modest and not too far out of line with trend increases since the mid 1980s, when other developments stimulated trade with Mexico. Thus, NAFTA seems to have shifted trade within the chemicals toward Mexico without significantly affecting overall trade, just as it did in textiles and apparel.

Given the lack of significant changes in employment and trade, it seems unlikely that NAFTA generated much change in job flows in the chemical industry. Figure 7.9 confirms this conjecture. Gross job flows in the chemical industry have been relatively stable near their long-run averages during the NAFTA period. Thus, there is little evidence, from either gross job flows or net employment change, that NAFTA caused much reallocation of jobs beyond the normal churning in this industry. Apparently the NAFTA changes were not large enough to bring about

Figure 7.8 Ratio of U.S.–Mexico Bilateral to U.S. Multilateral Trade in the Chemical Industry (1972–2001)

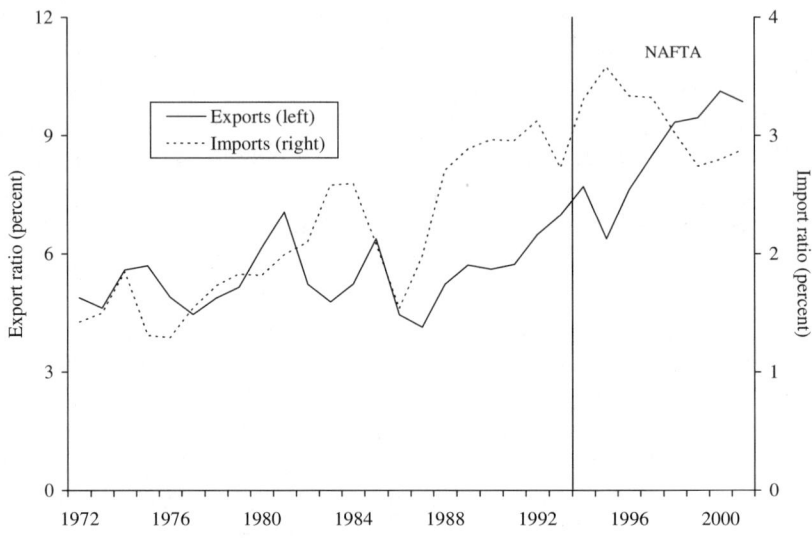

SOURCE: Census Bureau, Bureau of Economic Analysis

Figure 7.9 U.S. Gross Job Flows in the Chemical Industry (1973–2002)

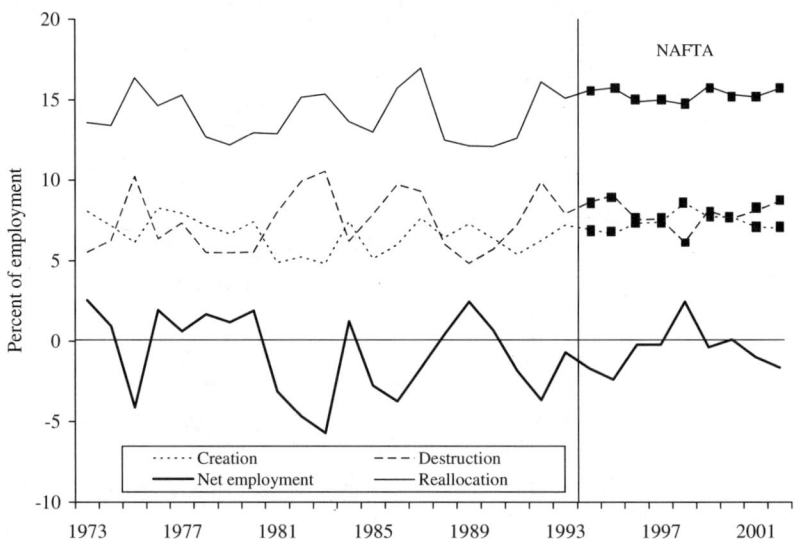

NOTE: ■ Indicates imputed data.
SOURCE: Authors' calculations; Bureau of Labor Statistics, Longitudinal Research Database.

significant employment adjustments overall. Furthermore, the shifts of trade in chemicals toward Mexico apparently occurred within establishments, rather than between establishments, and did not entail many job changes.

Automobiles

The automobile industry (SIC 371) dominates trade among Canada, Mexico, and the United States.[19] Automobiles and automobile products represent not only the largest component of all three bilateral trade relationships, but also the largest component in each direction for all six bilateral trade flows among these three countries. Overall, the auto industry accounts for 40 percent of North American trade (Weintraub and Sands 1998).

The liberalization of the North American automobile trade began in 1965 with the Canada–U.S. Automotive Products Trade Agreement (APTA), also known as the Auto Pact. This agreement increased the number of U.S. vehicles and components allowed to be sold in Canada. It led to the integration of the automotive industries in the United States and Canada, with Canadian plants taking over a disproportionate share of vehicle assembly, and U.S. sites largely responsible for research and development, product engineering, and the production of high-valued parts (Kumar and Holmes 1998). NAFTA represents an effort to extend this vertical integration to Mexico.

Prior to NAFTA, Mexican policy primarily had been directed toward preventing the integration of its auto industry with U.S. firms. The Mexican government issued a series of Auto Decrees, beginning in 1962, that segmented the domestic auto market and awarded rights to manufacture for each segment. The fifth Auto Decree, issued in 1989, liberalized domestic production but retained barriers to exports from the United States. Along with continued tariff protection, this decree included a "trade balancing" requirement for Mexican assemblers that mandated their export sales as a function of their import purchases. This provision made investment in Mexico the only viable way for U.S. auto firms to sell in the Mexican market. The Mexican government encouraged production for export with the 1989 *Maquiladora* Decree. *Maquiladora* plants, sited in Mexico near the U.S. border, manufactured and assembled products that were exported to the United States (Doh 1998).

Table 7.3 provides an overview of the changes in tariffs and trade rules for the automobile industry due to NAFTA.[20] NAFTA eventually eliminates all of the protectionist aspects of the Mexican Auto Decrees.

Table 7.3 NAFTA Changes for Automobiles

Country	Category	Change	Developments
CARS AND LIGHT TRUCKS			
Mexico	Tariff	Immediate reduction from 20% to 10% with elimination by 1998 for light trucks and by 2003 for cars.	U.S. light auto exports to Mexico increase from 17,000 units ($0.24 billion) in 1993 to 91,000 units ($1.3 billion) in 1996.
	Rule	Allow domestic sales by *maquiladora* plants.	Greater economies of scale because manufacturers no longer need to simultaneously manufacture same models in different countries.
	Rule	Eliminate trade balancing rules.	
	Quota	Eliminate import quotas.	
United States	Tariff	Immediate elimination of 2.5% tariff on cars; immediate reduction from 25% to 10% on light trucks and elimination by 2004.	Mexican light auto exports to U.S. increased from $11.1 billion in 1993 to $22.9 billion in 1996.
HEAVY AND MEDIUM TRUCKS			
Mexico	Tariff	Eliminate 20% tariff by 2003.	U.S. heavy and medium truck exports to Mexico increase.
	Rule	Eliminate trade balance and local content requirements by 1998.	
	Rule	Mexican companies can lease vehicles.	Mexican vehicle operation and maintenance markets opened to U.S. providers.
United States and Mexico	Rule	Liberalized restrictions on land transportation between United States and Mexico.	Mexican fleets must be modernized to meet U.S. safety and environmental standards, creating a new market for U.S. suppliers.

All Mexican tariffs and most nontariff barriers associated with North American trade in cars and trucks are to be eliminated. Likewise, all U.S. tariffs on cars and light trucks will be removed.

These changes create an essentially frictionless, integrated automobile market in North America. Given the dominance of U.S. automobile manufacturers in NAFTA countries, this integrated market suggests that the impact of trade on U.S. employment may be quite different in the automobile industry than in other industries that are not integrated. Conceivably, the liberalization of automobile trade between the United States and Mexico may actually increase both trade and employment in the industry if liberalization improves the cost efficiency and productivity of the industry, or if it stimulates total demand for automobiles.

Figure 7.10 plots the history of employment in the automobile industry since 1939. Automobile employment fluctuated widely between 600,000 and 1 million throughout most of the historical period. During the late 1950s and early 1960s employment declined but subsequently rebounded following APTA. During the 1980s and early 1990s, foreign competition, especially from Japan, and labor-saving technological innovations contributed to much slower employment growth. During the post-NAFTA period, however, employment rose significantly, and even its share of total manufacturing employment increased. Thus, the question arises: are the changes in NAFTA linked in any way to this surge in auto employment?

The importance of total foreign trade in the auto industry has not changed much during the NAFTA period, as can be seen in Figure 7.11. Multilateral exports and imports (left scale) were relatively flat during this period, and neither trade measure ended up much above its previous historical high. The recent slower growth of multilateral trade contrasts with the steady trend increase in both multilateral exports and imports during the prior two decades, particularly in imports, which peaked in the mid 1980s.

However, Figure 7.11 shows that bilateral trade with Mexico (right scale) has increased dramatically since the 1980s and especially during the NAFTA period. Bilateral imports from Mexico approximately tripled since NAFTA, from less than 2 percent to nearly 6 percent. Bilateral exports to Mexico also increased after NAFTA, approximately doubling from less than 2 percent to nearly 4 percent. The figure

Figure 7.10 U.S. Employment in the Automobile Industry (1939–2001)

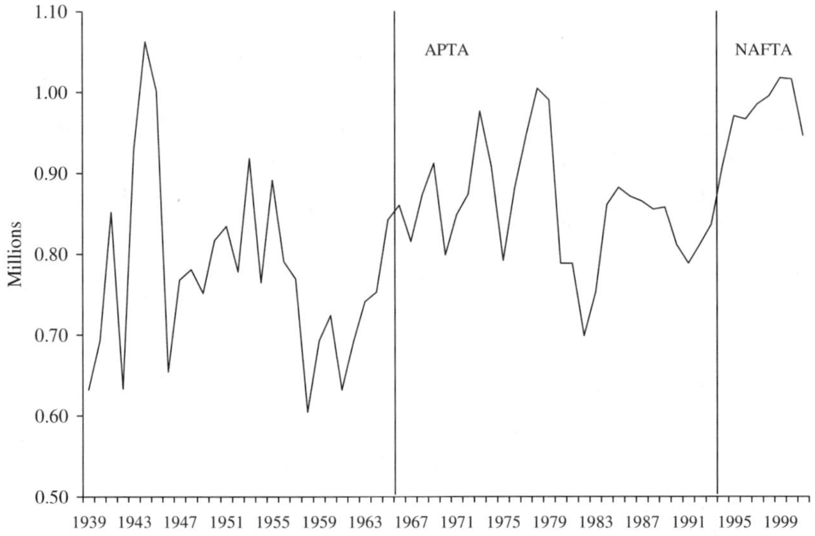

SOURCE: Bureau of Labor Statistics.

reveals that bilateral trade with Mexico began increasing long before NAFTA—at least since the late 1980s, or earlier—so NAFTA cannot be responsible entirely for the shift toward trade with Mexico in the auto industry. Nevertheless, the rate of increase jumped sharply for imports immediately following NAFTA, and for exports more recently, so there may be some effect of NAFTA in addition to the economic factors underlying the trend increase.

The trend increase in bilateral U.S.–Mexico trade has significantly altered the composition of trading partners for the auto industry, as shown in Figure 7.12. As recently as the late 1980s, bilateral exports to and imports from Mexico accounted for less than 5 percent each of multilateral trade. But, by 2001, bilateral exports accounted for nearly one-fourth of multilateral exports, and bilateral imports accounted for nearly one-fifth of multilateral imports. Consequently, the importance of both the exchange rate between the Mexican peso and U.S. dollar and of U.S. establishments involved in trade with Mexico has increased greatly for total multilateral trade in automobiles.

Figure 7.11 International Trade Shares in the Automobile Industry, U.S. Multilateral and Bilateral U.S.–Mexico (1972–2001)

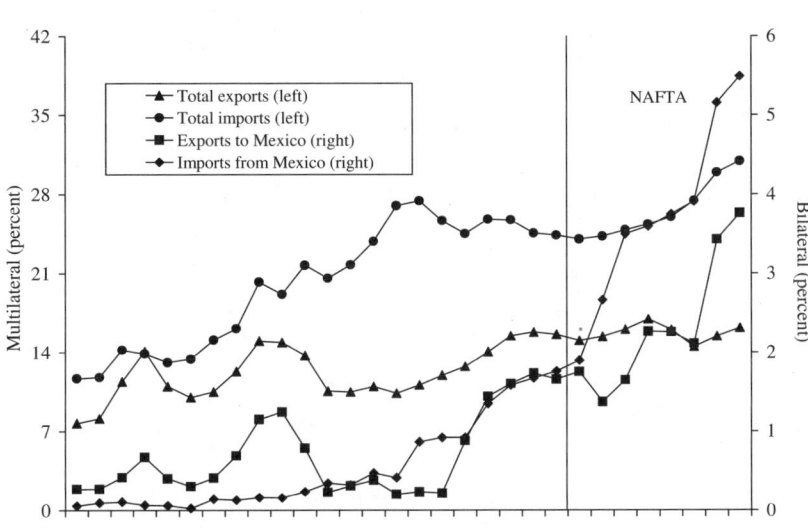

SOURCE: Census Bureau, Bureau of Economic Analysis.

The period immediately following NAFTA seemed to open trade. Exports of autos from the United States to Mexico rose 584 percent, to $1.3 billion, between 1993 and 1996 (an increase in units from 17,000 to 91,000). Trade also increased in the other direction, with U.S. imports of automotive products from Mexico rising from $11.1 billion in 1993 to $22.9 billion in 1996. This figure includes an increase in auto exports from Mexico to the United States from $3.7 billion in 1993 to $11.3 billion in 1996. Industry analysts estimate that, on average, over half of the value of the content of vehicles exported to the United States from Mexico is produced in the United States. Mexican imports in the mid 1990s helped American manufacturers when they faced capacity constraints, especially for sport utility vehicles and light trucks.[21]

NAFTA also seems to be affecting the division of production between the United States and Mexico in much the same way that the Auto Pact altered the division of production between Canada and the

Figure 7.12 Ratio of U.S.–Mexico Bilateral to U.S. Multilateral Trade in the Automobile Industry (1972–2001)

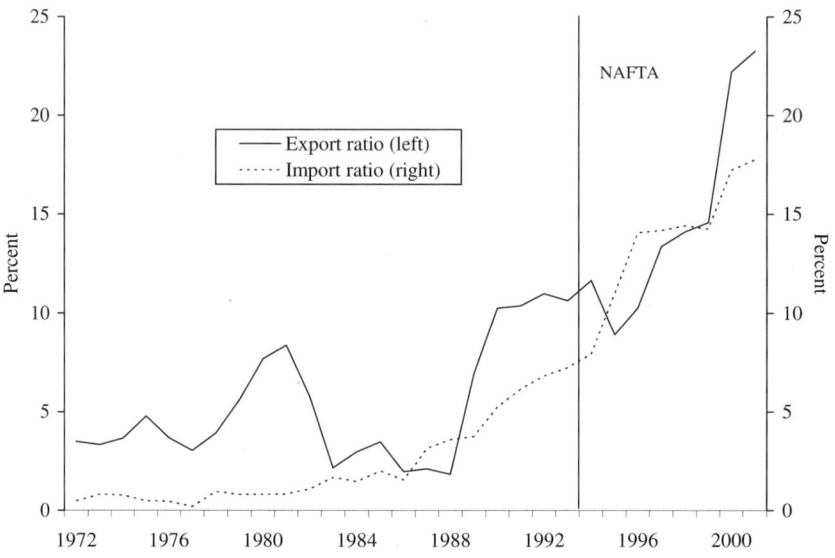

SOURCE: Census Bureau, Bureau of Economic Analysis.

United States. This restructuring enabled U.S. manufacturers to realize economies of scale in production. For example, the consolidation of production that can be achieved under NAFTA enabled Ford to relocate production of its Thunderbird and Cougar models from Mexico to Lorain, Ohio. Production at the Ford plant in Cautitlin, Mexico, was shifted to the Contour and Mystique models. This change in production patterns allowed Ford to realize economies of scale that it could not enjoy when forced to produce certain models simultaneously in the United States and Mexico.

Turning to the gross jobs flows of the automobile industry, depicted in Figure 7.13, we see little evidence of substantial changes during the NAFTA period. Relative to their history, gross job creation and destruction have been relatively stable since the mid 1980s when trade in automobiles began shifting toward Mexico, except for the usual increases during the two most recent mild U.S. recessions. In fact, job reallocation actually tended to decline throughout the NAFTA period before the U.S. slowdown in the early 2000s.

Thus, even though NAFTA probably had a very significant effect on the composition of foreign trade, the reorientation of trade toward Mexico does not appear to have had a significant effect on employment or job reallocation in establishments in the U.S. automobile industry. Despite significant increases in the shares of U.S. trade with Mexico, the data show little sign of much reshuffling of employment across U.S. auto plants through job creation and destruction. Perhaps because of the unique structure of the North American auto industry, which exhibits strong links between auto producers in each country and U.S. auto companies, or because of the role of unions in the automobile industry, trade liberalization does not induce the same kinds of job reallocation it does in other industries.

Net employment growth was relatively strong following NAFTA, however, and it may be that trade liberalization contributed in part to overall growth in the U.S. auto industry that increased the demand for labor. One should bear in mind that U.S. real GDP and household wealth grew spectacularly well during this period, and these develop-

Figure 7.13 U.S. Gross Job Flows in the Automobile Industry (1973–2002)

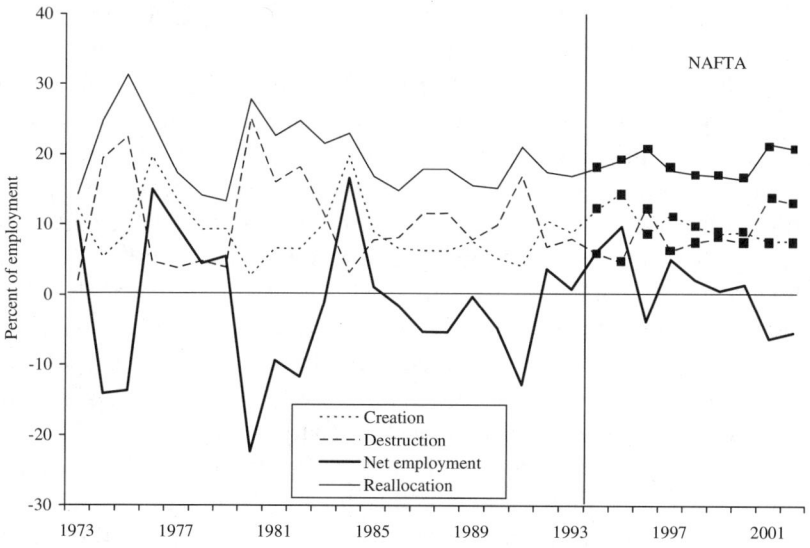

NOTE: ■ Indicates imputed data.
SOURCE: Bureau of Labor Statistics, Longitudinal Research Database.

ments may be the sole explanation for the strong growth in auto employment. Nevertheless, the technological and market-structure advantages offered by NAFTA for this industry likely helped boost overall auto employment somewhat on the margin.

Summary of Industry Results

Multilateral international trade increased in all three industries since the mid to late 1980s. It now accounts for nearly one-third of activity in the chemicals industry and nearly one-half of the activity in the other two industries. The increase in multilateral trade was greatest in textiles and apparel, where it increased by about one-half. However, there is very little evidence that multilateral trade increased more as a result of NAFTA, with the possible exception of textiles and apparel imports. Instead, it appears that multilateral trade is experiencing a trend increase for other reasons.

Bilateral trade between the United State and Mexico also increased in all three countries since the mid to late 1980s. However, these data seem to clearly point to a substantive influence of NAFTA on trade within the industries. In particular, NAFTA appears to have substantially altered the composition of trade by shifting U.S. exports and imports in these industries toward Mexico and away from other countries. Although the shares of bilateral U.S.–Mexico exports and imports are relatively small fractions of total industry activity, these bilateral exports and imports account for sizable fractions of total exports and imports in these industries. As of 2001, they account for about two-fifths in the auto industry, one-third in textiles and apparel, and about one-eighth in chemicals. Since NAFTA, the share of bilateral U.S.–Mexico trade doubled in the auto industry and increased almost as much in textiles and apparel.

These trade developments represent important examples of how changes in international factors can affect activity within an industry but without affecting overall industry activity. In this regard, NAFTA-related changes are analogous to the within-industry effects of real exchange rates studied earlier in this book. Attempts to observe the impact of NAFTA using industry-level (or more aggregated) data will have difficulty because, even at the level of industry detail examined here, the impact is subtle at best. To get a clear picture of the effects of

NAFTA, one must examine the trade and employment patterns for specific countries and domestic establishments.

Despite strong evidence of a reallocation of bilateral trade toward Mexico in these industries, we do not observe clear evidence of the impact of trade on employment and gross job flows in these industries. During the NAFTA period, employment rose in autos, fell in textiles and apparel, and was roughly unchanged in chemicals. Obviously, these divergent employment experiences are not explained well by either the multilateral or bilateral trade developments in these industries. But, even the gross job-flows data do not offer clear evidence that the within-industry reallocation of trade toward Mexico induced greater job reallocation, with the possible exception of the textiles and apparel industry.

Why hasn't the reallocation of trade toward Mexico induced by NAFTA produced clearer evidence of greater job reallocation? Two explanations seem the most promising. The most obvious one is that bilateral trade with Mexico is simply too small a share of total industry activity to have a large aggregate impact—even by the 2000s, bilateral trade (exports and imports) accounts for less than 10 percent of each industry's total activity. A second, and more subtle, explanation is that the reallocation of trade toward Mexico simply may have occurred at the individual establishment level rather than across establishments. In other words, most establishments that trade may have changed their trading partners but not the level of their total trade, rather than establishments that deal with Mexico expanding and establishments that deal with the rest of the world contracting. Corroboration of this hypothesis requires examining establishment-level bilateral trade data, which are not available (to our knowledge).

CONCLUSION

Major trade agreements, such as NAFTA, that liberalize trade by reducing tariffs and other nontariff barriers to trade can significantly affect both trade and labor-market flows. These trade agreements alter the cost of trade between countries significantly. In the case of NAFTA, the price changes were as much as 20 to 25 percent for tariffs, and the implicit cost reduction was even greater with regard to other trade barriers. Thus, in a sense, trade liberalization potentially has similar effects to those coming about through exchange rate variation. Unfortunately, however, it is difficult to identify the precise manner in which trade liberalization affects trade and employment demand. Trade agreements make discrete, and often large, changes in tariff rates and other barriers.

These difficulties were amplified in the case of NAFTA, particularly regarding trade between the United States and Mexico, because the agreement was primarily bilateral in nature. The United States and Canada already had enacted the Canadian Free Trade Agreement, so most of the changes affected trade between the United States and Mexico. NAFTA reduced tariffs and other barriers to trade between the United States and Mexico significantly. However, the proportion of U.S. trade with Mexico was often small compared with total U.S. trade, so the NAFTA changes could only have modest effects at best. Moreover, U.S. trade with both Mexico and the rest of the world had been increasing long before NAFTA. Thus, it is hard to attribute much of a role to NAFTA in U.S. net employment changes.

The bilateral nature of the NAFTA changes did seem to alter the composition of U.S. exports and imports, raising the share of trade with Mexico relative to the rest of the world. Even in this regard, the extent of the compositional shift was fairly small. Nevertheless, in principle, compositional changes in trade patterns across trading partners could have increased gross job creation and destruction among U.S. plants if exporters and importers were sufficiently segmented in their trading markets. The fact that we find little evidence of higher job reallocation among U.S. plants suggests either that the NAFTA changes were not significant for overall labor demand or that trade with foreign countries is not sufficiently segmented across plants to bring out shifts in labor demand among plants.

To sum up, in principle, trade liberalization can be linked to net and gross job flows by significantly altering the costs of exports and imports among trading partners. In practice, however, NAFTA does not appear to have induced much change in either net or gross job flows in the United States. Clearly, this conclusion is preliminary and tentative, as additional research is needed to more properly ascertain the connection between job flows and impediments to trade.

Notes

1. Whether the reallocation is mostly between or within industries depends on the degree to which the establishments producing intermediate goods are classified in the same industry as the final goods producers.
2. NAFTA also expanded upon the Maquiladora 9802 Program which, since 1966, has allowed U.S. firms to establish plants in northern Mexico that export to the United States without U.S. or Mexican restrictions on trade.
3. A few tariffs on U.S. exports of agricultural products to Mexico are to be phased out over a 15-year period rather the 10-year period scheduled for phasing out tariffs on industrial products. For a more complete description of the provisions of NAFTA, see the U.S. Department of Commerce's NAFTA homepage at: <http://www.mac.doc.gov/nafta/nafta2.htm>.
4. For example, Davis and Kowalczyk (1998) estimated that the average Mexican tariff rates in 1991 for products classified as Chemicals and Related Products was 11.1 percent, and for Manufactured Goods it was 13.2 percent while the average U.S. tariff rates for these products were 4.8 percent and 6.7 percent, respectively. See table 8.1, p. 238, in their article.
5. It is worth noting, however, that NAFTA may have had an effect on the policy response of the Mexican government to the 1995 financial and economic crises. In the wake of financial and economic crises in 1982, the Mexican government imposed quotas and duties of up to 100 percent on American products. It is conceivable that a similar policy may have been pursued in 1995 were it not for NAFTA. In fact, in response to the 1995 peso crises, the Mexican government raised tariff rates on goods from non-NAFTA countries.
6. These estimates and statistics, including the results of the DRI/McGraw Hill study, are cited in chapter 1 of the report by the Office of the U.S. Trade Representative (1997).
7. Other research on the effects of the Free Trade Agreement includes Gaston and Trefler (1997), who showed that the agreement accounted for only a small share of overall Canadian job losses between 1989 and 1993, and Hein and Sims (2000), who focused on the effect of the agreement on U.S. wine exports to Canada.
8. See U.S. Department of Commerce, NAFTA homepage, <http://www.mac.doc.gov/nafta; documents 3001.htm and 3002.htm>.
9. There are also issues of data availability. The gross job-flow data from the LRD currently are not available for years after 1993, but we estimate the data plotted in the graphs for the period 1994 to 2001 using industry-level gross job flow constructed with employment data from the Bureau of Labor Statistics. See Haltiwanger and Schuh (1999) for details.
10. Data on average tariff rates for selected industries in 1992 and 1996 are from the Office of the U.S. Trade Representative (1997), page 32. This document is also the source of the information in Tables 7.2 and 7.3.

11. For more about this and our other assessments about employment in these industries, see Murray (1995).
12. The National Bureau of Economic Research World Trade Database (WTDB), which is our main source of historical trade data, provides data for the textile and apparel industries combined only through 1992. Consequently, we supplement the WTDB with data for 1993 to 1999 that also combine the two separate industries.
13. Trade data for 2000 and 2001 come from the Bureau of Economic Analysis (BEA). The BEA trade data are classified by the new NAICS industry system and thus not exactly comparable to the trade data classified by SIC. To correct for this, we use NAICS-based data to impute estimates of the SIC-based data for these industries.
14. We calculate bilateral trade shares by dividing the value of the industry's imports (exports) between the U.S. and the specified country by the value of the industry's total multilateral imports (exports).
15. McClenahen (1999).
16. See website <http://atmi.org/newsroom/naftare1.html>.
17. Job flows through 1993 are from Davis, Haltiwanger, and Schuh (1996) and Schuh and Triest (1998). Gross job flows after 1993 are imputed using industry job-flow data constructed from BLS employment data on four-digit industries. See Haltiwanger and Schuh (1999) for more details. The imputation formula comes from a linear regression model of plant job flows on BLS industry-level job flows and total manufacturing net employment growth, similar in spirit to that used by Davis, Haltiwanger, and Schuh (1996). Net employment growth data after 1993 come from the BLS employment data and thus are not imputed.
18. See Morse (2001).
19. By "automobile" we mean motor vehicles and motor vehicle parts and equipment, a definition that includes trucks, buses, trailers, and motor homes.
20. For details, see Doh (1998).
21. See Office of the U.S. Trade Representative (1997), chapter 2.

8
Policy Implications

This book begins with a reference to the protests at the ministerial meetings of the WTO in Seattle in November 1999. It is noteworthy that these protests occurred when the United States was in the eighth year of a record-setting economic expansion and when the unemployment rate stood at 4.1 percent, the lowest rate in two decades. Of course, these protests were attended by a relatively small number of people, but concerns with the displacements caused by international trade were prevalent at that time. This is striking, for if ever we were to expect unalloyed support for free trade, we would expect it at a time of low unemployment during a boom that was fueled, in no small part, by the export performance of American firms.

Part of the puzzle regarding why opposition to globalization was so strong in the late 1990s when the unemployment rate was so low is resolved by the analysis of job reallocation we present in this book. The U.S. manufacturing sector is characterized by pervasive churning of jobs, and our econometric estimates suggest that the increase in the real exchange rate that accompanied the late 1990s boom contributed to this process. Job destruction results in the displacement of workers and the attendant loss of job-specific skills. While displaced workers probably have an easier time finding suitable new employment during a boom than during a bust, they are still likely to suffer significant economic and emotional losses. Job loss can be devastating to a worker with substantial job-specific human capital, and it may seem to threaten the worker's way of life. It is understandable that policies that seem to threaten job stability engender substantial opposition. Our emphasis on gross, rather than net, flows highlights the fact that job loss is much greater than previously thought, although job gain is much greater too.

Of course, international trade is only one of many factors that affect job churning. Technological change also contributes to new opportunities and new challenges that bring about job creation and destruction. But trade seems to hold a special place in terms of the public's willingness to have the government intervene. The Program on

International Policy Attitudes (PIPA) reports that, across time, polls regularly find that about two-thirds of respondents agree with statements like "The United States should tax foreign goods imported in this country in order to protect American jobs and wages." It would be hard to imagine a similar level of public support for quashing technological advance in order to preserve jobs.

In part, this difference of attitude may be because the benefits of technological change are readily apparent in the form of new products and production processes. In contrast, international trade generates benefits which are important but less obvious to the casual observer. Technological change may also seem inevitable, while trade seems more easily controlled by policy.

There is some evidence that the public is willing to support trade liberalization as long as it is accompanied by policies to attenuate the negative effects on displaced workers. For example, surveys conducted by PIPA have found that while only 18 percent of respondents favor free trade in the absence of programs to help workers who lose their jobs, 87 percent favor free trade if it were combined with major efforts to educate and retrain Americans to be competitive in the global economy.[1] The public apparently understands that trade is beneficial but that it entails significant adjustment costs.

One of the goals of this book has been to gain a better understanding of some of the adjustment costs which underlie the political opposition to free trade. This chapter begins with a brief summary of the main results presented in this book and then turns to a discussion of policies which might ameliorate the adjustment costs faced by workers. Exchange rate management, tariffs, and worker-assistance policies are discussed, but we argue that exchange rate management is largely infeasible and tariffs are counterproductive. Worker-assistance policies have a mixed record, but we believe that they are the most promising area for future policy initiatives. To be clear, we are proponents of trade liberalization, but we think it is desirable to address the adjustment cost issue both to build political support for free trade and for social welfare reasons.

SUMMARY OF MAIN FINDINGS

Increased Openness

Underlying the public concern about the effects of trade is the trend toward increased integration of the United States in the world economy. A simple but important fact documented in Chapter 2 is that openness has become pervasive across U.S. manufacturing industries. Although nearly all manufacturing industries have become more open over time, there are large differences in the importance of international trade across industries. There are also substantial differences across industries in the movements over time of trade-weighted industry-specific real exchange rates.

The increased volume of international trade is greatly beneficial and enables us to enjoy a higher overall standard of living than we could otherwise attain. However, the vulnerability of some workers to economic loss is heightened by trade liberalization and openness. Some workers lose out as a result of international competition, and an important goal of policy is to help insure workers against such potential losses.

The Importance of Gross Job Flows

Gross job flows in U.S. manufacturing are large. As Chapter 3 documents, in over half of the years of our sample, the rates of job creation and job destruction summed to over 20 percent. The relatively small changes in the number of manufacturing jobs masks the tremendous amount of job reallocation which is constantly occurring across establishments.

The magnitude of the rates of job creation and job destruction varies substantially both over time and across industries. Surprisingly, however, the heterogeneity in the gross job-flow rates is not associated with major industry groups. Even when we adopt a very fine categorization of industries (using four-digit SIC codes), we find that most of the variance in job creation and job destruction is within, rather than between, industries. So, it is not the case that only certain broad sectors are characterized by pervasive reallocation of jobs.

The high rates of job creation and job destruction are very relevant for understanding the adjustment costs associated with increased international trade. Job reallocation can occur in response to any change in relative prices, including those associated with trade liberalization and movements in real exchange rates. Reallocation can entail significant adjustment costs, even when there is little or no change in net employment. Workers lose the value of job-specific skills and often earn less at their new jobs. Moreover, the process of searching for a new job entails time, money, and psychic costs, and it may require geographical relocation.

The Sensitivity of Gross Job Flows to Real Exchange Rate Movements

The theoretical framework presented in Chapter 5 demonstrates that a change in the real exchange rate may simultaneously cause both job creation and job destruction, and Chapter 6 presents econometric results that suggest that real exchange rate movements have a substantial impact on job churning. The econometric model decomposes real exchange rates into trend and cyclical components. An appreciation of the cyclical component of the real exchange rate increases job destruction and reduces net employment growth, but it has essentially no effect on job creation. In contrast, an appreciation of the trend component of the real exchange rate increases both job creation and job destruction, but it has little effect on net employment growth.

Although trend real exchange rate changes have little effect on net employment, substantial adjustment costs are incurred as workers and other resources are reallocated across places of employment. But, this reallocation may enhance economic efficiency if the exchange rate movement results from differentials across countries in productivity growth or other factors affecting comparative advantage. In this case, the resulting job-market churning is similar to that which accompanies technological change: painful to workers whose jobs are destroyed but a necessary component of economic growth. Policies may be needed to help workers who suffer losses due to the decreased value of their human capital, but those policies should be aimed at facilitating rather than hindering reallocation.[3]

EXCHANGE RATE MANAGEMENT

It may be tempting for some to conclude from our analysis of the effects of real exchange rate movements on gross job flows that exchange rate management policies should be adopted to promote employment stability. This conclusion, however, does not follow from our results. First, it should be noted that exchange rate management is, at best, a difficult goal. Foreign exchange market intervention is not especially efficacious. Policies that are more effective in altering exchange rates, such as monetary policy, have consequences beyond those in foreign exchange markets. And fixed exchange rates are not fixed permanently; one can find many examples, such as in Europe in the early 1990s and in Latin America and Asia in the later part of the 1990s, where fixed exchange rates were abandoned under pressure from market forces.

Exchange rate management, to the extent that it can be successful, will mitigate otherwise temporary changes in exchange rates, for example, by serving to prick an unsustainable speculative bubble. But, our analysis suggests that, while this may be an important goal for some reasons, the effects of such short-term exchange rate movements on job creation and destruction are likely to be small.

The role of macroeconomic policies in generating movements in the cyclical component of real exchange rates is not fully understood and deserves further study. Cyclical appreciations of real exchange rates are associated with increased rates of job destruction, without an offsetting increase in job creation, and so may be desirable to avoid. Although it is possible that a fuller understanding of the relationship between macro policies, real exchange rate movements, and job destruction will eventually yield better policies, such improvements will be difficult to achieve. One stumbling block is that the relevant real exchange rates vary by industry due to differences in trading patterns. So, in any given time period, some industries may be experiencing effective appreciations while others are experiencing depreciations.

It is important to remember that the job destruction associated with cyclical real exchange rate fluctuations is just one of many forces affecting the demand for labor. Although increased openness increases the exposure of U.S. workers to potential job losses due to exchange rate appreciations, it may also decrease the degree of risk through other channels. For example, the impact of a domestic drop in the demand for goods and services will be dampened in an open economy with more stable global demand. For a large diversified economy such as the United States, it is possible that increased openness may actually help to dampen cyclical fluctuations.

TARIFFS AND INDUSTRIAL POLICY

An alternative policy prescription to shield workers from the effects of international competition is to provide protection, in the form of tariffs, quotas, or subsidies, to industries that seem to be the victim of stiff international competition. Railing against protectionism is an age-old duty of economists, who cite the costs to consumers of supporting inefficient producers. The analysis presented in this book offers another reason for casting doubt on the utility of protectionist policies: they are poorly targeted. Our analysis in Chapter 2 shows that there is pervasive heterogeneity across manufacturing sectors with respect to openness. Also, we show that job creation and job destruction can vary widely across establishments within narrowly defined industries.

The high degree of heterogeneity within industries in the exposure to trade argues for caution in considering trade-related policies aimed at particular industries. It is difficult to fine-tune policies so that they affect some detailed-level industries and not other closely related industries. Moreover, such policies may create allocative inefficiencies by directing resources toward activities in which the United States no longer has a comparative advantage. In some cases, policies designed to protect an industry suffering from competition from abroad may actually harm closely allied industries which are successfully competing with their foreign competitors.

A case-in-point is the imposition of steel tariffs by the United States in March 2002. Large domestic producers had a substantial cost disadvantage relative to foreign producers. The cost disadvantage was partly due to the run-up in the real exchange rate during the 1990s boom years. Other factors, however, such as underfunded pension liabilities, also contributed to the cost disadvantage. And global steel-making overcapacity was putting financial pressure on steel makers in many countries.

Although some major domestic steel manufacturers have been helped by the tariff, it is quite ironic that other domestic steel manufacturers were actually hurt by the tariff. Some of the most adversely affected plants have been domestic steel mills that process imported steel products because the tariff increased the price of their inputs into production. One result of this unintended consequence has been political pressure to grant exemptions from the tariffs, and exemptions from the 30 percent tariff on hot-rolled steel were quickly granted to South Korean and Australian producers, with a combined market share of nearly 20 percent, who shipped their steel for further processing to mills located in the United States (King 2002). Firms that use imported steel that is not exempt from the tariff will likely become less competitive with foreign rivals, and job destruction may result. The end result is that some domestic steel jobs will have been saved, although perhaps only temporarily, at the expense of jobs in other industries.

Additional spillover effects from the imposition of tariffs may come from the reaction of other countries. Soon after the steel tariffs were announced by the Bush administration, press reports indicated that retaliatory measures were being considered by the European Union and by Japan, reinforcing fears that the United States may have sparked a new round of trade wars that could prove especially damaging during a period of worldwide economic weakness.[4] Even if a full-blown trade war does not break out, protectionist actions such as these hurt efforts to maintain, much less expand, a liberalized world trading system. The effects of rising protectionist barriers will be felt widely, not least among those in the developing world who could most benefit from access to markets in industrial countries (Stevenson 2002).

An argument sometimes made in favor of tariffs is to preserve jobs in an industry that is temporarily not competitive, for example during a period when the dollar is temporarily higher than normal. Cyclical appreciations of the real exchange rate, which our econometric results show are associated with increased job destruction but no offsetting increase in job creation, may be largely independent of any changes in long-run comparative advantage. But the argument in favor of using tariffs to prevent job destruction associated with temporary movements in real exchange rates presumes that we are able to distinguish between permanent and temporary changes. In practice, we are largely unsuccessful at doing so within the time frame in which policy must be formulated. Moreover, any tariffs imposed in response to a real appreciation which is perceived as temporary may be politically difficult to remove after the appreciation is reversed.

It is also difficult to gauge what changes in real exchange rates would be needed to return domestic establishments to profitability. For example, we do not know when, if ever, the dollar will depreciate against the currencies of other steel-producing countries to the point where the domestic steel industry is again profitable. So, it is not apparent that the steel tariffs will have a positive long-run impact, and the short-run effect of higher production costs and retaliation from other countries is decidedly negative. Although tariffs seem to enjoy political support, the 2002 steel tariffs demonstrate why most economists think increased tariffs are a bad policy option.

Trade liberalization agreements can be viewed as the antithesis of the policy of using tariffs to protect vulnerable industries. Our analysis of the effects of NAFTA is instructive here. As discussed in Chapter 7, there were special concerns about the effect on the textile and apparel sector of reducing protection from Mexican goods because this sector seemed especially vulnerable to competition from low-wage Mexican workers. But employment in the textile industry was declining over the past half-century for reasons more closely associated with technological change than with international trade. Furthermore, as reported in Chapter 7, the textile trade association stated that trade with Mexico was "truly mutually rewarding." Thus, while it is possible that some establishments in the textile sector were hurt by trade liberalization, the overall effect may have been beneficial, even for this industry.

As pointed out in Chapter 7, trade liberalization and permanent changes in real exchange rates involve similar shifts in relative prices, and both can be expected to result in job reallocation. The practice of phasing in tariff reductions as trade agreements are implemented is likely to have the beneficial result of allowing the reallocation to proceed gradually and relatively predictably. Adjustment costs would then likely be lower than they would be with immediate implementation.

WORKER ASSISTANCE POLICIES

Exchange rate management and tariffs are unattractive candidates for buffering workers from the dislocating effects of trade. To protect the welfare of displaced workers, as well as to maintain political support for free trade, however, it is important to identify more desirable policies for reducing adjustment costs incurred by workers. Policies aimed at directly aiding displaced workers seem to be the most promising direction for policy initiatives, although, as we discuss below, difficult issues arise in designing such policies.

Currently, the main policy aimed at helping workers who suffer unemployment due to international trade is the Trade Adjustment Assistance (TAA) Act, established under the Trade Act of 1974. This policy applies to workers who can demonstrate that their job loss was largely due to increased imports. Its most recent version extends the period of time workers can collect unemployment insurance if they are enrolled in an approved training program. A similar program was created specifically for workers whose job loss can be largely traced to the effects of NAFTA. These trade adjustment assistance programs, however, are not viewed as successful. The bipartisan U.S. Trade Deficit Review Commission surveyed the state workforce agencies that administer the TAA programs and reported that 19 state agencies found the programs "inadequate" and another 19 reported that these programs needed improvement. Furthermore, the program includes disincentives for undertaking training and, even if this were not the case, there is little evidence that the training is effective (Froning 2001).

It is difficult to design programs that buffer workers from adjustment costs associated with international trade. How to effectively target such programs is particularly problematic. In practice, it is often impossible to determine whether job displacement is due to international trade, technological change, shifts in intranational comparative advantage, changes in consumer tastes, mistakes by an establishment's or firm's management, or some other factor. The econometric analysis presented in Chapter 6 is able to statistically identify a link between real exchange rate movements and gross job flows, but it does not allow us to determine exactly which particular jobs are destroyed or created due to a change in real exchange rates. Providing greater compensation for job displacement due to trade-related factors than that due for other reasons is likely to lead to efforts by affected workers and firms to make the case that they are "victims" of international trade.

From a broader welfare perspective, it is hard to make the case that job displacement due to trade-related factors should be treated differently from job displacement resulting from other factors not under workers' control. In either case, workers suffer an economic loss that it would be desirable to insure against. Perhaps the best case for special policies targeted at trade-related displacement is that such policies may be needed to win political support for trade liberalization,[5] but this argument is not entirely convincing. Such policies may publicize the role of trade in job destruction by explicitly labeling some job losses as trade related, and they may also leave some workers bitterly disappointed when they experience job loss which is ruled not to be trade related, but which they perceive to be due to international competition. More general policies aimed at helping workers suffering losses from job displacement may be more effective at promoting political support for free trade. Clearly, additional research is needed on this topic.

In addition to the targeting problem, incentive issues arise in designing programs to assist displaced workers. The magnitude of the economic loss observed to be suffered by displaced workers is partly dependent on choices made by the workers. Those who search most intensively for a new job, and who are most flexible regarding type of work, working conditions, and location, will tend to be reemployed sooner and with a smaller loss of earnings compared to displaced workers who search less intensively or who are more discriminating regarding nonpecuniary job attributes. Because search intensity is very difficult to measure, and the choices open to workers are generally not observable, policies cannot be conditioned on these aspects of behavior. As a result, policy designers need to take into account the possible distortions to behavior which worker assistance policies may generate.

A promising alternative to TAA has recently been proposed by Lori Kletzer and Robert Litan (2001). They proposed that two benefit programs, wage insurance and subsidies for health insurance, be available to all displaced workers, not just those displaced for reasons related to international trade. Wage insurance would replace, for eligible workers, some fraction of their wage loss for up to two years, beginning when workers found a new job. Kletzer and Litan argued that the most effective form of job training occurs on the job and this program would effectively subsidize retraining on the job. Subsidizing health insurance would help alleviate an important source of anxiety due to job loss.

These ideas are catching on. The Senate passed a bill in May 2002 that, along with providing the president with fast-track trade authority, also includes a pilot trade-specific wage insurance program that compensates 50 percent of the wage loss of qualifying workers (up to $5,000 maximum per year) for two years from the date of unemployment and that pays 70 percent of health insurance costs for workers displaced due to import competition.[6]

CONCLUSION

Worker assistance programs are aimed toward reducing the adjustment costs associated with trade. The analysis presented in this book supports the view that adjustment costs are significant and should be addressed, but it also offers some hope they are not an insurmountable barrier to garnering support for free trade. The adjustment costs facing a particular worker include the loss of job-specific skills she suffers when she moves from one establishment to another, and these can be disaggregated into establishment-specific skills and industry-specific skills. We have shown in Chapter 3 that there is pervasive heterogeneity in job creation and destruction across establishments within an industry. Thus, workers may be able to maintain jobs that take advantage of industry-specific skills, even when moving from one establishment to another. This could minimize the amount of retraining needed for displaced workers. It would also mean that the most relevant type of retraining is that undertaken by an establishment for its employees, as opposed to off-site retraining aimed at increasing employment potential for workers in a particular industry.

Another consideration concerning adjustment costs has to do with timing. Adjustment costs are likely higher for any displaced worker at a time when many other displaced workers are also looking for employment. Thus, large exchange rate swings may generate job destruction simultaneously across sectors. But, as discussed in Chapter

2, there is actually quite a bit of heterogeneity in industry-specific exchange rates. Therefore, we may not see as much of a simultaneous effect of a given change in the trade-weighted dollar exchange rate as we would expect if we were not aware of this diversity in the bilateral trade relationships across industries.

The analysis in this book has not addressed the issue of the geographic location of job creation and job destruction. Moving from one location to another represents another substantial adjustment cost, and perhaps barriers to workers' willingness to move to new opportunities. Regional development issues also arise. Geographic areas which specialize in economic activities in which the United States does not have a comparative advantage would suffer a decline as trade is liberalized. Such issues clearly warrant further study.

One difficulty in designing effective programs to address the costs borne by displaced workers is our lack of knowledge regarding the displacement process. We are able to statistically identify a link between real exchange rate movements and job destruction, but we know relatively little about the characteristics of the jobs destroyed and the workers displaced. The development of micro-level data sets containing matched information on establishments and workers holds the promise of increasing our understanding of the displacement process and may allow the development of programs better targeted at reducing the adjustment costs associated with trade. We return to this point, and develop it more fully, in the next chapter.

One must recognize, however, that targeting programs to address adjustment costs associated with international trade is likely to remain very difficult. It is both more feasible, and also arguably more desirable, to address the problems of labor-market adjustment more generally, without trying to determine if displacement occurs due to factors associated with international trade or instead due to technological change, intranational shifts in comparative advantage, or some other factor. The primary argument in favor of separate policies to deal with trade-related displacement is political—that such policies are needed to build support for free trade. But it seems likely that political opposition to free trade could also be muted by policies that address the more general problem of adjustment costs faced by displaced workers. This discussion points to the need for a deeper understanding of the sources of the political opposition to free trade and what policies would be effective in attenuating it.

In conclusion, the traditional case for free trade is strong, but political reality, as well as economic considerations of costs and benefits, demand an accounting of adjustment costs as part of the calculus of determining the net benefits from trade. Adjustment costs are better understood through an analysis of gross job flows than by studying changes in net employment alone. Therefore, analyses like the ones presented in this book should be a key part of the way we approach our understanding of the effects of trade on labor markets.

Notes

1. See <http://www.americans-world.org/digest/global_issues/intertrade/summary.cfm>.
2. Davis, Haltiwanger, and Schuh (1996) pointed out that the importance of idiosyncratic factors makes it difficult to design and evaluate targeted industrial and commercial policies.
3. All of the arguments in this subsection also apply equally to the sensitivity of gross job flows to changes in trade restrictions and agreements.
4. Examples include Winestock and King (2002) and King and Zaun (2002).
5. This point is made by Bhagwati (1988) and by Fung and Staiger (1996).
6. Workers would need to be over 50 years old and earn less than $50,000 per year to qualify for the wage insurance program. Qualifying workers would be given the option of participating in the program in lieu of signing up for ordinary TAA benefits.

9
Directions for Future Research

This book is part of a new and growing literature that embarks on the ambitious task of analyzing the effects of international factors on gross, rather than net, labor-market flows. Our contribution focuses on gross job flows while others, like Kletzer (1998a), analyze gross worker flows. As we argue throughout the book, gross flows research offers a more complete evaluation of the labor-adjustment costs associated with changes in international factors than does research that considers net labor-market flows.

The study of gross labor-market flows is a complex and ongoing endeavor. Our efforts to incorporate international dimensions are merely one aspect of a much broader research program. Thus, our work is one of many steps toward the goal of understanding how labor markets work and what factors—international and others—influence them. While the analysis presented in this book represents an important step toward a more complete understanding of the intricate relationship between international factors and labor markets, there are questions we are unable to address, largely due to limitations imposed by the unavailability of data.

In the remainder of this chapter, we discuss how the development of new data sets would enable researchers to obtain a more complete and accurate understanding of the connection between labor markets and international factors. We emphasize the importance of developing joint measures of gross job flows and gross worker flows at firms and establishments, as well as the importance of generating micro-level international trade data for these sites. This new data development would enable researchers to undertake a much more precise analysis of labor adjustment costs, in general and especially those associated with international factors. A deeper understanding of these adjustment costs is needed before we can confidently draw firm and reliable conclusions about net welfare gains from trade. A fuller assessment of the source of adjustment costs and their size will also serve as a critical input to the design of improved government policies.

MATCHING JOB AND WORKER FLOWS

Recent research has taken an important step toward a more complete evaluation of the costs of adjustment to international factors by moving beyond net changes and examining the substantial gross flows that pervade labor markets. Studies such as this book, which look at the effects of international factors on gross job flows, along with complementary studies of the effects of international factors on gross worker flows, reveal that international factors generate far more churning in labor markets than was previously demonstrated. But there are still many unknown dimensions of gross labor flows.

Future research on this issue must take the additional step of studying gross job and worker flows jointly. Neither our study, nor studies based only on worker flows, provide a complete picture of the effects of international factors on labor markets. The main reason, as we noted earlier, is that gross job and worker flows are not the same because jobs and workers are heterogeneous. In reality, jobs are heterogeneous within establishments, a fact we are forced to ignore because of data limitations. Thus, in principle, jobs within an establishment can be created or destroyed, necessitating workers, changing establishments. Moreover, heterogeneous workers can match with or separate from establishments for many reasons other than changes in international factors.

Another reason to study gross job and worker flows jointly is that they are determined jointly. Our analysis is partial equilibrium in that it focuses on labor demand, as are studies of worker flows that try to infer labor demand from worker dislocations. At a minimum, future research must study labor-market flows in a general equilibrium setting that includes labor supply and especially human capital accumulation decisions, such as investment in firm-specific capital.

Studying job and worker flows jointly makes longitudinal issues important. To ascertain the ultimate consequences of job- and worker-flow activity, one must follow the fortunes of individual workers and jobs over time. For dislocated workers, for example, we want to know how long they are unemployed, what unemployment benefits they receive, where they move, what job(s) they accept in the future, what training they receive or invest in, and what their subsequent wage profile is. Likewise for jobs that are destroyed because of international factors, we want to know whether the job was permanently or temporarily destroyed, whether it was replaced by a substitute job in the same establishment or another establishment, and whether it was matched to another (presumably lower wage) worker.

DATA DEVELOPMENT

Perhaps the single most critical shortcoming to the analysis of net welfare gains from trade is the unavailability of sufficient data for the task at hand. Data deficiencies primarily arise in two areas: matched job- and worker-flow data, and plant- and firm-level export and import data.

Labor Data

Development of microeconomic longitudinal databases linking specific workers and employers with detailed information about each is an absolute necessity. In the United States, there is not yet an equivalent of the French database used by Abowd, Corbel, and Kramarz (1999). Davis, Haltiwanger, and Schuh (1996, chapter 8) advocated the development of such databases through the combination of several existing databases from the U.S. Census Bureau and U.S. Bureau of Labor Statistics (BLS). There has been some encouraging progress on this issue since then, but more is required.

The fundamental limitation to the development of a satisfactory database has been the lack of a coordinated focus on longitudinal data collection. The Census Bureau tends to focus on employers, collecting data with rich detail on firm and establishment characteristics but little information on worker characteristics. In contrast, the BLS tends to focus on workers, collecting rich detail on worker characteristics but relatively little information on employer characteristics. Unfortunately, the sampling techniques and employer identification techniques used by the Census and BLS are not exactly the same so it is difficult to link data from the two agencies. Nevertheless, efforts have been made to develop linked employer–employee databases that could be used to provide a better understanding of the effects of international factors on gross labor flows.

One of the most promising extant data sources is the BLS 202 data set, which contains information on nearly all U.S. employers who participate in the unemployment insurance (UI) system and the employees who work for them. Although the definition and tracking of employers is not fully satisfactory, the BLS 202 UI database offers the opportunity to construct job and worker flows jointly, as in Burgess, Lane, and Stevens (2000). In addition, these data are being used by the BLS to produce regular statistics on job and worker turnover.[1] However, the BLS 202 UI data cannot track all worker flows among states of the labor force, as can be done with the Current Population Survey (CPS) data. But, CPS data do not track individual workers for long enough periods of time or provide enough reliable details about employers. And the Displaced Worker Survey (DWS), which pertains to only a portion of the CPS, has many limitations, as pointed out by its users.

Pioneering work has begun to combine Census and BLS data sources. Haltiwanger, Lane, and Spletzer (1999) combined five different Census and BLS data sets, but limitations on data availability and matching significantly reduced the scope of the panel. Recently, an even more comprehensive effort has begun to bear fruit. The Census Bureau's ambitious Longitudinal Employer–Household Dynamics Program has yielded a longitudinal data set melding the BLS 202 UI data with Census Bureau economic and demographic data that emulates the French database. The analysis of the relationship between human capital, technology, and productivity by Abowd et al. (2002) using this database demonstrates its potential for related analyses of international factors and gross labor flows.

However, acquiring all the necessary information for evaluating the characteristics of workers and firms or establishments involved in gross labor flows may require more than combining existing data sources. Instead, it will likely be necessary to develop new sources of data designed to measure the relevant issues. Efforts to understand the influence of workplace practices and information technology are an excellent example of this kind of response. Black and Lynch (2001) used data from a special Census telephone survey called the Educational Quality of the Workforce National Employers Survey (EQW-NES) that recorded "information on how employers recruit workers, organize work, invest in physical capital, and utilize education and training investments" p. 436). Many of these data are closely related to the proper measurement of labor-adjustment costs. Other data could be acquired in a similar fashion, though it would be best to have this information on a longitudinal basis rather than a one-time survey.

Despite the important progress in developing matched employee–employer databases, it remains a patchwork approach to achieving the desired goal. The real innovation most needed is a fundamental change in the approach to data collection. New surveys must be designed and data collection efforts marshalled to develop longitudinal databases that are well-suited to the needs of researchers, economic and other. This will require either innovative new cooperation and joint funding among government agencies—perhaps stimulated by new congressional legislation—or private organizations to rise up and fill the void.

International Trade Data

This pioneering work developing gross flows data is encouraging, but there remains a second fundamental shortcoming of existing data on exports and imports. A half century ago, when the development of U.S. economic data was in its heyday, international trade amounted to less than one-tenth of GDP. By the turn of the twenty-first century, it amounted to more than one-fourth. Perhaps because U.S. international trade used to be relatively unimportant, and almost surely because international trade poses special measurement problems, existing trade data are inadequate for the kind of longitudinal data analysis required to properly assess the impact of international factors on gross labor flows.

The core problem is that it generally is not possible to identify the firms and establishments that originally produce output for export or those that ultimately consume or distribute the output that is imported. Two factors generate this problem. One is that U.S. collection of foreign trade data centers on the ports where goods and services enter and exit the country rather than the firms and establishments engaged in trade.[2] The other factor is that the U.S. data collection agencies do not track interfirm or interestablishment trade well in the domestic economy.[3] This deficiency is exacerbated by the fact that, for both exports and imports, goods and services are often distributed through multiple firms or establishments (often in multiple industries) between the port of entry or exit and the final or original domestic destination. As a result, it is extremely difficult to identify the foreign trade of particular establishments or firms that export and import.

For exporters, the difficulties are somewhat less severe. The Census Bureau obtains export data from the Shipper's Export Declaration (SED), which now makes some effort to identify some characteristics of the original exporting firm. The State Export Data Series is constructed using information from the origin of movement (OM) and exporter location (EL), which was introduced beginning in the 1980s.[4] However, this information does not identify the origin of production of the exported output, much less the firm or establishment. Often the producer and exporter are not the same, and the exporter does not necessarily keep track of the distribution trail. In fact, original producers' output even may be exported without their knowledge. Unfortunately, the Census Bureau discontinued two data programs that generated this kind of information.[5]

Despite these limitations, some efforts by the Census Bureau yield information about exporting firms and establishments. One is the annual Profile of U.S. Exporting Companies.[6] The other is data from the economic censuses. The Census Bureau's Longitudinal Research Database (LRD) contains export data for some plants in the database, which has been used by Bernard and Jensen (1995).

For importers, the problem is far more severe. Neither the LRD, nor any other microeconomic database we are aware of, contains information about imports at the plant level. In the U.S. data system, after imports arrive at the port of entry their subsequent destination is not tracked to specific firms or establishments. The type of product and country of origin provide some implicit information about destination and use of imports, but implicit information is inherently approximate.

One critical distinction regarding imports that cannot be made is whether imports are input materials or final products. Changes in exchange rates have opposite effects on firms and establishments depending on these two import types. Another critical distinction is whether imports are capital goods for investment in domestic production. The import product type data are informative here, but they are not able to identify which firms and establishments are installing these imported capital goods. Finally, a complicating development is the globalization of U.S. corporations and the emergence of multinational corporations. These changes raise the degree of difficulty in measuring the effects of international factors on domestic labor markets.

The inability to track exports and imports to specific firms and establishments severely limits the accuracy with which we can attribute job- and worker-flow movements to international factors. Perhaps it is inherently too difficult to fully track international trade to individual employment locations. But, improvements in the statistical system can be made that would improve our ability to be able to accurately observe the effects of trade on labor markets.

Consequently, we advocate the development of data and procedures to link the international trade data to the firms and establishments that are the original producers of exports and final users of imports. Such efforts will require the collection of more information on trade between domestic firms and establishments. One approach to achieving part of this goal would be to obtain the employer identification (EI) number from the original producer of exported output using the SED by requiring exporters to track the origin. In fact, almost any modification to achieve the desired goal will require the tracking of similar kinds of identifying information.

MEASURING LABOR-ADJUSTMENT COSTS

Historically, researchers have underestimated the magnitude of labor-adjustment costs. A key reason is the lack of adequate data, as we pointed out in the preceding section. If progress can be made toward developing more adequate data sets, then progress can be made in calculating more complete estimates of labor-adjustment costs. In this section, we raise some of the issues and questions that could be addressed with such data.

Most studies of labor-adjustment costs focus on net employment change rather than on the gross flows of jobs and workers in dynamic market economies. However, gross flows are much larger than net flows. Thus, the first, and perhaps most straightforward, question is simply whether the direct costs of adjustment are proportional to net flows or gross flows. If the latter, then adjustment costs associated with job creation and destruction will be much larger than existing estimates of adjustment costs based on net employment change. Some adjustment costs, such as worker training associated with job creation and severance pay due to job destruction might be (linearly) proportional to the gross flows. But other costs, such as advertising associated with job creation and hiring, may have scale economies, and there may be fixed costs, such as those associated with personnel departments.

A second critical area of measurement is the evolution of human capital of the specific workers who are involved in job- and worker flows. The critical question is: When a job is destroyed and a worker is laid off, how much firm-specific human capital is destroyed? The answer to this question is fundamental to assessing how much that particular worker's *permanent* income is reduced, not just how much income is lost during spells of unemployment.[7] Calculation of this change requires information on the worker's lifetime wage profile and job tenure, as well as education and occupation.

Another aspect of adjustment costs is the cost of job and worker relocation, which does not appear to have been measured in the literature at all. For dislocated workers, there are search costs associated with finding a new job. These may not be large in cases where workers do not have to move out of their local labor markets, but when they must move to another geographic location the costs could be much larger. In the worst cases, such as the episode of crisis in steel-producing regions during the early 1980s, the net worth of workers can plummet when economic depression slashes property values—the primary saving vehicle for many blue-collar workers. For firms that shut down lines of operation, or even entire plants, and rebuild in other regions, the costs may be large too, as the U.S. auto industry discovered during the 1970s and 1980s.[8] Many firms find that, when they change the geographic location of their operations, their workers will not relocate with them, forcing them to hire and train an entirely new workforce.

There is yet another area of labor-adjustment cost that is probably very real but not measurable even with the new data we propose, so we only mention it in closing. Job destruction, regional economic deterioration, and worker geographic relocation can bring significant social and even psychological costs to displaced workers and their families. Unfortunately, these costs typically are viewed as outside the domain of economic analysis and therefore typically are not included in assessments—empirical or theoretical—of labor-adjustment costs.

SUMMARY

A major contribution of our research is to raise the point that international factors have a much more intensive and extensive impact on the labor market than previously believed. This naturally raises the question whether the costs of labor adjustment might be much more intensive and extensive than previously thought. However, our research does not answer that question because it is only the first step toward being able to address the issue—studying gross rather than net flows. In particular, we find that changes in real exchange rates and trade policies have economically significant effects on gross job creation and destruction.

We suspect that these internationally generated gross job flows influence gross worker flows as well. However, we have not demonstrated that they do or, if so, how. If international factors do affect worker flows, they likely also affect human capital investment, wages, and worker welfare. And, if so, the labor-adjustment costs associated with changes in international factors are probably more intensive and extensive than previously thought. However, the lack of adequate data precludes the study of both job and worker flows, and thus limits our ability to draw conclusions about labor-adjustment costs at present. More research and measurement are needed in these areas.

At present, in the absence of all necessary information, we can only surmise that the net welfare gains to free trade, and to freer trade, may be different than previously estimated. However, if data are collected and research is conducted along the lines suggested in this chapter, there is encouraging room for significant improvement in our understanding of the magnitude and nature of labor-adjustment costs and net welfare gains from trade.

Notes

1. The BLS is using the data to construct quarterly gross job flows for the entire economy, which are expected to be released in late 2003. New data from the Job Openings and Labor Turnover Survey (JOLTS) have also been developed using 2002 data. For more information, see <http://stats.bls.gov/jlt/home.htm>.
2. The classification of exports as "free alongside ship" (f.a.s.) and imports as "customs, insurance, and freight" (c.i.f.) reflects this approach
3. This yields the so-called double-counting problem where the sales of one domestic producer becomes the inputs of another producer. Current data do not fully and adequately account for this hurdle in constructing value added.
4. For more information, see <http://www.census.gov/foreign-trade/aip/elom.html>.
5. These were "Exports from Manufacturing Establishments" from 1983 to 1991 and "Selected Characteristics of Manufacturing and Wholesaling Establishments That Export" in 1991 and 1992. Note that the former occurred during the large run up of the dollar and vocal debate about its effects.
6. For more information, see <http://www.census.gov/foreign-trade/aip/edbrel-9899.pdf>.
7. Incidentally, if the destruction of a job-worker match also destroys human capital, then calculations of lost income during unemployment should not use the pre-unemployment wage but rather the post-unemployment wage. This latter method will reduce the estimate of adjustment costs somewhat, but is unlikely to offset the full present value of lost income that appears to occur with much job displacement.
8. This capital relocation issue is closely tied to the labor relocation decision but quite complex and beyond the scope of our discussion.

Appendix A
Standard Industrial Classification (SIC) System

The U.S. Office of Management and Budget developed the SIC system to group industries into categories based upon their major product. This system defines 20 two-digit manufacturing industries, SIC 20 to SIC 39. These 20 industries are further subdivided into 143 three-digit manufacturing industries ranging from SIC 201 to SIC 399. These industries are, in turn, further subdivided into 447 four-digit industries ranging in number from SIC 2011 to SIC 3999. Table A.1 presents the SIC numbers and the industry names for the 20 two-digit SIC manufacturing industries.

Table A.1 Two-Digit SIC Industries

SIC	Nondurable goods industries	SIC	Durable goods industries
20	Food and kindred products	24	Lumber and wood products
21	Tobacco manufacturers	25	Furniture and fixtures
22	Textile mill products	32	Stone, clay and glass products
23	Apparel and other textile products	33	Primary metal products
26	Paper and allied products	34	Fabricated metal products
27	Printing and publishing	35	Machinery, except electrical
28	Chemicals and allied products	36	Electrical machinery
29	Petroleum and coal products	37	Transportation equipment
30	Rubber and plastics products	38	Instruments and related products
31	Leather and leather products	39	Other durable goods

To give a sense of the further disaggregation of industries at the three-digit and four-digit level, we consider the two-digit industry Furniture and Fixtures (SIC 25). This industry is disaggregated into a set of five three-digit industries: SIC 251, Household Furniture; SIC 252, Office Furniture; SIC 253, Public Building and Related Furniture; SIC 254, Partitions, Shelving, Lockers, and Office; and SIC 259, Miscellaneous Furniture and Fixtures. Each of these three-digit groups is comprised of one or more four-digit groups. For example, SIC 251 is comprised of six four-digit groups: SIC 2511, Wood Household Furniture, except Upholstered; SIC 2512, Wood Household Furniture, Upholstered; SIC 2514, Metal Household Furniture; SIC 2515, Mattresses, Foundations, and Convertible Beds; SIC 2517, Wood Television, Radio, Phonograph, and Sewing Machine Cabinets; and SIC 2519, Household Furniture, Not Elsewhere Classified.

For a full online listing of SIC industries, refer to the U.S. Department of Labor website: <http://www.osha.gov/oshstats/sicser.html>.

Appendix B

A Formal Economic Model of the Effect of Exchange Rate Changes on Job Creation and Job Destruction

This appendix presents a more formal version of the model described in Chapter 5.[1] The model begins with a specification of the cost function for the pth establishment in industry i as

$$C(W_p, G_p; Q_p) = W_p^{\alpha} G_p^{(1-\alpha)} Q_p$$

where W_p is the wage paid by that establishment, G_p is the unit cost of its non-labor input, and Q_p is its output. By Shepard's lemma, the demand for labor by this establishment, L_p, is the partial derivative of the cost function with respect to wages, that is

$$L_p = \frac{\partial C(W_p, G_p; Q_p)}{\partial W_p} = \alpha W_p^{\alpha-1} G_p^{(1-\alpha)} Q_p.$$

The total differential of the logarithm of the above equation is

(B1) $\widehat{L_p} = -(1-\alpha)\widehat{W_p} + (1-\alpha)\widehat{G_p} + \widehat{Q_p}.$

where we use the notation that, for any variable Z, $\widehat{Z} = d \ln Z$.

We assume that the demand for the product of the pth establishment in industry i is

(B2) $Q_p = A_p Y^{\beta} \prod_{j=1}^{k} \left[E_j^{-\mu\Omega_i} Y_j^{*\beta\Omega_i} \right]^{\omega_j^i}$

where A_p is an idiosyncratic demand shock facing this establishment, E_j is the real exchange rate with country j, (representing the price of the establishment's product divided by the domestic-currency price of the potential substitute product sold by competitors from country j), Y is a measure of domestic income, and Y_j^* is a measure of income in country j. The idiosyncratic shocks mentioned in the chapter are the realizations of the variable A_p. The model described in the chapter assumes that both the trade weights, ω_j^i, and the openness parameter, Ω_i (with $0 \leq \Omega_i \leq 1$), are common to all establishments in industry i and, therefore, the product $\omega_j^i \Omega_i$ shows the openness of all establishments in industry i with respect to trade with country j. The total differential of the logarithm of Equation (B2) is equivalent to

(B3) $\widehat{Q_p} = \widehat{A_p} + \beta\widehat{Y} - \mu\Omega_i \sum_j \omega_j^i \widehat{E_j} + \beta\Omega_i \sum_j \omega_j^i \widehat{Y_j^*}.$

To simplify notation, define the difference in the logarithm of the trade-weighted exchange rate for all establishments in industry i as

$$\widehat{E_i} = \sum_{j=1}^{k} \omega_j^i \widehat{E_j}$$

and the difference in the logarithm of the trade-weighted foreign output as

$$\widehat{Y_i^*} = \sum_{j=1}^{k} \omega_j^i \widehat{Y_j^*}.$$

Using these definitions, and substituting Equation (B3) into Equation (B1), we get the labor-demand equation for the pth establishment

(B4) $\widehat{L_p} = -(1-\alpha)\widehat{W_p} + (1-\alpha)\widehat{G_p} + \widehat{A_p} + \beta\widehat{Y} - \mu\Omega_i \widehat{E_i} + \beta\Omega_i \widehat{Y_i^*}.$

This is the log-difference of the labor-demand schedules presented in the figures in Chapter 5. Note that the coefficient on the log-difference of the wage is negative (that is, the labor-demand schedules are downward sloping) and that the schedules shift with a change in either the idiosyncratic shock, A_p, or the aggregate shocks, represented by the log-difference in the exchange rate, but also by the log-difference in overall foreign or domestic output. There is a positive effect of a depreciation of the trade-weighted real exchange rate ($\widehat{E_i} < 0$) on labor demand, all else equal.

In the model, we assume that all establishments within the ith industry pay the same wage, W_i, so $W_p = W_i$ for all establishments in industry i. We can weaken the assumption that the wage is the same across all industries by assuming some substitutability among workers in the ith industry and workers in the rest of the economy such that the labor-supply equation facing the pth establishment in the ith industry is

$$L_p = \left(\frac{W_i}{\Gamma^\varepsilon}\right)^\gamma,$$

where Γ is the prevailing wage in the "rest of the economy," γ is a measure of labor-supply elasticity $(\gamma > 0)$, and ε is a measure of the cross-elasticity of labor supply between the ith industry and the rest of the economy, with $\varepsilon \geq 0$. This specification gives us the total differential of labor supply facing the pth establishment,

$$\widehat{L_p} = \gamma\left(\widehat{W_i} - \varepsilon\widehat{\Gamma}\right).$$

Assume that $\widehat{G_p}, \widehat{Y},$ and $\widehat{Y_i^*}$ are all equal to zero, in order to focus on the role of the real exchange rate and note that all establishments in industry i pay the same wage, to obtain a simple form of the labor-demand Equation (B4)

$$\widehat{L_p} = \widehat{A_p} - (1-\alpha)\widehat{W_i} - \mu\Omega_i\widehat{E_i}.$$

Define φ_p^i as the relative employment size of the pth establishment in the ith industry, an industry with n establishments, where

$$\sum_{p=1}^{n} \varphi_p^i = 1.$$

Then the industry-wide change in employment is

$$\widehat{L_i} = \sum_{p=1}^{n} \varphi_p^i \widehat{L_p}.$$

Define the weighted average of the proportional change in the demand shock among the n establishments in industry i, $\widehat{A_i}$, as

$$\widehat{A_i} = \sum_{p=1}^{n} \varphi_p^i \widehat{A_p}$$

Set overall labor-demand in the ith industry equal to labor supply in that industry to solve for $\widehat{W_i}$ as a function of $\widehat{E_i}, \widehat{\Gamma},$ and $\widehat{A_i}$, and then use these values to solve for $\widehat{L_p}$, to obtain

(B5) $\quad \widehat{L_p} = \left(\widehat{A_p} - k\widehat{A_i}\right) - k\varepsilon\gamma\widehat{\Gamma} - (1+k)\mu\Omega_i\widehat{E_i}$

where $k = (1-\alpha)/(1-\alpha+\gamma)$ and $1 \geq k \geq 0$. The pth establishment will exhibit job creation if $\widehat{L_p} > 0$ and job destruction if $\widehat{L_p} < 0$. This solution shows that job creation or destruction by a particular establishment depends upon an idiosyncratic shock specific to that establishment, $\widehat{A_p}$, an aggregate shock specific to the industry of which the establishment is a member, $\widehat{A_i}$, and the change in value of aggregate variables, $\widehat{E_i}$ and $\widehat{\Gamma}$. The likelihood that an establishment exhibits job destruction rises with $\widehat{E_i}$, that is, with a larger appreciation of the exchange rate.

The rates of job creation and job destruction in an entire industry can be calculated as the weighted average of the rates of job creation and job destruction for the establishments in that industry. Call the set of establishments that expand employment in a given period $M+$ and those that contract employment $M-$. Define

$$\Phi_+ = \sum_{p \in (M^+ \cup M^-)} \varphi_p \text{ and } \Phi_- = \sum_{p \in (M^+ \cup M^-)} \varphi_p$$

where $\Phi_+ \geq 0, \Phi_- \geq 0$ and $\Phi_+ + \Phi_- = 1$. Continuing with our assumption that $\widehat{G_p}$, $\widehat{Y}$, and $\widehat{Y_i}$ are all equal to zero, the industry rates of job creation and job destruction are

$$C_i = \sum_{p \in M+} \varphi_p \left[\left(\widehat{A_p} - k\widehat{A_i} \right) - k\varepsilon\gamma\widehat{\Gamma} - (1+k)\mu\Omega_i \widehat{E_i} \right]$$

$$= -\phi_+ \left(k\varepsilon\gamma\widehat{\Gamma} + (1+k)\mu\Omega_i \widehat{E_i} + k\widehat{A_i} \right) + \sum_{p \in M+} \varphi_p \widehat{A_p}$$

$$D_i = -\sum_{p \in M-} \varphi_p \left[\left(\widehat{A_p} - k\widehat{A_i} \right) - k\varepsilon\gamma\widehat{\Gamma} - (1+k)\mu\Omega_i \widehat{E_i} \right]$$

$$= \phi_- \left(k\varepsilon\gamma\widehat{\Gamma} + (1+k)\mu\Omega_i \widehat{E_i} + k\widehat{A_i} \right) + \sum_{p \in M-} \varphi_p \widehat{A_p}.$$

These results suggest that an appreciation of the exchange rate is associated with less job creation and greater job destruction, holding constant other factors. These results also suggest that for two industries that are identical but for their respective values of openness (Ω), the effect of the exchange rate on both job creation and job destruction is more pronounced in the industry that is more open.

Note

1. This model is presented in Klein, Schuh, and Triest (2003).

Appendix C
Data Sources

The data used in this book come from the following sources.

1) *Gross job flows.* Data on gross job creation, destruction, and reallocation were developed by Davis, Haltiwanger, and Schuh (1996) and updated by the U.S. Census Bureau. The data are available annually and quarterly for the period 1972 to 1993 at the four-digit SIC industry level. The data can be downloaded from http://www.bsos.umd.edu/econ/haltiwanger/download.htm.

2) *Multilateral trade.* Data on multilateral exports and imports were developed by Abowd (1990) and updated by Feenstra (1996, 1997). The data are available annually for the period 1972 to 1994 at the four-digit SIC industry level. The data can be downloaded from http://data.econ.ucdavis.edu/international/home.html.

3) *Other manufacturing data.* Data on sales (shipments), prices, wages, productivity, and other manufacturing activity come from the NBER-CES Manufacturing Industry Database developed by Bartelsman and Gray (1996) and Randy Becker. The data are available annually for the period 1958 to 1996 at the four-digit SIC industry level. The data can be downloaded from http://www.nber.org/nberces.

4) *Bilateral trade.* Data on bilateral exports and imports come from the World Export and Import Database developed by Statistics Canada using United Nations data and distributed by the NBER and University of California at Davis. See Feenstra, Lipsey, and Bowen (1997) and Feenstra (2000) for documentation. The data are available annually for the period 1970 to 1997 at the four-digit SIC industry level. The data and Feenstra paper can be downloaded from http://data.econ.ucdavis.edu/international.

5) *International data.* Data on nominal bilateral exchange rates, aggregate producer prices, and real GDP (volume index) by country are from International Monetary Fund's International Financial Statistics (IFS). The data are available annual and quarterly for various sample periods depending on the country. The data were obtained via Haver Analytics and supplemented by various IFS yearbook publications.[1]

6) *Other U.S. macro data.* Data on interest rates, inflation, manufacturing employment, aggregate multilateral exchange rates, and other U.S. macroeconomic variables come from Haver Analytics.

Job creation rates and job destruction rates are calculated from establishment-level net employment changes. We choose to conduct our analysis at the industry level rather than at the establishment level because this allows us to match the job flow data with industry-level international trade data and four-digit industry data on real exchange rates that we constructed (following the methodology in Gourinchas 1998).

NOTATION AND DATA DEFINITIONS

Table C.1 reports the notation and definitions of variables. The openness variable is defined as

$$\widetilde{\Omega}_{it} = (1/5) \sum_{s=1}^{5} \left[\frac{X_{i,t-s} + M_{i,t-s}}{Y_{i,t-s} + X_{i,t-s} + M_{i,t-s}} \right].$$

The industry-specific multilateral real exchange rate is defined as

$$E_{it} = \sum_{j=1}^{J_i} \omega_{ijt} E_{ijt},$$

where j indexes trading partners (countries), J_i denotes the set of partners, ω_{ijt} denotes trade share weights, and E_{ijt} denotes bilateral real exchange rates. The trade share weights are defined as

$$\omega_{ijt} = (1/2) \sum_{s=1}^{2} \left[\frac{X_{ij,t-s} + M_{ij,t-s}}{\sum_{j=1}^{J_i} X_{ij,t-s} + M_{ij,t-s}} \right].$$

Note

1. The yearbook data are required because the latest price index data do not have a sufficient number of decimal places for many countries that experienced hyperinflation.

Table C.1 Notation and Data Definitions

Variable	Definition	Units	Data source[a]
C	Gross job creation	%	1
D	Gross job destruction	%	1
E_j	Bilateral exchange rate	FCU/$	5
E	Multilateral exchange rate	Index	4,5
i^f	Federal funds rate	%	6
M	Multilateral imports	$	2
M_j	Bilateral imports	$	4
N	Net employment growth $(C - D)$	%	1
π	Inflation, GDP deflator	%	6
P^Q	Final goods (producer) price	Index	3
P^*	Foreign final goods (producer) price	Index	5
S	Total sales (shipments)	$	3
W_i	Production worker compensation	$	3
X	Multilateral exports	$	2
X_j	Bilateral exports	$	4
Y	Domestic sales $(S - X)$	$	3
Y^*	Foreign real GDP volume	Index	5

NOTE: For P^*, the consumer price is used when the producer price is not available.
[a] See appendix text for description of sources.

References

Abowd, John M. 1990. "The NBER Immigration, Trade and Labor Markets Data Files." NBER working paper no. 3351. Cambridge, MA: National Bureau of Economic Research.

Abowd, John M., Patrick Corbel, and Francis Kramarz. 1999. "The Entry and Exit of Workers and the Growth of Employment: An Analysis of French Establishments." *The Review of Economics and Statistics* 81(2): 170–187.

Abowd, John M., John C. Haltiwanger, Julia Lane, and Kristin Sandusky. 2002. "Within and between Firm Changes in Human Capital, Technology, and Productivity." Unpublished paper. Presented to the Census Advisory Committee of Professional Associations Meeting, April 18–19, Arlington, VA.

Abowd, John M., and Francis Kramarz. 1997. "The Costs of Hiring and Separations." NBER working paper no. 6110. Cambridge, MA: National Bureau of Economic Research.

Baldwin, Robert E. 1994. "The Effects of Trade and Foreign Direct Investment on Employment and Relative Wages." *OECD Economic Studies* (23): 7–54.

Baldwin, Robert E., John H. Mutti, and J. David Richardson. 1980. "Welfare Effects on the United States of a Significant Multilateral Tariff Reduction." *Journal of International Economics* 10(3): 405–423.

Bartelsman, Eric J., and Wayne Gray. 1996. "The NBER Productivity Database." NBER technical working paper no. 205. Cambridge, MA: National Bureau of Economic Research.

Bentivogli, Chiara, and Patrizio Pagano. 1999. "Trade, Job Destruction and Job Creation in European Manufacturing." *Open Economies Review* 10(2): 165–184.

Bernard, Andrew, and Bradford Jensen. 1995. "Exporters, Jobs and Wages in U.S. Manufacturing, 1976–1987." *Brookings Papers on Economic Activity, Microeconomics*: 67–112.

Beveridge, Stephen, and Charles R. Nelson. 1981. "A New Approach to Decomposition of Economic Time Series into Permanent and Transitory Components with Particular Attention to Measurement of the Business Cycle." *Journal of Monetary Economics* 7(2): 151–174.

Bhagwati, Jagdish. 1988. *Protectionism*. Ohlin Lectures No. 1. Cambridge, MA and London: MIT Press.

Black, Sandra E., and Lisa M. Lynch. 2001. "How to Compete: The Impact of Workplace Practices and Information Technology on Productivity." *The Review of Economics and Statistics* 83(3): 434–445.

Blanchard, Olivier, and Peter Diamond. 1990. "The Cyclical Behavior of the Gross Flows of U.S. Workers." *Brookings Papers on Economic Activity* (2): 85–143.

Bleakley, Hoyt, Ann E. Ferris, and Jeffrey C. Fuhrer. 1999. "New Data on Worker Flows during Business Cycles." *New England Economic Review* (July/August): 49–76.

Blinder, Alan S. 1988. "The Challenge of High Unemployment." *American Economic Review* 78(2): 1–15.

Branson, William, and Jamie Love. 1988. "United States Manufacturing and the Real Exchange Rate." In *Misalignment of Exchange Rates: Effects on Trade and Industry*, Richard Marston, ed. Chicago, IL: University of Chicago Press, pp. 241–276.

Burfisher, Mary E., Sherman Robinson, and Karen Thierfelder. 2001. "The Impact of NAFTA on the United States." *Journal of Economic Perspectives* 15(1): 125–144.

Burgess, Simon, and Michael Knetter. 1998. "An International Comparison of Employment Adjustment to Exchange Rate Fluctuations." *Review of International Economics* 6(1): 151–163.

Burgess, Simon, Julia Lane, and David Stevens. 2000. "Job Flows, Worker Flows, and Churning." *Journal of Labor Economics* 18(3): 473–502.

Caballero, Ricardo J., and Mohamad L. Hammour. 1996. "On the Timing and Efficiency of Creative Destruction." *Quarterly Journal of Economics* 111(3): 805–852.

Campa, Jose, and Linda Goldberg. 1997. "The Evolving External Orientation of Manufacturing: A Profile of Four Countries." *Federal Reserve Bank of New York Economic Policy Review* 3(2): 53–81.

———. 2001. "Employment versus Wage Adjustment and the U.S. Dollar." *Review of Economics and Statistics* 83(3): 477–489.

Coughlin, Cletus C., and Howard J. Wall. 2001. "NAFTA and the Changing Pattern of State Exports." Unpublished paper. Federal Reserve Bank of St. Louis, March.

Davidson, Carl, Lawrence Martin, and Steven Matusz. 1999. "Trade and Search Generated Unemployment." *Journal of International Economics* 48(2): 271–299.

Davidson, Carl, and Steven Matusz. 2001a. "On Adjustment Costs." Unpublished paper. Michigan State University, East Lansing, MI.

———. 2001b. "Trade and Turnover: Theory and Evidence." Unpublished paper. Michigan State University, East Lansing, MI.

Davis, Donald, and Carsten Kowalczyk. 1998. "Tariff Phase-Outs: Theory and Evidence from GATT and NAFTA." In *The Regionalization of the World*

Economy, Jeffrey A. Frankel, ed. A National Bureau of Economic Research Project Report. Chicago: University of Chicago Press, pp. 227–258.

Davis, Steven J., and John C. Haltiwanger. 1992. "Gross Job Creation, Gross Job Destruction, and Employment Reallocation." *Quarterly Journal of Economics* 107(3): 819–863.

———. 1999. "Gross Job Flows." In *Handbook of Labor Economics,* Vol. 3B, Orley Ashenfelter and David Card, eds. Amsterdam, New York, and Oxford: Elsevier Science, North Holland, pp. 2711–2805.

———. 2001. "Sectoral Job Creation and Destruction Responses to Oil Price Changes." *Journal of Monetary Economics* 48(3): 465–512.

Davis, Steven J., John C. Haltiwanger, and Scott Schuh. 1996. *Job Creation and Destruction.* Cambridge, MA: MIT Press.

Deardorff, Alan. 1994. Comment on "Trade and Jobs in U.S. Manufacturing" by Sachs, Jeffrey D. and Howard J. Shatz. *Brookings Papers on Economic Activity* (1): 1–69.

Del Boca, Alessandra, and Paola Rota. 1998. "How Much Does Hiring and Firing Cost? Survey Evidence from a Sample of Italian Firms." *Review of Labour Economics and Industrial Relations* 12(3): 427–449.

de Melo, Jaime, and David Tarr. 1990. "Welfare Costs of U.S. Quotas in Textiles, Steel and Autos." *The Review of Economics and Statistics* 72(3): 489–497.

Dewatripont, Mathias, André Sapir, and Khalid Sekkat, eds. 1999. *Trade and Jobs in Europe: Much Ado about Nothing?* New York: Oxford University Press.

Dixit, Avinash. 1989. "Entry and Exit Decisions under Uncertainty." *Journal of Political Economy* 97(3): 620–638.

Doh, Jonathan P. 1998. "The Impact of NAFTA on the Auto Industry of the United States." In *The North American Auto Industry under NAFTA,* The Significant Issue Series, Sidney Weintraub and Christopher Sands, eds. Washington, DC: The Center for Strategic and International Studies, pp. 15–47.

Dominguez, Kathryn M., and Jeffrey Frankel. 1993. *Does Foreign Exchange Intervention Work?* Washington, DC: Institute for International Economics.

Economic Report of the President. 1998. Washington, DC: U.S. Government Printing Office.

———. 2000. Washington, DC: U.S. Government Printing Office.

———. 2002. Washington, DC: U.S. Government Printing Office.

Fallick, Bruce C. 1996. "A Review of the Recent Empirical Literature on Displaced Workers." *Industrial and Labor Relations Review* 50(1): 5–16.

Fallick, Bruce C., and Charles A. Fleischman. 2001. "The Importance of Employer-to-Employer Flows in the U.S. Labor Market." Federal Reserve

Board FEDS working paper no. 2001–18. Board of Governors of the Federal Reserve System, Washington, DC.

Feenstra, Robert C. 1996. "NBER Trade Database, Disk 1: U.S. Imports, 1972–1994: Data and Concordances." NBER working paper no. 5515. Cambridge, MA: National Bureau of Economic Research.

———. 1997. "NBER Trade Database, Disk 3: U.S. Exports, 1972–1994, with State Exports and Other U.S. Data." NBER working paper no. 5990. Cambridge, MA: National Bureau of Economic Research.

———. 2000. "World Trade Flows, 1980–1997." Unpublished working paper, University of California Davis, Davis, CA.

Feenstra, Robert C., and Gordon H. Hanson. 2003. "Global Production Sharing and Rising Inequality: A Survey of Trade and Wages." In *Handbook of International Trade*, Kwan Choi and James Harrigan, eds., Oxford: Basil Blackwell, pp. 146–185.

Feenstra, Robert C., Robert E. Lipsey, and Harry P. Bowen. 1997. "World Trade Flows, 1970–1992, with Production and Tariff Data." NBER working paper no. 5910. Cambridge, MA: National Bureau of Economic Research.

Foote, Christopher. 1998. "Trend Employment Growth and the Bunching of Job Creation and Destruction." *Quarterly Journal of Economics* 113(3): 809–834.

Freeman, Richard. 1995. "Are Your Wages Set in Beijing?" *Journal of Economic Perspectives* 9(3): 15–32.

Froning, Denise H. 2001. "Trade Adjustment Assistance: A Flawed Program." Heritage Foundation, Heritage Lectures No. 714, July 31, Washington, DC.

Froot, Kenneth A., and Paul Klemperer. 1989. "Exchange Rate Pass-through When Market Share Matters." *American Economic Review* 79(3): 637–654.

Fung, K.C., and Robert W. Staiger. 1996. "Trade Liberalization and Trade Adjustment Assistance." In *The New Transatlantic Economy*, Matthew B. Canzoneri, Wilfred J. Ethier, and Vittorio Grilli, eds. Cambridge: Cambridge University Press, pp. 265–294.

Furusawa, Taiji, and Edwin L.-C. Lai. 1998. "Adjustment Costs and Gradual Trade Liberalization." *Journal of International Economics* 49(2): 333–361.

Gaston, Noel, and Daniel Trefler. 1994. "Protection, Trade, and Wages: Evidence from U.S. Manufacturing." *Labor Relations Review* 47(4): 547–566.

———. 1997. "The Labour Market Consequences of the Canada–U.S. Free Trade Agreement." *Canadian Journal of Economics* 30(1): 18–41.

Goldberg, Linda, and Joseph Tracy. 2000. "Exchange Rates and Local Labor Markets." In *The Impact of International Trade on Wages,* Robert C. Feenstra, ed. NBER conference volume. Chicago: University of Chicago Press, pp. 269–308.

Goldberg, Linda, Joseph Tracy, and Stephanie Aaronson. 1999. "Exchange Rates and Employment Instability: Evidence from Matched CPS Data." *American Economic Review* 89(2): 204–210.

Golub, Stephen. 1999. *Labor Costs and International Trade.* Washington, DC: AEI Press.

Gourinchas, Pierre-Olivier. 1998. "Exchange Rates and Jobs: What Do We Learn from Job Flows?" In *NBER Macroeconomics Annual 1998,* Ben S. Bernanke and Julio J. Rotemberg, eds. Cambridge, MA: MIT Press, pp. 153–207.

———. 1999. "Exchange Rates Do Matter: French Job Reallocation and Exchange Rate Turbulence, 1984–1992." *European Economic Review* 43(7): 1279–1316.

Grossman, Gene M. 1986. "Imports as a Cause of Injury: The Case of the U.S. Steel Industry." *Journal of International Economics* 20(3/4): 201–223.

———. 1987. "The Employment and Wage Effects of Import Competition in the United States." *Journal of International Economic Integration* 2(1): 1–23. Also published as NBER working paper no. 1041, September 1988. Cambridge, MA: National Bureau of Economic Research.

Hall, Robert E. 1999. "Labor Market Frictions and Employment Fluctuations." In *Handbook of Macroeconomics,* Vol. 1B, John B. Taylor and Michael Woodford, eds. Amsterdam, New York, and Oxford: Elsevier Science, North Holland, pp. 1137–1171.

Haltiwanger, John C., Julia I. Lane, and James R. Spletzer. 1999. "Productivity Differences across Employers: The Roles of Employer Size, Age, and Human Capital." *American Economic Review, Papers and Proceedings* 89(2): 94–98.

Haltiwanger, John C., and Scott Schuh. 1999. "Gross Job Flows between Plants and Industries." *New England Economic Review* (March/April): 41–64.

Hamermesh, Daniel S. 1989 "What Do We Know About Worker Displacement in the U.S.?" *Industrial Relations* 28(1): 51–59.

———. 1993. *Labor Demand.* Princeton, NJ: Princeton University Press.

Hamermesh, Daniel S., and Gerard A. Pfann. 1996. "Adjustment Costs in Factor Demand." *Journal of Economic Literature* 34(3): 1264–1292.

Hanson, Gordon H., and Ann Harrison. 1999. "Trade Liberalization and Wage Inequality in Mexico." *Industrial and Labor Relations Review* 52(2): 271–288.

Hein, Dale, and Eric N. Sims. 2000. "The Impact of the Canada–United States Free Trade Agreement on U.S. Wine Exports." *American Journal of Agricultural Economics* 82 (February): 173–182.

Holt, Charles, Franco Modigliani, John Muth, and Herbert Simon. 1960. *Planning Production and Work Force.* Englewood Cliffs, NJ: Prentice Hall.

Hoon, Hian Teck. 2001a. "Adjustment of Wages and Equilibrium Unemployment in a Ricardian Global Economy." *Journal of International Economics* 54(1): 193–209.

———. 2001b. "General-Equilibrium Implications of International Product-Market Competition for Jobs and Wages." *Oxford Economic Papers* 53(1): 138–156.

Irwin, Douglas. 1996. *Against the Tide: An Intellectual History of Free Trade.* Princeton, NJ: Princeton University Press.

Jacobson, Louis S., Robert J. LaLonde, and Daniel G. Sullivan. 1993a. *The Costs of Worker Dislocation.* Kalamazoo, MI: W.E. Upjohn Institute for Employment Research.

———. 1993b. "Earnings Losses of Displaced Workers." *The American Economic Review* 83(4): 685–709.

King, Neil, Jr. 2002. "U.S. Firms Cry Foul at Procedure for Giving Steel-Tariff Exemptions." *The Wall Street Journal*, March 19, p. A2.

King, Neil, Jr., and Todd Zaun. 2002. "Japan Joins EU in Plans to Slap Tariffs on Imports of U.S. Steel." *The Wall Street Journal*, May 17, p. 1.

Klein, Michael W., Scott Schuh, and Robert Triest. 2003. "Job Creation, Job Destruction, and the Real Exchange Rate." *Journal of International Economics* 59: 239–265.

Kletzer, Lori G. 1998a. "International Trade and Job Loss in U.S. Manufacturing, 1979–91." In *Imports, Exports, and the American Worker*, Susan M. Collins, ed. Washington, DC: The Brookings Institution, pp. 423–472.

———. 1998b. "Job Displacement." *The Journal of Economic Perspectives* 12(1): 115–136.

———. 2000. "Trade and Job Loss in U.S. Manufacturing, 1979–94." In *The Impact of International Trade on Wages*, Robert C. Feenstra, ed. Chicago: University of Chicago Press, pp. 349–393.

———. 2001. *Job Loss from Imports: Measuring the Costs.* Washington, DC: Institute for International Economics.

Kletzer, Lori G., and Robert Litan. 2001. "A Prescription to Relieve Worker Anxiety." Institute for International Economics Policy Brief No. 01-2.

Kloek, Teun. 1981. "OLS Estimation in a Model Where a Microvariable is Explained by Aggregates and Contemporaneous Disturbances are Equicorrelated." *Econometrica* 49(1): 205–207.

Knetter, Michael. 1989. "Price Discrimination by U.S. and German Exporters." *American Economic Review* 79(1): 198–210.

Krueger, Anne O. 1999. "Trade Creation and Trade Diversion under NAFTA." NBER working paper no. 7249. Cambridge, MA: National Bureau of Economic Research.

Krugman, Paul. 1988. *Exchange Rate Instability*. Cambridge, MA: MIT Press.

Kumar, Pradeep, and John Holmes. 1998. "The Impact of NAFTA on the Auto Industry in Canada," In *The North American Auto Industry under NAFTA*, The Significant Issue Series, Sidney Weintraub and Christopher Sands, eds. Washington, DC: The Center for Strategic and International Studies, pp. 137–138.

Leahy, Michael P. 1998. "New Summary Measures of the Foreign Exchange Value of the Dollar." *Federal Reserve Bulletin* 84(10): 811–818.

Magee, Christopher, Carl Davidson, and Steven Matusz. 2001. "Trade, Turnover, and Tithing." Unpublished paper, September, Michigan State University, East Lansing, MI.

Magee, Stephen P. 1972. "The Welfare Effects of Restrictions on U.S. Trade." *Brookings Papers on Economic Activity* (3): 645–701.

Matusz, Steven J., and David Tarr. 2000. "Adjusting to Trade Reform." In *Economic Policy Reform: The Second Stage*, Anne O. Krueger, ed. Chicago: University of Chicago Press, pp. 365–403.

Mazur, Jay. 2000. "Labor's New Internationalism." *Foreign Affairs* 79(1): 79–93.

McClenahen, John S. 1999. "Textiles: Weave a Case for Relief." *Industry Week* 248(18): 8.

Melitz, Marc J. 2002. "The Impact of Trade on Intra-industry Reallocations and Aggregate Industry Productivity." NBER working paper no. 8881. Cambridge, MA: National Bureau of Economic Research.

Morse, Dan. 2001. "U.S. Textile Makers Unravel under Debt, Import Pressures." *The Wall Street Journal*, December 28, p. A2.

Mortensen, Dale T., and Christopher A. Pissarides. 1994. "Job Creation and Destruction in the Theory of Unemployment." *Review of Economic Studies* 66: 397–415.

———. 1999a. "Job Reallocation, Employment Fluctuations, and Unemployment." In *Handbook of Macroeconomics,* Vol. 1B, John B. Taylor and Michael Woodford, eds. Amsterdam, New York, and Oxford: Elsevier Science, North Holland, pp. 1171–1228.

———. 1999b. "New Developments in Models of Search in the Labor Market." In *Handbook of Labor Economics*, Vol. 3B, Orley Ashenfelter and David Card, eds. Amsterdam, New York, and Oxford: Elsevier Science, North Holland, pp. 2567–2627.

Moulton, Brent. 1990. "An Illustration of a Pitfall in Estimating the Effects of Aggregate Variables on Micro Units." *Review of Economics and Statistics* 72: 334–338.

Murray, Lauren. 1995. "Unraveling Employment Trends in Textiles and Apparel." *Monthly Labor Review* 118(8): 62–72.

Office of the United States Trade Representative. 1997. "Study of the Operation and Effect of the North American Free Trade Agreement." Report of the President to Congress pursuant to Sec. 512 of the NAFTA Implementation Act, PL103-182.

Oi, Walter. 1962. "Labor as a Quasi-Fixed Factor of Production." *Journal of Political Economy* 70: 538–555.

Revenga, Ana. 1992. "Exporting Jobs? The Impact of Import Competition on Employment and Wages in U.S. Manufacturing." *Quarterly Journal of Economics* 107(1): 255–284.

———. 1997. "Employment and Wage Effects of Trade Liberalization: The Case of Mexican Manufacturing." *Journal of Labor Economics* 15(3): S20–S43.

Ricardo, David. 1963. *The Principles of Political Economy and Taxation.* Homewood, IL: Irwin Publishing Company.

Richardson, J. David. 1995. "Income Inequality and Trade: How to Think, What to Conclude." *Journal of Economic Perspectives* 9(3): 33–55.

Riordan, Michael H., and Robert W. Staiger. 1993. "Sectoral Shocks and Structural Unemployment." *International Economic Review* 34(3): 611–629.

Sachs, Jeffrey, and Howard Shatz. 1994. "Trade and Jobs in U.S. Manufacturing." *Brookings Papers on Economic Activity*, (1): 1–78.

Schuh, Scott, and Robert Triest. 1998. "Job Reallocation and the Business Cycle: New Facts for an Old Debate." In *Beyond Shocks: What Causes Business Cycles?*, Jeff Fuhrer and Scott Schuh, eds. Boston: Federal Reserve Bank of Boston, pp. 271–337.

Sener, Fuat. 2001. "Schumpeterian Unemployment, Trade, and Wages." *Journal of International Economics* 54(1): 119–148.

Stevenson, Richard W. 2002. "Seeking Trade, Africans Find Western Barriers." *New York Times,* May 26, p. 3.

Takacs, Wendy E., and L. Alan Winters. 1991. "Labour Adjustment Costs and British Footwear Protection." *Oxford Economic Papers* 43(3): 479–501.

Thurow, Lester. 1992. *Head to Head: The Coming Economic Battle among Japan, Europe, and America.* New York: William Morrow.

Trefler, Daniel. 2001. "The Long and Short of the Canada–U.S. Free Trade Agreement." NBER working paper no. 8293. Cambridge, MA: National Bureau of Economic Research.

Tybout, James R., and M. Daniel Westbrook. 1995. "Trade Liberalization and the Dimensions of Efficiency Change in Mexico Manufacturing Industries." *Journal of International Economics* 39(1): 53–78.
Wagner, Helmut, ed. 2000. *Globalization and Unemployment.* Heidelberg: Springer-Verlag Berlin.
Weintraub, Sidney, and Christopher Sands. 1998. *The North American Auto Industry under NAFTA.* The Significant Issue Series. Washington, DC: The Center for Strategic and International Studies.
Winestock, Geoff, and Neil King Jr. 2002. "EU to Target GOP's Swing States in Payback for Bush Steel Tariffs." *The Wall Street Journal,* March 27, p. A2.
Wood, Adrian. 1995. "How Trade Hurt Unskilled Workers." *Journal of Economic Perspectives* 9(3): 57–80.

The Authors

Michael W. Klein is Professor of International Economics at the Fletcher School, Tufts University, and a research associate of the National Bureau of Economic Research. He has been a visiting scholar at the International Monetary Fund, the Board of Governors of the Federal Reserve, the Federal Reserve Bank of New York, and the Federal Reserve Bank of Boston. Along with his research concerning the effects of international factors on U.S. labor markets, he also has published research on exchange rate policy, foreign direct investment, international capital mobility, import pricing, and the political business cycle. He holds a B.A. from Brandeis University, and a Ph.D. in Economics from Columbia University.

Scott Schuh is an assistant vice president and economist for the Federal Reserve Bank of Boston. Previously, he served as an economist for the Board of Governors of the Federal Reserve System and the Council of Economic Advisers under President Reagan, worked as a research associate at the U.S. Bureau of the Census, and taught at Johns Hopkins University. His research focuses on the implications of microeconomic heterogeneity for macroeconomic behavior. With Steven Davis and John Haltiwanger, he coauthored the award-winning and critically acclaimed book *Job Creation and Destruction*, which analyzed new data on employment changes at U.S. manufacturing plants. His research on employment, investment, and monetary policy is published in various scholarly journals. He holds a B.A. from California State University–Sacramento, and a Ph.D. from Johns Hopkins University.

Robert K. Triest is an assistant vice president and economist in the research department at the Federal Reserve Bank of Boston. Before joining the Bank, he was an assistant professor of economics at Johns Hopkins University and an associate professor at the University of California–Davis. Triest's research publications have focused on topics in labor economics and public economics. He holds a Ph.D. in economics from the University of Wisconsin.

Index

The italic letters f, n, and t following a page number indicate that the subject information of the heading is within a figure, note, or table, respectively, on that page.

Adjustment costs. *See* Labor-market adjustment costs
American Textile Manufacturers Institute (ATMI), 129
APTA (Canada–U.S. Automotive Products Trade Agreement, 1965), 137
Auto Decrees (Mexico), 137
Auto Pact (1965), 137
Automobile industry, 137–44, 138t, 140f, 141f, 142f, 143f
    employment within, 139, 140f, 142–44
    gross job flows, 37–38, 37t, 142–43, 143f
    integration of, 137, 139
    international trade shares, 140–41, 141f, 142f
    labor productivity of, 142
    NAFTA and, 138–39, 138t, 141–44

Ball and roller bearings industry, 65
Bilateral trade, 122
Blinder, Alan, 50
Bureau of Economic Analysis (U.S. Census Bureau), 25f, 134f, 136f, 141f, 142f
Bureau of Labor Statistics, U.S., 125f, 134f, 140f
    data collection, 165–66
    Displaced Worker Surveys (DWS), 79, 166
    Job Openings and Labor Turnover Survey (JOLTS), 172n1
    Longitudinal Research Database, 136f, 143f
Bush, George W., 6

Campa, Jose, 17, 31n4, 63t, 69–72, 82n21, 95n9, 110n2
Canada
    openness to trade, 17
    See also Free Trade Agreement; NAFTA
Canada–U.S. Automotive Products Trade Agreement (APTA, 1965), 137
Capital account flows, 22
Census Bureau, U.S.
    Bureau of Economic Analysis, 25f, 134f, 136f, 141f, 142f
    data collection, 165
    Educational Quality of the Workforce National Employers Survey (EQWNES), 166–67
    Longitudinal Employer–Household Dynamics Program, 166
    Longitudinal Research Database (LRD), 33–34, 47n3, 168
    Profile of U.S. Exporting Companies, 168
    Shipper's Export Declaration (SED), 168
Chemicals and allied products industry, 132–37, 132t, 134f, 136f
    employment within, 133, 134f
    gross job flows, 135, 136f, 137
    international trade shares, 133, 134f, 135, 136f
    NAFTA and, 132t, 133–37
    wages, 132
Commerce Department, U.S., 119
Comparative advantage, 15
Competition, international
    determinants of, 113
    divergence of exposure to, 9–10

Competition international (cont.)
  free trade as, 15
  openness and, 9
  reallocation of resources and, 1
CPS (Current Population Survey), 166
Current account, 31n6
  exchange rates and, 15, 16, 25–26, 25f, 32n12
Current Population Survey (CPS), 166

Data development, 165–69
Data sources, 21f, 28f, 29f
Davis, Steven J., 5, 33, 54, 55, 73, 103, 108, 109, 161n2, 165
Diminishing marginal product, 85
Displaced Worker Surveys (DWS), 79, 166
DRI/McGraw-Hill, 119

Educational Quality of the Workforce National Employers Survey (EQWNES), 166–67
Energy prices, 108
EQWNES (Educational Quality of the Workforce National Employers Survey), 166–67
Exchange rate management, 153–54
Exchange rates
  current account and, 15, 16, 25–26, 25f, 32n12
  See also Real exchange rates
Export share, defined, 122

Fabricated metal products industry, 65–66, 71
Federal Reserve Board, 23f
Federal Reserve's broad index, 23, 26, 28–29, 28f, 29f
France, gross job flows in, 75
Free trade
  adjustment costs of, 2–4, 12
  benefits of, 1–2, 12
  as competition, 15
  support for, 4, 13n3, 50, 81n11

Free Trade Agreement (FTA), 113, 120, 147n7
Furniture and fixtures industry, 71

G-10 index, 23, 26, 28–29, 28f, 29f, 32n13
GATT (General Agreement on Tariffs and Trade), 113
Germany, impact of real exchange rate on employment growth, 69
Goldberg, Linda, 17, 31n4, 63t, 69–72, 72, 79–80, 82n21, 95n9, 110n2
Gore, Al, 116
Gross job flows, 2–3
  across industries, 42–46, 45t
  automobile industry, 37–38, 37t, 142–43, 143f
  chemicals and allied products industry, 135, 136f, 137
  France vs. U.S., 75
  manufacturing industry, 38–39, 40f–41f, 42, 151–52 (*See also specific manufacturing* industry)
  textile and apparel industries, 129–31, 130f
  worker flows comparison, 54, 55
  See also Job creation; Job destruction; Job reallocation; Labor-market flows
Gross job flows, determinants, 63t, 73–78
  real exchange rate movements, 39, 40f–41f, 74–77, 88–91, 103, 105–8, 109–10, 152, 159–60
Gross job flows, economic model of the effect of exchange rates on, 83–94, 175–78
  aggregate shocks, 88–91, 89f
  idiosyncratic shocks, 84–86, 87f, 88
  regression analysis, 98–102
  regression results, 102–3, 104t, 105–8, 106t, 107t
  trend vs. cyclical movements, 97–98, 100–101, 109–10

Haltiwanger, John C., 5, 33, 54, 55, 73, 103, 108, 109, 161n2, 165
Health insurance, subsidized, 159
Heckscher-Olin-Samuelson (HOS) trade model, 50–51

IMF (International Monetary Fund) International Financial Statistics, 123f
Import competition
 developing vs industrial nations, 67–68
 worker flows and, 79
Import penetration ratio, defined, 122
Industry demand, 108
Industry life cycle, 42
Industry openness, measure of, 18
International trade
 job reallocation and, 4–6
 unemployment and, 50–52
International Trade Commission (ITC), 61, 64
International trade data, 167–69
 double-counting problem, 167–68, 172n3

Japan, impact of real exchange rate on employment growth, 69
Job creation
 adjustment costs of, 100
 calculation of, 36
 impact of real exchange rate movements on, 103, 105–8
 See also Gross job flows
Job destruction, 34
 adjustment costs of, 100
 calculation of, 36
 impact of real exchange rate movements on, 39, 40f, 42, 76–77, 103, 105–8, 110
 See also Gross job flows; Worker dislocation
Job flows. See Gross job flows

Job Openings and Labor Turnover Survey (JOLTS), 172n1
Job reallocation
 defined, 8, 34
 across and within industries, 7–9
 adjustment costs of, 58
 international trade and, 4–6
 manufacturing industry, 55, 149
 NAFTA and, 145
 See also Gross job flows
Job reallocation, determinants
 exchange rates, 5–6, 7, 8–9, 10–11, 103, 105–8
 trade policy, 5–6, 7–8, 12
JOLTS (Job Openings and Labor Turnover Survey), 172n1

Labor, trade liberalization and, 115
Labor-market adjustment costs, 56–61, 100
 determinants of, 170–71
 measurement of, 56–61, 169–71, 172n7
 regional development and, 160
 turnover, 59–60, 81n14
 worker dislocation, 34, 59, 60–61, 149
Labor-market churning. See Job reallocation
Labor-market flows, 52, 53f, 54–55
 See also Gross job flows; Worker flows
Labor-market flows, future research, 163–71
 data development, 165–69
 matching job and worker flows, 164–65
 measuring labor-market adjustment costs, 169–71
Labor-market flows, studies of international determinants
 gross job flows, 63t, 73–78
 worker flows, 78–80

Labor markets, studies of international
    determinants, 50–61, 62t–63t,
    72–80
  adjustment costs, 56–61
  labor-market flows, 52, 53f, 54–55
  trade and unemployment, 50–52
Labor productivity
  automobile industry, 142
  textile and apparel industries, 126
  trade liberalization and, 120
Leather and leather products industry, 71
Leather tanning industry, 65

Manufacturing industry
  gross job flows, 38–39, 40f–41f, 42,
    151–52
  job reallocation within, 55, 149
  net employment and, 55, 64–65
  openness of, 151
Maquiladora 9802 Program, 147n2
Maquiladora Decree (1989), 137–38
Maquiladora plants, 137–38
Marginal product of labor, 85
Mexican financial crisis, 118, 122–23,
    123f
  NAFTA and, 147n5
Mexico
  Auto Decrees, 137
  economic growth of, 122–23, 123f
  See also NAFTA
Multilateral trade, 122

NAFTA, 11, 113, 117–18
  implementation schedule, 121, 147n3
  Mexican financial crisis and, 147n5
  opposition to, 116
NAFTA, economic effects of, 145–46
  automobile industry, 138–39, 138t,
    141–44
  chemicals and allied products
    industry, 132t, 133–37
  job reallocation, 145
  research on, 118–21
  textile and apparel industries, 125t,
    126–31
  U.S.–Mexico bilateral trade, 144
National Bureau of Economic Research
    World Trade Database (WTBD),
    146n12
Net employment
  calculation for rate of change of, 36
  impact of real exchange rate
    movements on, 103, 105–8, 109
  manufacturing industry, 55, 64–65
Net employment, studies of international
    determinants, 61, 62t–63t, 64–72
  Branson and Love, 62t, 65–66
  Burgess and Knetter, 62t, 68–69
  Campa and Goldberg, 63t, 69–72
  Goldberg and Tracy, 63t, 72
  Grossman, 62t, 64–65
  Revenga, 62t, 66–67
  Sachs and Shatz, 67–68
Non-electrical machinery industry,
    65–66
North American Free Trade Agreement.
    See NAFTA

Office of Management and Budget, U.S.,
    173
Openness, 17–22
  defined, 180
  across industries, 18f, 19–22, 20t, 21t
  measurement of, 17–18
  real exchange rates and, 91–92, 107,
    108, 109

Paint industry, 133
Petroleum and coal products industry, 71
Photography equipment industry, 65
PIPA (Program on International Policy
    Attitudes), 13n3, 149–50
Plaza Accord (1985), 24
Primary metal products industry, 65–66,
    71
Program on International Policy
    Attitudes (PIPA), 13n3, 149–50

Protectionism, 6, 117
  steel industry, 154–56
  textile and apparel industries, 124, 125
  See also Tariffs

Radio and television industry, 65
Real exchange rates, 31*n*8
  determinants of, 24–26
  gross job flows and, 39, 40*f*–41*f*, 74–77, 88–91, 103, 105–8, 109–10, 152, 159–60
  industry-specific, 27–30, 28*f*, 29*f*, 31*n*8, 180
  job destruction and, 39, 40*f*, 42, 76–77, 103, 105–8, 110
  job reallocation and, 103, 105–8
  net employment and, 103, 105–8, 109 (*See also* Net employment, studies of international determinants)
  openness and, 91–92, 107, 108, 109
  tariff-inclusive, 92–93
  trend vs. cyclical movements of, 105–8, 109–10
  volatility of, 16, 22–26, 23*f*
  worker flows and, 80
  See also Exchange rates
Real exchange rates, multilateral, 23, 23*f*, 26–27
  See also Federal Reserve's broad index; G-10 index
Ricardo-Viner (RV) trade model, 51

Schuh, Scott, 5, 33, 54, 55, 73, 76, 103, 109, 161*n*2, 165
Seattle (Washington), 1
Shipper's Export Declaration (SED), 168
SIC (Standard Industrial Classification) system, 173–74, 173*t*
Smoot-Hawley Tariff Act (1930), 117
Standard Industrial Classification (SIC) system, 173–74, 173*t*
Steel industry, 64, 154–56

Sterilized intervention, 31*n*9

TAA (Trade Adjustment Act, 1974), 157
Tariffs
  benefits of, 155–56
  disadvantages of, 12, 154–55
  See also Protectionism
Technological change, 150
Textile and apparel industries, 124–31, 125*t*, 128*f*, 130*f*
  employment, post-NAFTA, 126–27, 129–31, 130*f*
  employment, pre-NAFTA, 125–26, 125*f*
  gross job flows, 129–31, 130*f*
  international trade shares, 127, 128*f*, 129
  labor productivity of, 126
  protectionism, 124, 125
  wages, 124
Trade account. *See* Current account
Trade Adjustment Act (TAA, 1974), 157
Trade Adjustment Assistance program, 12
Trade agreements, multilateral, 113, 117
  See also NAFTA
Trade deficit. *See* Current account
Trade liberalization
  economic effects of, 114–17
  labor productivity and, 120
  public support for, 150
  wage inequality and, 120
Trade share weight, defined, 180
Trade surplus. *See* Current account
Transportation equipment industry, 65–66
Turnover, adjustment costs of, 59–60, 81*n*14

Unemployment, international trade and, 50–52
United Kingdom
  impact of real exchange rate on employment growth, 69
  openness to trade, 17

United States
    current account, 31n6
    See also Free Trade Agreement;
        NAFTA; specific industries
U.S. International Trade Commission,
    119
U.S. Trade Deficit Review Commission,
    157

Wage inequality, trade liberalization and,
    120
Wage insurance, 158–59, 161n6
Worker assistance policies, 157–59, 160
Worker dislocation, 2–3, 103
    adjustment costs, 34, 59, 60–61, 149
    calculation of, 82n29
    See also Job destruction
Worker flows
    gross job flows comparison, 54, 55
    import competition and, 79
    real exchange rates and, 80
    studies of international determinants,
        63t, 78–80
    See also Labor-market flows
WTBD (National Bureau of Economic
    Research World Trade Database),
    146n12
WTO (World Trade Organization)
    creation of, 117
    demonstrations against, 1, 116–17,
        149

About the Institute

The W.E. Upjohn Institute for Employment Research is a nonprofit research organization devoted to finding and promoting solutions to employment-related problems at the national, state, and local levels. It is an activity of the W.E. Upjohn Unemployment Trustee Corporation, which was established in 1932 to administer a fund set aside by the late Dr. W.E. Upjohn, founder of The Upjohn Company, to seek ways to counteract the loss of employment income during economic downturns.

The Institute is funded largely by income from the W.E. Upjohn Unemployment Trust, supplemented by outside grants, contracts, and sales of publications. Activities of the Institute comprise the following elements: 1) a research program conducted by a resident staff of professional social scientists; 2) a competitive grant program, which expands and complements the internal research program by providing financial support to researchers outside the Institute; 3) a publications program, which provides the major vehicle for disseminating the research of staff and grantees, as well as other selected works in the field; and 4) an Employment Management Services division, which manages most of the publicly funded employment and training programs in the local area.

The broad objectives of the Institute's research, grant, and publication programs are to 1) promote scholarship and experimentation on issues of public and private employment and unemployment policy, and 2) make knowledge and scholarship relevant and useful to policymakers in their pursuit of solutions to employment and unemployment problems.

Current areas of concentration for these programs include causes, consequences, and measures to alleviate unemployment; social insurance and income maintenance programs; compensation; workforce quality; work arrangements; family labor issues; labor-management relations; and regional economic development and local labor markets.